March 31, 1958.

61

James N~~~~~.

EARLY ENGLISH CHRISTIAN POETRY

EARLY ENGLISH CHRISTIAN POETRY

Translated into
Alliterative Verse

by

CHARLES W. KENNEDY

Murray Professor of English Literature, Emeritus
Princeton University

With Critical Commentary

LONDON
HOLLIS & CARTER
1952

MADE AND PRINTED IN GREAT BRITAIN BY
THE BROADWATER PRESS LTD, WELWYN GARDEN CITY, HERTS, FOR
HOLLIS AND CARTER LTD
25 ASHLEY PLACE, LONDON, S.W.1
First published 1952

To
ELIZABETH

"More is thy due than more than all can pay"

PREFACE

OLD English poetry, the vernacular poetry written in England from the seventh century to the Norman Conquest, has been jestingly described as a small body of verse almost completely surrounded by scholars. It is a mild witticism and, like many others, an exaggeration. Yet it suggests a truth. The modern English reader is cut off from first-hand acquaintance with this poetry by the language in which it was written. In vocabulary and paradigm the English of the Anglo-Saxons differs so markedly from modern English, or even from the English of Chaucer, that it presents the difficulties of a foreign tongue. To read a page of Cynewulf in the original the modern English reader must learn Old English almost as he would learn Modern German.

Moreover, although this early verse has been vividly illumined by the critical studies, in England, of such modern scholars as Napier, Wyatt, Gollancz, R. W. Chambers, Tolkien, and Sisam, and on this side of the water Bright, Klaeber, Cook, Tupper, Lawrence, C. F. Brown, and Malone (to mention only a few in a distinguished company), the results of their labours are likely to have reached the modern reader only indirectly or as caviare to the general. And in the occasional book that is addressed to the general reader it is not always that a scholar is so happy in eloquent interpretation of this ancient literature as is Margaret Williams in *Word-Hoard*.

It is perhaps not altogether strange, then, if many a reader comes to feel that a body of poetry presenting these difficulties, and lying so aloof from modern life, is not for him. Even if through translations he succeeds in attaining some acquaintance with the primitive chivalry of *Beowulf*, or the Germanic heart-break of the *Wanderer*, or the stoic courage and loyalty of *Maldon*, the lines often ring in his ears with a sound of far-off voices chanting a way of life long past and gone.

And yet, in the corpus of Old English poetry, the Christian poems still utter a wisdom which has its immortality, and applies to the twentieth century as to the seventh. The poems of Caedmon and Cynewulf, and many another singer now unknown, were deeply rooted in the culture of the medieval Church, and eloquently expressive of its faith. This is a body of verse that has the timeless vitality of Christianity itself. It preserves its interest and its appeal not only for students of the past, but for all who find the world's hope in the Christian faith.

It has been my endeavour in this volume to translate for the general reader the best of this Christian poetry. The selections have been chosen to suggest its wide range of theme and many-sided expression of medieval Christianity, its convinced faith, and its enduring hope. The verse medium employed is an imitative four-stress alliterative line suggesting the original, but making a less restricted use of alliterative patterns.

No one, I think, can ever be more aware than the translator himself how much escapes his utmost endeavour. For he has intimate knowledge both of his own work and of the original he seeks to interpret. He best knows what has slipped away "as a bird from the hand of the fowler". In the end he can only lay down his pen and let the work speak for itself.

For these translations I have used the following texts: for the *Fall of Lucifer*, *Lamentations of the Fallen Angels*, and *Fall of Man*, G. P. Krapp's edition of the Junius Manuscript, Columbia University Press, 1931; for the *Advent Lyrics*, the *Ascension*, and the *Last Judgment*, A. S. Cook's edition of the *Christ* of Cynewulf, Ginn & Co., 1909; for *St Andrew's Mission to Mermedonia*, G. P. Krapp's edition of the *Andreas*, Ginn & Co., 1906; for *St Helena's Finding of the Cross*, the *Panther*, the *Whale*, and the *Phoenix*, A. S. Cook's edition of the Old English *Elene*, *Phoenix*, and *Physiologus*, Yale University Press, 1919; for the *Dream of the Cross*, G. P. Krapp's edition of the Vercelli Book, Columbia

University Press, 1932; for the Cambridge *Doomsday*, E. V. K. Dobbie's edition of the *Anglo-Saxon Minor Poems*, Columbia University Press, 1942.

I have arranged the metrical translations of these texts, chapter by chapter, in a sequence that begins with the Rebellion of Lucifer and ends with the Last Judgment. It is perhaps unnecessary to point out that the original texts are not united in any such sequence, but are of varying dates and authorship and are widely scattered among the many poems of four different manuscripts. But the order in which the poems are presented here is a natural one, and serves conveniently to emphasize the range and significance of the themes that are reflected in this early religious verse. Each of the poems translated is discussed in detail in the foreword to the chapter in which it is included.

For assistance in various ways in connection with my work on this volume I take this opportunity to express grateful thanks to the following:

to Mr Douglas Jerrold, who some six years ago suggested to me the pleasant labour of this book, and to Mr Ernest Short of Hollis and Carter Ltd, for their kindly patience during an unavoidable delay in my completion of the work;

to my colleague, Professor Donald Stauffer of Princeton, for his continuous and helpful interest in the progress of the book;

to the Princeton University Research Fund for the grant which provided secretarial assistance.

Finally, there is one other to whom, in this work as in all else, I owe the deepest debt of all, which is acknowledged in the dedication but goes beyond words.

C. W. K.

25 March 1951
Princeton, New Jersey

TABLE OF CONTENTS

INTRODUCTION

OLD ENGLISH CHRISTIAN POETRY

THE greatest single source of inspiration for the vernacular poetry written in England from the seventh century to the Norman Conquest was found in the faith and culture of the Christian Church. The Germanic settlers had, of course, brought with them to England race memories and ancient records of their Continental way of life. The primitive magic of their Charms, the confused traditions of *Widsith*, the material of Scandinavian folk-lore and chronicle from which the *Beowulf* was descended, elements such as these were links still binding them to their Continental past. But in England, from the seventh century, the chief source of culture lay in the growing strength and ascendancy of the Christian faith.

As the Church became more and more firmly established, it was natural that its inspiration should be felt in the beginnings of Early English vernacular poetry. Not only the Vulgate and the Apocrypha, but the antiphons of Advent, the services of Christmas and Easter, the lections appointed for Holy Saturday, the Latin hymnology, all such ecclesiastical influences played a direct and important part, as time went on, in shaping some of the finest of this verse. In addition to the influence of Scripture and liturgy, similar creative pressures were present in themes of the Hexaëmeral tradition, religious homilies, lives of the saints, commentaries of the Church Fathers, and various symbolisms recognized by the Church, and fixed in the conventions of Christian art and letters. From such sources grew a vital poetry written in an age that called men to conversion, and to a conviction that the Kingdom of God is not of this world.

The Christian faith had obtained a foothold in Britain during the period of the Roman occupation. Indeed, the fact that the Bishops of London, of York, and of Lincoln were present at the Council of Arles in 314, and that the British Church was repre-

3

sented at the Council of Rimini in 359, would seem to indicate that by the fourth century the British Church held a recognized place in the councils of Western Christianity. But the withdrawal of the Roman legions, and the Germanic invasions, weakened the strength of British Christianity and interrupted its contacts with the developing life of the Roman Church.

It was the landing of Augustine and his missionary band in Kent in 597, and the personal interest of Pope Gregory the Great, that began the relatively continuous and systematic Christianization of England. It is probable that the way had been prepared for Augustine's conversion of Ethelbert of Kent through the influence of his Frankish Queen Berhta, a granddaughter of Clotaire the Great, who had brought with her from the Continent her Christian faith, retaining her personal chaplain Liuthard and using the ancient Church of St Martin at Canterbury as an oratory.

The Christianizing influence exerted from Canterbury was paralleled in the North by Irish missionaries who carried on the work begun in Scotland under Columba. Early in the second half of the sixth century Columba had left Ireland and established himself on the island of Iona where he built a monastery and a church, and thereafter devoted himself to the conversion of the northern tribes. The monastery on Iona became a mother house of many foundations spreading the Celtic faith. The conversion in 627 of Edwin, King of Northumbria and overlord of the other kingdoms except Kent, seemed to promise a firm establishment of the new faith in northern England. But Edwin's death some six years later, followed by the rise to power of Penda of Mercia and the heathen reaction, was a severe blow. It was Aidan of the monks of Iona whose missionary zeal, radiating from his see at Lindisfarne, ultimately became a determining influence in establishing Christianity in Northumbria. By this same Celtic influence the work of conversion was later carried forward in Mercia, and a movement of pagan reaction gradually overcome among the East Saxons.

From these two sources, Roman and Celtic, the work of converting Britain was carried forward, though for a time a rift existed between the two movements. Between the Celtic Christianity and that of Rome lay certain points of difference in matters such as the manner of tonsure and the methods of reckoning Easter, and in details of the rite of baptism. It was not until the Synod of Whitby in 664 that firm decisions were reached on these points of difference. As a result of these decisions, and perhaps even more of the subsequent wise and authoritative ecclesiastical administration of Theodore, Archbishop of Canterbury, the English Church was finally brought together in allegiance to Rome.

It is in the pages of the *Ecclesiastical History of the English People* of Bede, the gentle scholar who for a lifetime "delighted to learn or teach or write" at the School of Jarrow, that we find the most vivid and extended contemporary picture of this spread of Christian culture through England. Even if Bede's *History* by modern standards is not in all respects critical, it is still an invaluable mirror of the time, simply and clearly written with an artist's sense of design, a Churchman's judgment as to what is important and what is not, and a scholar's understanding assessment of the human scene.

There is moreover in this Christian chronicler a very charming shrewdness which from time to time is visible in his narrative. It is inevitable that in the course of such extensive social change as was represented in the Christianization of England there should have been occasions when the self-seeker found it convenient to line up shoulder to shoulder with the altruist. A glimpse of one such instance is recorded in Bede's account of the conversion of King Edwin of Northumbria, and the counsel given by two of his advisers. The story is told in all charity, and yet one could not easily have a more vivid portrayal of the two types of judgment and motive that come into play when a people is confronted, as was England in the seventh century, by sweeping changes in the national life. Cefi, a materialist chief-bishop

B

of the pagan faith, on worldly grounds urges Edwin to turn to the new religion. For no one had served the old gods more faithfully than had he, yet many had received more and greater favours from Edwin than he. He knows that if the old gods had had any power they would have done more for him. "Therefore, if you find that this new preaching has more good and more power, let us hasten to accept it without delay."

It is an unnamed councillor of Edwin who has left to us one of the most unforgettable comments on man's earthly life that our literature contains. His words suggest only too tragically the pagan longing for something more certain and more fitting by which to measure human aspiration and human hope: "O King, this present life of men on earth, in comparison with the time that is unknown to us, seems to me as if you were sitting at a banquet with your ealdormen and thanes in the winter time with the fire burning and the hall warmed, and outside the storms of winter rain or snow were raging; and there should come a sparrow swiftly flying through the hall, coming in by one door and flying out through another. During the time it is inside it is not touched by the storm of winter; but, that little moment of quiet having passed, it soon returns from winter back to winter again, and is lost to sight. So this mortal life seems like a short interval; what may have gone before or what may come after it, we do not know. Therefore, if this new teaching has brought any greater certainty, it seems fitting that it should be followed."[1]

It was the Christianization of England that established the great Schools of Canterbury and Jarrow and York with their libraries of carefully accumulated and treasured manuscripts. From these centres, through England's monastic and Cathedral foundations, spread the Latin learning and culture of the Church. Benedict Biscop, in 669 Abbot of St Peter's, Canterbury, five years later established the monastery of St Peter at Wearmouth, and subsequently the famous School of Jarrow at which Bede

---

[1] Bede, *Ecclesiastical History*, Book II, Chapter 13.

was educated. Benedict made a number of journeys to Rome, gathering manuscripts for the Library at Jarrow, and bringing back with him from the Continent workers in stained glass to adorn the buildings of the two foundations.

By the eighth century the School at York had risen to prominence and, toward the end of the century, under Alcuin had become one of the great centres of learning in Europe. Alcuin's searches in Rome added manuscripts to the York Library, which already possessed widely recognized distinction. Among the authors represented by works in the York collection, and mentioned by Alcuin, were Aristotle, Cicero, Virgil, Pliny, Lucan, Statius, Lactantius, Ambrose, Orosius, Augustine, Boethius, Cassiodorus, Gregory, Bede, and others, among them Alcuin himself. The School suffered a serious blow when in 781 he left to enter the service of Charlemagne. Though he returned to England for a short time in 790, and again in 794, he left England finally for the Continent in 795, and spent his last years at the Abbey School of St Martin in Tours, surrounded by the students who sought him out, and the many scholars who followed his name.

It is during this period of the seventh and eighth centuries when this scholarship of Latin Christianity was gradually spreading through England, that we see the rise and flowering of English religious poetry in the vernacular. It seems likely, indeed, that these same cultural influences stimulated the rewriting of older poetry rooted in the Germanic traditions of the Continent. It is probable that behind the *Beowulf* lay an older Continental epic, or series of epic lays, which later in England a Christian poet reshaped into the poem as we know it. Certainly, the outcropping of ancient pagan material here and there through the Christian overlay is an outstanding characteristic of the poem. In the *Seafarer* also the difference in style between the realism of the first half, and the moralizing mood of the second half, has led some scholars to suggest that a later poet may have added the second part in an attempt to shape the poem into a religious allegory contrasting the transient joy and pain of earthly life with the everlasting bliss of the heavenly vision.

However this may be, it was by this vital and growing Christian faith that the poems of Caedmon and Cynewulf, and their followers, were kindled. All the themes inherent in the new religion: the Rebellion of Lucifer and the Fall of Man; the Redemption of Man through the Incarnation, Passion, Resurrection, and Ascension; the apocalyptic visions of the Last Judgment, the horrors of hell, and the joys of heaven; all this vast panorama of human destiny became the subject matter of a poetry, uneven in merit perhaps, but rarely uninspired, and at its best marked by an extraordinary elevation of poetic mood.

This body of religious verse is preserved mainly in four priceless Old English manuscripts apparently to be dated in the late tenth or early eleventh century: the *Beowulf* MS., the Junius MS., the Exeter Book, and the Vercelli Book.[1] The *Beowulf* MS.[2] had in the early seventeenth century been part of the famous collection of Sir Robert Cotton. In 1731 it escaped destruction in the Ashburnham House fire, but suffered damage with subsequent progressive deterioration and some impairment of the text. The manuscript was later gone over, each leaf separately inlaid, and the whole rebound.[3] It is this manuscript that, in addition to the *Beowulf*, contains the *Judith*, a spirited versification, unfortunately incomplete, of the story of Judith and Holofernes.

The Junius MS. contains four poems on Old Testament

---

[1] There are a few religious poems scattered here and there in other manuscripts of which the most important are the following: The *Be Domes Daege* (MS. 201) and the *Solomon and Saturn* (MSS. 41 and 422) in the Library of Corpus Christi College, Cambridge; the *Menologium* (Cotton Tiberius B. 1), a versified chronology of the Christian year, in the British Museum; and metrical translations of the Psalms in the Bodleian Library (MS. Junius 121), and in the Paris Psalter manuscript (Fonds Latin 8824) in the Bibliothèque Nationale.

[2] British Museum, Cotton Vitellius A xv.

[3] An autotype edition based on both the manuscript and Thorkelin's transcripts of 1787 was published in 1882 by the Early English Text Society.

themes: The *Genesis*, *Exodus*, *Daniel*, and *Christ and Satan*. About 1651 it came into the possession of a Francis Dujon, librarian to Lord Arundel and known in literature as Junius, who had an edition of it printed in 1654. Because of an apparent similarity between the four poems and Bede's description of Caedmon's writings, the contents of the Junius MS. were rather too quickly credited to Caedmon. The manuscript is now in the Bodleian Library, Oxford, where it is catalogued as MS. Junius 11.[1]

Of the four great codices the Junius MS. is the only one that is illustrated. It contains forty-eight drawings, apparently of the Winchester School, in the first ninety-six pages of *Genesis*, including spirited illustrations of the Fall of Lucifer and the Temptation and Fall of Man. Under the second drawing of the series is a portrait labelled "Ælfwine". It is possible that this was intended to represent the patron of the work and can be identified with the Ælfwine who became Abbot of Newminster near Winchester in 1035.

The Exeter Book has belonged to the Chapter Library of Exeter Cathedral since 1072. It is mentioned in the list of gifts made to the Cathedral by the Leofric who in 1046 became Bishop of Devonshire and Cornwall. Written on vellum in a fine liturgical hand, the manuscript contains no drawings except a set of about sixty large initial letters. At some time the manuscript suffered considerable damage and an uncertain number of leaves at the beginning have been lost. How great was the loss is difficult to estimate; it may have been considerable.[2] Of the four great manuscripts the Exeter Book is outstanding in the variety and range of its verse, some of which constitutes the very finest of the religious poetry. Two of the signed poems of Cynewulf are here, the *Ascension* and *Juliana*, in addition to the

[1] A facsimile reproduction of the MS., with an introduction by Gollancz, was published in 1927.

[2] A facsimile edition of the Exeter Book was published for the Dean and Chapter in 1933 with descriptive chapters by R. W. Chambers, Max Förster, and Robin Flower.

Advent Lyrics, two poems on Judgment Day, the *Life and Death of St Guthlac*, and the most graceful of all the religious poems, the *Phoenix*.

It is a tantalizing mystery how the Old English manuscript now known as the Vercelli Book found its way from England to Italy, where it has long been the property of the Library of the Cathedral Church at Vercelli. Any explanation of its presence there must rest on conjecture. Of the various suggestions made, the most plausible connects the manuscript with the name of an Italian Cardinal, Guala Bicchieri, who in 1208 was sent as Papal Legate by Pope Innocent III first to France, and later to England. On the accession of Henry III of England, Cardinal Guala was honoured by the new monarch with a benefice of the Church of St Andrew at Chesterton, in Cambridgeshire. On his return to Italy he founded the Cathedral Church in Vercelli, and dedicated it to St Andrew. Since the Vercelli Book contains the *Andreas*, a long and important poem dealing with a mission of St Andrew, it may well be that it was this poem that brought the Anglo-Saxon manuscript into the possession of an Italian Cardinal whose ecclesiastical life was so intimately connected with an English Church of St Andrew at Chesterton and an Italian Church of St Andrew at Vercelli. Like the Exeter Book the Vercelli MS. has two signed poems of Cynewulf, the *Elene*, a poem of the Finding of the Cross, and the *Fates of the Apostles*. It contains also an *Address of the Soul to the Body* and the lovely *Dream of the Rood*.

It is once more Bede in the *Ecclesiastical History*[1] who tells us of the beginnings of the religious verse of which so much has been preserved in these manuscripts. He is writing of the monastery at Whitby founded in 658 by Oswy of Northumbria and, under the Abbess Hilda, established as a double foundation, a sisterhood of nuns and a fraternity of monks, of the Benedictine order. It was near this monastery, Bede tells us, that a cowherd named Caedmon was suddenly and miraculously

[1] Book IV, Chapter 24.

endowed with the poetic gift, and composed the short poem now known as Caedmon's *Hymn*. Until he was of advanced years, Caedmon had lived in secular life and, according to Bede, "had never learned any poetry; and therefore sometimes at a banquet when for the sake of merrymaking it was agreed that all should sing in turn, when he saw the harp coming towards him he would rise up from table and go out and return home". When he had done this on a certain occasion, and had gone out to the stables where it was his duty to care for the cattle that night, he fell asleep there, and in a vision was divinely granted power to compose poetry and wrote the *Hymn*.

In the morning the overseer, hearing of the matter, took him to the Abbess Hilda and informed her of what had happened. There in the presence of many learned men Caedmon repeated the verses he had composed in order that they might judge the nature and the origin of his sudden talent. When they gave him a passage of sacred history and asked him to versify it if he could, he went away and brought it back the next day composed in excellent verse. Then they all recognized the grace of God in the man, and Hilda urged him to leave secular life and take monastic vows, receiving him into the monastery and bidding that he be instructed in the whole course of sacred history. Thereafter he composed many poems, none of any light or trivial matter, but only those that pertained to religion.

One of the most significant details in this account is Bede's reference to a general agreement that "for the sake of merry-making all should sing in turn" to the accompaniment of a harp passed from hand to hand. If we remember that, according to Bede, Caedmon's embarrassed withdrawal from the merry-making happened not once only but "sometimes", and that it apparently took place in a hamlet or on a farm near the monastery, and not in the monastery itself, the statement suggests the extent to which this early vernacular verse was memorized and sung among the people, as was the poetry of the popular ballads centuries later. Bede's statement, moreover, makes unmistakable the close association of the harp with the recitation of the vernacular verse, and the custom of passing the harp from hand to hand implies a general ability on the part of many to manage at least a few simple chords of accompaniment.[1] The harp was undoubtedly of the small type portrayed in the drawing of Tubal-Cain in the Junius manuscript. The instrument there shown is a short, twelve-stringed harp held on or between the knees of a seated figure, the sloping top resting below the minstrel's chin. It is interesting in this survey of the religious verse to remember that the first of the five references to the harp in the text of *Beowulf* is a mention of its use in Hrothgar's hall to accompany a minstrel's recitation of the Christian story of Creation.

This vernacular verse in which Caedmon began to write his religious poems at Whitby was composed in a four-stress, alliterative metre, with no fixed limit upon the number of unstressed syllables. The stressed syllables naturally carried the alliteration, and the Old English ear recognized both consonant and vowel alliteration. Any vowel was considered as alliterating with any other vowel. The line was divided into two half-lines of two stresses each by a definitely marked pause, or caesura.

Rhyme was little used, though not unknown. Not only end rhyme but also internal rhyme are found in occasional brief passages in a few poems; in the eighty-seven lines of the so-called *Riming Poem* both internal rhyme and end rhyme are used throughout. But the employment of rhyme in Old English verse is infrequent, and in its place alliteration supplies the fundamental decorative device.[2] Stanzaic division in poems is even more rare,

[1] Professor J. C. Pope, in his sensitive and illuminating study of Old English alliterative verse (*The Rhythm of Beowulf*, Yale University Press, 1942) shows the prevalence of the "rest" in the rhythmic pattern of the Old English poetic line, and makes it clear that one use of the harp was to maintain and stress poetic rhythm during recitation of the vernacular verse by accenting these "rests" in the line with chords struck on the harp.

[2] If the stressed syllables of a line are numbered from 1 to 4, the five alliterative patterns most frequently found may be indicated as follows: (1) 1A, 2A: 3A; (2) 1A: 3A; (3) 2A: 3A; (4) 1A, 2B: 3A, 4B; and (5) 1A, 2B: 3B, 4A.

though *Deor's Lament* and *Wulf and Eadwacer* show somewhat un-usual attempts at something like strophic pattern through the use of recurring refrain.

An illustration of this meter in simple form, as it was used in the earliest of this Christian verse, may be found in the nine lines of the *Hymn* inspired by Caedmon's dream-vision at Whitby:

Nu sculon herigean   heofonrices weard,
meotodes meahte   and his modgeþanc,
weorc wuldorfaeder   swa he wundra gehwaes,
ece drihten,   or onstealde.
He aerest sceop   eorþan bearnum
heofon to hrofe,   halig scyppend;
þa middangeard   moncynnes weard,
ece drihten,   aefter teode
firum foldan,   frea aelmihtig.

It is meet that we worship   the Warden of heaven,
The might of the Maker,   His purpose of mind,
The Glory-Father's work   when of all His wonders
Eternal God   made a beginning.
He earliest stablished   for earth's children
Heaven for a roof,   the Holy Shaper;
Then mankind's Warden   created the world,
Eternal Monarch,   making for men
Land to live on,   Almighty Lord!

In this vernacular metre Caedmon, received into the monas-tery at Whitby and by Hilda's bidding instructed in Scripture and doctrine, began to write the religious poems that Bede de-scribes. The *Ecclesiastical History* lists the themes that Caedmon versified. Included among them were the Creation and the whole story of Genesis, the Exodus of the Israelites from Egypt, the Incarnation, Passion, Resurrection, and Ascension, the Coming of the Holy Ghost, the teaching of the Apostles, the terrors of Judgment Day, the horrors of hell, and the sweetness of the heavenly life. Caedmon's versifications of these themes were so delightful to hear that even his instructors wrote them down and learned them, as he recited them. Bede tells us that certain others in England after Caedmon attempted to write religious poems, but that no one of them was able to equal him. When this statement was made the Cynewulfian poetry, of course, was yet to be written.

The opinion that the Junius manuscript contains the poetry of Caedmon has not stood up well under scholarly study of the manuscript and its contents. Indeed, the evidence of the poems themselves suggests that they are of widely varying dates, and by a number of different authors. For one thing, the *Genesis* is not one poem but a combined text of two. An earlier *Genesis*, (*A*), begins with the Rebellion of Lucifer and the Creation, and continues a versification of the Biblical Genesis through the Sacrifice of Isaac. But there is a break in this earlier *Genesis* at line 235 and a loss of most of the original material dealing with the Temptation and Fall of Man. The loss extends from the description of the four rivers of Paradise to the appearance of God in the Garden after the Fall, with the subsequent arraignment and sentencing of Adam and Eve. In order to fill this gap and supply the story of the Fall of Man, there had at some time been inserted 617 lines of a later *Genesis*, (*B*). Moreover, as will be seen,[1] this inserted story of the Fall of Man has a much more dramatic narrative style than *Genesis A*, and reveals linguistic and metrical characteristics that stamp it as a translation of an Old Saxon poem. The discovery of an Old Saxon poetic fragment in the Vatican Library corresponding to twenty-five lines of the inserted *Genesis B* made the old Saxon origin of this portion of the poem unmistakable. Caedmon, therefore, could not have written the whole of *Genesis* as we have it. The ascription to him of the other Junius poems seems likewise dubious. If any of the poetry in the Junius MS. can be attributed to his pen, it may possibly be the *Genesis A*.

[1] See Foreword, Chapter I.

When Francis Dujon published the first edition of the Junius poems, he described them as the monk Caedmon's "paraphrase" of Scripture. We shall see later how far the versified story of the Fall of Man went beyond a paraphrase of the Biblical Genesis. Nor can the word be properly applied to the other poems of the Junius MS. The *Exodus*, for example, gives evidence of being a carefully designed composite of themes derived from the liturgy for Holy Saturday. In its main narrative divisions the poem deals with the march of the Israelites to the Red Sea, the pursuit by the Egyptians, the divided waters and the Crossing, the destruction of the pursuing Egyptians and the hymn of Moses. Only a portion of the Biblical Exodus serves as material for the narrative, namely, Exodus xiii 17-xiv 31 and Exodus xv 1-21. Because of this very partial dependence on the Vulgate, and the numerous additions to the Vulgate material, it was thought for a time that a Latin poem of Avitus on the Crossing of the Red Sea, the *De Transitu Maris Rubri*, furnished an additional source.

It is probable, however, that the shaping influence in *Exodus* was not the *De Transitu* of Avitus, though the poem may well have been known to the Old English author, but the liturgy of the services for Holy Saturday, the ceremonies devoted in the medieval Church to the baptism of catechumens.[1] The introductions into the *Exodus* of extensive passages dealing with Noah's Flood and the Sacrifice of Isaac are puzzling by their seeming irrelevance. But the liturgy of Holy Saturday suggests a key to this juxtaposition of subject matter. The ritual included the reading of twelve "prophecies" or lections appointed for use throughout the ceremony. Among these were the stories of the Flood and the Crossing of the Red Sea, accepted symbols of baptism, and the narrative of the sacrifice of Isaac, a type of the heroic sacrifice required by the Christian warfare in which the catechumens were enlisting through baptism. If it can be assumed that a poet, deeply moved by the rich symbolisms of these

[1] See Bright, "The Relation of the Caedmonian *Exodus* to the Liturgy", *Modern Language Notes*, XXVII 97–103.

baptismal services, and under their influence, undertook a poem which would have as its chief theme the Crossing of the Red Sea, but with a subsidiary interweaving of other symbolic themes present in the ritual, we have an explanation of the unusual structure of the poem, and an evidence of liturgical influence in this early verse to parallel that which later shaped the *Advent Lyrics*.[1]

The third of these Caedmonian poems, the *Daniel*, based upon the Vulgate text of Daniel i-v, is an episodic narrative poem of the general type of *Genesis A*. A break in the manuscript leaves Belshazzar's Feast, and the poem, incomplete. The main episodes in which the poet is indebted to the Vulgate original are the capture of Jerusalem by Nebuchadnezzar, the setting up of the golden image and refusal of the three youths to worship, the ordeal of the fiery furnace, Nebuchadnezzar's madness and recovery, and Belshazzar's Feast and the prophetic writing on the wall. Two passages in the *Daniel* are of particular interest. Lines 279–332 are a variant version of the prayer of Azarias preserved in the Exeter Book. It seems likely that both versions go back to some common original. Lines 362–408 are a versification of a Latin canticle preserved among the Vespasian hymns, the *Cantus trium puerorum*. The presence of this passage in the *Daniel* may possibly indicate the liturgical use of the canticle.

The remainder of the Junius text has long been known as *Christ and Satan*. The lines divide into three entirely separate and distinct sections: the *Lamentations of the Fallen Angels*, the *Harrowing of Hell*, and a fragment of a poem on Satan's temptation of Christ based on the Biblical account in Matthew iv 1–11.[2] It seems probable that these three poetic sections, so clearly distinct and independent, are in fact three separate poems. The *Lamentations* are translated and discussed in Chapter I where they take their place in the stream of Hexaëmeral tradition. It is noteworthy that there is considerable similarity be-

---

[1] See Foreword, Chapter II.
[2] For a careful study of the structure of this section of the Junius MS., see Clubb, "Christ and Satan", *Yale Studies in English*, LXX 1925.

tween the material of the *Lamentations* and certain passages in the Cynewulfian *Life of St Guthlac*.[1] The long speech of the hermit-saint to the demons who persecute him, and its resemblance to passages in the *Lamentations*, seem to suggest the dependence of both poems, in this detail, on some unknown common original.

The *Harrowing of Hell* must derive, as its ultimate source, from the Apocryphal *Gospel of Nicodemus*, a fourth-century story of the Descent into Hell which was widely known throughout the Middle Ages. Its characteristic themes are found not only in *Christ and Satan*, but in the Exeter Book *Harrowing of Hell*, and in lines 558–85 of Cynewulf's *Ascension*. In this portion of the *Christ and Satan* the theme of the Descent is followed by shorter divisions of the text dealing with the Resurrection, Ascension, and Last Judgment.

The work of Cynewulf,[2] the second of the known religious poets, was written in the second half of the eighth century, in all probability some time between 750 and 783. Cynewulf's writing gives pervasive evidence of the ecclesiastical learning of a monastic Churchman combined with the literary sophistication of a conscious poetic art. Under his stimulus and the influence of his followers and imitators a Cynewulfian school of religious poetry dominated the second half of the eighth century and the first quarter of the ninth. The facts of Cynewulf's career somewhat reverse those of Caedmon's. Of Caedmon, the man, we know at least what Bede tells us, but, aside from the brief *Hymn*, we cannot speak with surety about his verse. On the other hand, we know definitely of four poems written by Cynewulf: the *Juliana*, *Ascension*, *Elene*, and *Fates of the Apostles*. Yet of the poet himself we know nothing. He is the shadow of a name.

We are able to identify these four poems as the work of Cynewulf by the presence of runic letters that spell his name interwoven in the text near the end of each poem. In the *Juliana* and *Elene* the name is spelled *Cynewulf*. In the *Ascension* and *Fates*

---

[1] See *Guthlac A*, 529–656.
[2] For an informative study see Sisam, *Cynewulf and His Poetry*, Oxford, 1933.

of the Apostles the *e* is omitted, and the form is *Cynwulf*. In these signatory passages, except in *Juliana*, the runes serve both as letters and as words. The runic letters catch the reader's eye, forming the poet's name. The word value of the runes, that is, their names, is a part of the text itself.[1] In the *Juliana* the runes are used as letters only, or possibly, in the case of the first six runes, as letters combined to spell words.

It is characteristic of the poet and of the age that the signatures which enable us to assign these four poems to Cynewulf with certainty were made not from a literary, but from a religious motive. It was not primarily a pride of authorship that led the poet to end these poems with his name in runic letters, but a desire that his readers may pray for him and pray for him *by name*. His motive is made clear in subjective passages that precede and follow two of the signatures, lines 715–29 of *Juliana*, and 88–91 and 105–9 of the *Fates of the Apostles*.

In the *Juliana* passage the runes, as was the poet's practice, are inset in a brief section descriptive of Judgment Day. When his name has been woven into the text the poet writes: "Then (at Judgment Day) I shall have need of mercy, that the saint may intercede for me with the Highest King. My need admonishes me, and great sorrow of heart; and I entreat every man who may recite this poem to remember me *by name* fervently and zealously, and to pray God that the Ruler of heaven, the Lord of might, may give me help on the Great Day, the Father and Spirit of comfort in the dread hour, the Judge of deeds and the dear Son when the Trinity, sitting in glory, in unity shall decree to every man throughout the radiant creation a reward accord-

---

[1] Certain letters in the modern English alphabet can be used as words, and therefore can be woven into a text in the manner of the Cynewulfian signatures. With a little licence in the use of Y, the Christian name Cyril will illustrate Cynewulf's method: "When an architect copies a well-designed building, it is easy to C Y there R sure to be dimensions which his trained I will warn him not to alter by even an L." For detailed discussion of Cynewulf's runic signatures see Carleton Brown, "The Autobiographical Element in the Cynewulfian Rune Passages", *Englische Studien*, xxxviii, 196–233.

ing to his works." Having completed his poetic account of the
martyrdom of St Juliana, and looking forward to the day when
his own spirit shall depart "to an unknown country", Cynewulf
asks for the prayers of his readers, and the intercession of the
saint whose story he has told.

In the *Fates of the Apostles* we find the same explanation of
the Cynewulfian signature, in this instance in somewhat more
extended form. Having written of the "fates" of the twelve
Apostles, Cynewulf adds a subjective passage requesting their
intercession for him: "Now I entreat any man who may be
pleased with this poem to beseech that holy band (the Apostles)
for help and peace and solace in my sadness. Truly, I shall have
need of kindly friends on that journey when, all alone, I go to
my long home." The poet's name, however, has not yet been
stated. Therefore, Cynewulf begins his runic signature with the
introductory words: "Here may a shrewd man who delights in
verse find out who wrote this poem." The rune passage follows,
ending with the statement: "Now mayest thou know who, in
these words, was unknown to men." The poet is now in position
to request that his readers pray for him *by name*: "May he remember it (the name), whoever may be pleased with this poem, and
ask aid and comfort for me. For I must make a journey out of this
world, far hence, alone, to visit a land I myself know not where."

The poet, of whose sensitive spirit we receive such intimate
glimpses in these signatures, and elsewhere in his verse, was the
great religious poet of the second half of the eighth century in
England. His four signed poems, with other poems that may be
his and the poems of other writers who moulded their style on
his, form a body of poetry that gives distinction to his period and
the years immediately following. Of the work of this Cynewulfian school a number of poems are translated in this volume:
the *Elene* and the *Ascension*, both signed by Cynewulf, the *Advent
Lyrics*, *Dream of the Cross*, and *Last Judgment*, which may or may
not be his, and the *Phoenix* and the *Mission of St Andrew*, which are
more probably the work of other poets writing under Cyne-

wulf's influence, or in continuance of the Cynewulfian tradition. These poems are all discussed in detail at their appropriate place in these translations.

Though no record exists to tell us of Cynewulf the poet, his
poems disclose the man. By the testimony of others we know
nothing of him. By his self-revelation we know much. Even the
variant spellings of his name in the runic signatures enable us to
make a conjecture as to the dating of his poems, and as to his
identity. In general use, the name Cynewulf was first spelled
Cyn*i*wulf. But the *i* tended to shift to an *e* about 750, and the *e* to
disappear entirely toward the end of the century. If one could
rely on this evidence, the *Elene* and *Juliana* could hardly have
been written before the middle of the eighth century, or the
Ascension and *Fates of the Apostles* much before 800. But usage in
proper names is often uncertain, and subject to locally varying
factors. The spellings of the signatures certainly suggest dates for
Cynewulf's signed poems in the second half of the eighth century. But it is not possible to be more precise. And it is noteworthy that this linguistic evidence at once comes into conflict
with autobiographical suggestions. For it is in the *Elene*, which
by this spelling test should be one of the earlier poems, that the
poet dwells on his age and speaks of himself as near death.

If we can assume that all Cynewulf's signed poems were written before 783, it is possible that he may have been the Bishop
Cynewulf of Lindisfarne who retired from office in 779 or 780,
and died some three years later. Of the various conjectures as to
the poet's identity this one seems the most probable. For the
poet was almost certainly an Anglian, and there is much in his
verse that suggests the scholarship and faith of the professional
ecclesiastic speaking with authority. The signed poems, moreover, give repeated evidence of intentional emphasis on Christian dogma. Stress on Trinitarian doctrine is made explicit in
both the *Juliana* and the *Ascension* by reference to the Trinity as
Three Persons in one God.[1] *Juliana* contains an affirmation of

[1] *Juliana*, 721–9; *Christ*, 773–4.

the Oneness of the Trinity.[1] The Son is the Only Begotten, co-eternal with the Father.[2] By the Incarnation and Passion mankind was redeemed,[3] of which redemption the symbol is the Cross.[4] The *Ascension* follows Gregory in an assertion that our Lord ascended *with our body*,[5] and exhorts to belief in this doctrine.[6] In this same poem Cynewulf contrasts the humble and loving mercy of the Incarnation and the stern and righteous justice with which Christ shall come again to judge all souls at Doomsday.[7] Man shall be judged according to his works,[8] and in accordance with his record of thought, word, and deed, will be assigned to glory, to purgatorial fire,[9] or to hell. This stress upon dogma, and upon the religious obligations of baptism, repentance, and confession, while there is still time, is a pervasive influence in this religious poetry, finding appropriate expression not only in the signed poems of Cynewulf himself, but in the work of those who carried on the Cynewulfian tradition.

Yet in spite of its intimate reflection of liturgy and doctrine and the Latin scholarship of the Church Fathers, this verse does not constitute a narrowly cloistered or ascetic poetry. In a great period of conversion such as England had known the progress of the Christian faith made sharp contacts with the daily life of the people. This was inevitable. And as a result of these contacts the religious poems, whatever their specific subject, were shot through with swift flashes of intimate acquaintance with the life of the world, and vivid suggestions of the daily observations and concerns of men. In Cynewulf's *Ascension*, for example, the conventional list of God's gifts to men is expanded by the poet's addition of some of the skills and occupations of contemporary English life. Brief pastoral similes were expanded in the *Phoenix*, in one instance producing a charming vignette of pastoral life through the four seasons. The busy stir of individuals gathered in a common purpose is reflected in such scenes as the

[1] *Juliana*, 726–7.   [2] *Christ*, 464–5.   [3] *Elene*, 179–81; *Christ*, 613–18.
[4] *Elene*, 1220–7.   [5] *Christ*, 755.   [6] *Christ*, 751–5.
[7] *Christ*, 785–91; 820–5.   [8] *Christ*, 782–5.   [9] *Elene*, 1295–1316.

hurrying groups that load St Helena's ships for the voyage, or the cannibal horde that crowds to the capture of St Andrew, or the sorrowing host that stands on the seashore weeping after the saint as his sail fades on the sea-line, or the armed host besieging a walled city that shapes Cynewulf's effective metaphor of the assaults of Satan in the *Juliana*.

Nor have monastery walls shut out from these poems a sense of landscape derived from the daily life of the people. The road that Abraham and Isaac take to the place of sacrifice is over "the high downs", and there is terror in the lonely landscape of *St Guthlac* until the fiends are driven out. There is a sense of far-off Eastern beauty and wonder in the charmingly elaborated landscape of the *Phoenix*, and a delight in the fragrant spices, sweetest blooming on earth, from sprigs of which the Phoenix weaves its funeral nest. A love of birds, and wild things of the wood, entered into the adornment of brief, lovely scenes in *St Guthlac*, that have parallels centuries later in the legend of St Francis of Assisi. In many a passage of this poetry the sea is present, as if over the next rise one might see the blue. And it is a sea of moods and deceptive might. Its reflections vary from the smiling Mediterranean expanses of St Helena's voyage to the cold, gray, stormy surges of the gale which the poet introduces into the story of St Andrew's voyage with the Lord whose seamanship he so greatly admired. And for Cynewulf's skilful pen, the sea furnishes the detail from which he fashions the well-wrought metaphor of man's earthly life with which the *Ascension* closes.

Most of all, the vitality of this religious verse grows from the fact that the Old English poets sang of what they believed, and of its supreme importance. The Caedmonian and Cynewulfian poetry was a poetry of firm convictions rooted in the Christian faith. Even the structure of these poems sometimes seems to show this influence. Just as the Apostles' Creed begins with an affirmation of belief in the "Maker of heaven and earth", so not infrequently the Cynewulfian poems, whatever their theme, will pause for brief, earnest recitals of the wonder and wisdom of the Creation. And as the Creed includes an affirmation of faith in the Christ "who shall come again to judge both the quick and the dead", so many of these poems end in brief epilogues descriptive of the Last Judgment and the life to come. Indeed, not infrequently poems that are described as episodic narratives are shaped by a controlling inner unity that corresponds to a sequence in the Creed. In the Caedmonian *Harrowing of Hell*, for example, the lines dealing with the Descent into Hell are followed by passages that deal in succession with the Resurrection, Ascension, and Last Judgment. Thus we have here a series of four united topics that have their corresponding parallels in a united series of affirmations in the Apostles' Creed.

With the early decades of the ninth century and the ever increasing inroads of the Danes, Northumbrian ascendancy in letters was drawing to a close. There is a small amount of religious poetry that seems to be late, presumably of this period. The *Genesis B* is probably of the ninth century, as may be also the poetical dialogues of *Solomon and Saturn*. The spirited narrative of *Judith* is perhaps as late as the early tenth century. Some scholars indeed have seen in it a kind of allegory of England's struggles against the Danes. Of the same general period would seem to be the Cambridge Corpus Christi *Doomsday* and the *Menologium*, a versified calendar of the months according to the various religious festivals of the Christian year.

But the century of the early raids, and later wide-spread conquests, of the Danes, with attendant plundering and destruction of churches and monastic foundations, was hardly a time propitious for the writing of verse, or its preservation. In the general devastation much that had been written must have been destroyed. And an era was ending. The stream of poetic composition that had been fed by the Christian culture of the monasteries and the great northern Schools of Jarrow and Durham and York dwindled in the bitter decades of heathen war, and the age of Northumbrian poetry came to a close. When the West

Saxons were finally able to throw back the Danish hordes and exact the terms of Wedmore in 878, a change was at hand. There was the beginning of a new ascendancy in the power of Wessex, and a shift of influence in letters from the northern Schools to the Court at Winchester, from the ecclesiastical learning of Bede and Alcuin to the humanism of Alfred. And with the dawning of the new age came an attendant change in the literary genius of the time from poetry to prose.

CHAPTER I

THE LOSS OF PARADISE

FOREWORD

THE Old English poetic account of the Rebellion of Lucifer, Fall of Man, and Loss of Eden is found in portions of the first and last poems in the Junius MS. These sections are the first 964 lines of *Genesis*, and the first 364 lines of *Christ and Satan*. Lines 1–91 of *Genesis* deal with the Rebellion and Fall of Lucifer. This material is supplemented by a series of dramatic "laments" of the fallen angels found in *Christ and Satan*. Lines 92–964 of *Genesis* are devoted to the story of Creation, and the Fall of Man. A second, and more spirited, version of the Rebellion of Lucifer is included in this section of *Genesis* (ll. 246–321), where it forms an organic and dramatic prelude to the tragic story of the loss of Eden.

The text of the Old English *Genesis*, a poem of 2,936 lines, is the work of at least two poets, possibly more. In 1875 Sievers[1] suggested that lines 235–851 are an interpolation into the original text, and that these lines are a translation into Old English from an Old Saxon poem composed by the author of the *Heliand*, or an imitator. Sievers' theory was in large measure verified by the discovery eighteen years later in the Vatican Library of an Old Saxon poetic fragment which corresponds precisely to lines 791–817 of the Old English *Genesis*.

Genesis divides, therefore, into two parts: lines 1–234 and 852 to the end, usually known as *Genesis A* or the *Earlier Genesis*; and the interpolated lines 235–851 known as *Genesis B* or the *Later Genesis*. Evidence is lacking for a precise dating of either poem, but scholars somewhat generally agree that *Genesis A* can be assigned to the end of the seventh or beginning of the eighth century; and *Genesis B* to the ninth.

Even the most casual reading of the epic narrative of the Fall of Man as set forth in the 617 lines of *Genesis B*, or the dramatic lamentations of Lucifer in *Christ and Satan*, will serve to prove that this poetic material goes far beyond paraphrase of the Biblical Genesis. We have here to do with creative poetry, vivid in detail and dramatic in mood, dealing with a wealth of material gradually brought together by medieval scholars and churchmen into a stream of association known

[1] *Der Heliand und die angelsächsische Genesis.*

27

as the Hexaëmeral tradition. This stream of tradition, moreover, was fed not only by the writings of scholars, but also by the poetic fancies and ingenious inventions of popular legend. This may be the case in the Old English prose dialogue of *Solomon and Saturn* where we are told that the substance of which Adam was created consisted of eight elements, each element one pound by weight: earth for his flesh, fire for his blood, wind for his breath, sky for his varying moods, gift-bounty for his fat and his growth, blossoms for the beauty of his eyes, dew for his sweat, and salt for his tears.

The Hexaëmeral tradition grew from material of various sources. Through the early Christian centuries a body of commentary grew up around the Hexaëmeron, or six days of the Creation, as recounted in the Biblical *Genesis*. A series of Lenten homilies by Bishop Basil of Caesarea on the Hexaëmeron was an early Christian work devoted exclusively to this theme. A similar *Hexaëmeron* by Ambrose, various homilies and commentaries of Gregory the Great, Bede's *Commentary on Genesis*, an Old English *Hexaëmeron* often attributed to Ælfric, such works as these illustrate the material that went to swell the Hexaëmeral stream. An apocryphal *Vita* of Adam and Eve added scope and detail to the story. As the tradition grew it widened until it had drawn into a kind of religious trilogy the associated themes of the Rebellion of Lucifer, the Creation, and the Fall of Man.

The Junius MS. contains a series of drawings illustrative of these themes. Although the series was never completed as planned, it extends beyond the story of Adam and Eve as far as the chronicle of Abraham. Both the Rebellion of Lucifer and the Fall of Man receive vivid illustration in these drawings. The Junius MS., therefore, has unique distinction as a combined literary and artistic preservation of a highly dramatic early rendering of the Loss of Eden. The setting forth of this material reaches highest poetic level, and receives most expanded treatment, in *Genesis B*. If the phrase be used with appropriate reservations it can be said that we are here dealing with an Old English "Paradise Lost".

The question has been frequently raised whether Milton knew this early treatment of the theme he used for his great work. The Junius MS. had been given by Archbishop Ussher to Francis Junius about

1651, and was published by him in Amsterdam in 1655. It is possible that Milton in some way learned of the contents of the Old English *Genesis B* during the twelve years that intervened before the publication of *Paradise Lost*, for there are here and there resemblances in detail and phrasing between the two poems. But, as his biographer Masson suggests,[1] it can well be that such likenesses as exist imply little more than strong conception of the same material by two independent poetic imaginations drawing from the same stream of tradition.

The question is perhaps academic. The really striking result of a comparison of the dramatic structure and motivation of the two poems is to be found, not in the similarities, but in the differences that exist between *Genesis B* and *Paradise Lost*, as well as between *Genesis B* and the Biblical Genesis. With all his elaborations and expansions the temptation scene as set forth by Milton can, on the whole, be reconciled with the account contained in the Biblical Genesis. The motivation of the temptation and fall in *Genesis B* is fundamentally different.

In the Biblical account the serpent, "more subtle than any beast of the field", approaches Eve with the question: "Yea, hath God said, Ye shall not eat of every tree of the garden?" Eve answers that they may eat of the fruit of the trees of the garden with the exception of the tree "which is in the midst of the garden" or, in the words of God's prohibition, "the tree of the knowledge of good and evil". In the day that they eat of that tree they shall "surely die". But the serpent asserts: "Ye shall not surely die. For God doth know that in the day ye eat thereof, then your eyes shall be opened, and ye shall be as gods, knowing good and evil." Beyond this assertion the Biblical account gives us no further detail of the serpent's seduction. We are simply told that "when the woman saw that the tree was good for food, and that it was pleasant to the eyes, and a tree to be desired to make one wise, she took of the fruit thereof, and did eat, and gave also to her husband with her, and he did eat."

In the temptation scene of *Paradise Lost*[2] Eve is tempted by Satan speaking through the mouth of the serpent, and with every device of specious argument and false logic that seduction can employ. But one point stands out clearly. The wearing by Satan of the serpent's form is

[1] *Life of Milton*, VI 557, note.   [2] *P.L.*, IX, 494–1004.

essential to Milton's development of the temptation of Eve. For when Eve marvels that the serpent, hitherto mute and without power of reason, now can address her in human discourse, the serpent replies that this fact is in itself proof of the desirable qualities of the forbidden fruit. For he, the serpent, has eaten of the fruit, and death has not come. Instead, his intelligence has been increased to human, and he has gained human powers of speech. If he, therefore, having eaten, has lived and by the operation of the fruit has been exalted to human powers, so also shall Eve eat and live, and receive increase of wisdom from human to godlike. Such, briefly, is a part of Satan's argument, and his assumption of the disguise of serpent form is essential to that argument.

It is interesting to note how differently the temptation is visualized in *Genesis B*. There a follower of Satan appears to Adam and Eve, not in the serpent's form, but disguised as an angelic messenger claiming to have been sent by God to revoke His ban upon the fruit of the forbidden tree. It is true the serpent is mentioned in the text (491), and receives parallel representation in the drawings of *Genesis B*. In each instance, before his appearance to Adam and Eve, he is twined in the branches of the tree about to pluck the forbidden fruit which he is later to offer to Eve. But in his appearance to Adam, and subsequently to Eve, the tempter has assumed angelic form and claims to be a messenger sent from God. Eve, at least, is completely deceived. Speaking to Adam (657-9), she refers to the tempter as a "good angel of God", and states that she can "see by his attire" that he is a messenger of the King of heaven.

The assumption of angelic form by agents of evil is, of course, by no means confined to the poem we are considering. It is a wily device employed by demons in legends of the saints, among others the Old English *Juliana*, and it is found in the apocryphal *Vita* of Adam and Eve. There, in order to persuade Eve to cease from doing penance in the waters of the river Tigris, Satan assumes angelic disguise, in that instance employed to allege falsely the remission of a penance, as in *Genesis B* it is used to allege falsely the revoking of a prohibition.

The operation of this dramatic device in *Genesis B* produces a temptation scene that differs markedly from those of Milton and the

Biblical Genesis. For in these accounts Eve sins knowingly and of free choice. In the Old English poem she is deceived into wrong-doing. The Old English text leaves us in no doubt on this point. In *Genesis B*, unlike the accounts in *Paradise Lost* and the Bible, the tempter first approaches Adam. By Adam he is quickly and stubbornly rejected, even though Satan's messenger represents himself as one coming "in God's service" to inform Adam and Eve that they may now eat of the fruit that was formerly forbidden. Adam's immediate reply is to recall God's warning that he be not beguiled, or ever tempted, to the tree of death. That warning came from God Himself. Of this tempter who claims to be God's messenger he knows nothing.[1]

It is only after this failure with Adam that the tempter in anger turns to Eve. Adam, he says, has scornfully rejected a new command sent by God. God's anger will be roused against them both, and disastrous evil will befall their children in time to come. The demon convinces Eve that Adam has wilfully set himself in stubborn disobedience to God, and that because of his scornful refusal they will incur grievous punishment, unless Eve can prevail on him to accept the heavenly messenger and his new command. In that case, the tempter promises not to report Adam's insolence. By the tempter's appearance, and by his attire, Eve is persuaded that he is what he claims to be, and accepts his words as true.

Therefore, she herself eats of the forbidden fruit in obedience to this new command and summons all her powers to persuade Adam, lest he be lost. The tempter had promised that she would receive increased powers to see afar, and to hear afar, through the operation of the fruit. For a brief period after she has eaten he confers upon her these powers. Her vision of God and His angels in glory, and the melody she hears of the hymns of heavenly rapture, she cites as evidence of the rightness of her act, in urging Adam to join her in acceptance of the new command. And in what she does there is no intention of wrong-doing. She did it all, the poet tells us, through "holdne hyge", a loyal heart.[2]

Here then is a temptation that has deceived the mind and puzzled the will. What are we to make of this presentation of the story of the Fall of Man, differing so markedly from the Biblical and Miltonic

[1] *Genesis*, 531–9.   [2] *Genesis*, 708–11.

accounts? What has become of man's disobedience in this version of the legend? Some such questions must have arisen in the mind of the poet himself, when he looked back over his poem, for he cries out in amazement: "It is a great wonder that the Eternal Lord God would ever permit so many of His servants to be misled by lies that came as good counsel!"[1]

The poet of *Genesis B* has visualized the cosmic evil of man's fall with a simple intensity of pity and fear that touches the heart. The absence of intellectual and moral subtleties, and the stark drama of the deception of innocence by malevolence and fraud, focuses the reader's attention on the lurking forces of destruction hidden in the choices of human life. The poem is likely to linger long in the memory of all who read it.

One mark in *Genesis B* of the Old Saxon background of this version of the Fall of Man is the Germanic quality of the poet's characterization of Lucifer. Early in the poem the poet tells the story of Lucifer's Rebellion and Fall as a prelude to the Fall of Man. The Saxon poet has dramatized Lucifer's revolt by the symbolization most vivid to the Germanic mind in visualizing Lucifer as a proud and arrogant prince guilty of disloyalty to his overlord. The *comitatus* relationship of retainer and leader implying on the one hand generosity and protection, and, on the other, loyalty and service, is here implicit as a symbol of the enormity of Lucifer's crime. His insubordination and presumption ring out in the defiant question: "Why should I fawn for His favour, or bow in submission? I may be God as well as He."

Once again a little later in the poem we feel the influence of the *comitatus* ideal. Lucifer after his fall is shackled hand and foot to the floor of hell. His strength is bound but his pride is still unbroken. Even in his bondage he seeks vengeance against the Almighty by injury to man. But in his helplessness he is forced to appeal to his followers for one to be his agent in this revenge. There is a Germanic irony in the fact that his appeal is couched in terms of *comitatus* duty, the loyalty he has himself rejected: "If ever of old to any thane I dealt out gifts of princely treasure, he could not repay me at any better time than now."

[1] *Genesis*, 595–8.

Genesis B subordinates in Lucifer the tragic sense of loss and vanished glory. The spirit of Satan here is still the spirit of rebellion. We must turn to certain of the lamentations in *Christ and Satan* to feel the enormity of his loss take hold on his heart. Nowhere in the Junius poems does the poignant memory of departed glory receive more vivid expression than in certain brief passages of *Christ and Satan*. Here again we are dealing with the material of tradition, for an interest in the state of mind of Lucifer after his fall was reflected in medieval commentaries and homilies, as for example in Gregory's 34th homily on the Gospels.

In Lucifer's lamentations in *Christ and Satan* the descriptions of his abasement in hell, though vigorously written, are often fashioned from details of physical horror. But once or twice in the lamentations the verse rises above this plane, and Lucifer's tragedy is spiritually conceived, and interpreted in terms of the celestial glories he once knew and has forfeited, rather than in terms of the tortures of damnation in which he is engulfed: "Alas," he cries, "that I may not reach with my hands to the heavens above, nor thither lift up mine eyes, nor hear with my ears the pealing trumpet sound, because from His seat I would have driven God's Son."[1]

Here is no massing of the details of physical terror to denote the depth of Lucifer's fall: no dragons and adders, no blast of frost or blazing flames, no hell-floor burning with poison, no moaning and gnashing of teeth. In their stead are the hands that strain upward and touch nothing. Eyes that look upward and see nothing. Ears that listen and hear no sound. Instead of the clear voice of the heavenly trumpet an unbroken silence. These are convincing images of eternal loss. Here the poet attains a sense of ruin that is infinite and inexpressible, suggested with a stress and elevation of phrasing unusual in such pictures in Old English verse.

There is another passage similar in dignity and power of imagery which should be coupled in memory with the passage just quoted. It is found near the end of *Christ and Satan* in a fragment dealing with the temptation of Christ by Satan as set forth in Matthew iv 1–11. It is in form an expansion of Christ's spurning of Satan that goes beyond the Scriptural passage. The lines are marked by a rhythm of exalted phras-

[1] *Christ and Satan*, 168–73.

ing suggestive of that found in the poetic imagery employed in God's questioning of Job in the great thirty-eighth chapter of the Book of Job. There God asks: "Where wast thou when I laid the foundations of the earth? declare if thou hast understanding. Who hath laid the measures thereof, if thou knowest? or who hath stretched the line upon it? Whereupon are the foundations thereof fastened? or who laid the corner-stone thereof?" So here Christ sends Satan back to measure the vast spaces of hell that he may know the power of Almighty God against whom he had rebelled:

> Know how broad and boundless, how bitter is hell.
> Measure it with your hands; take hold on its bottom;
> Explore till you know its limitless expanse.
> Measure it from above even to the abyss;
> Measure how broad the black mist stretches.
> When your hands have measured the height and the depth,
> The compass of hell, the grave-house grim,
> Then shall you find you have fought against God!"[1]

In such passages as these we have the ultimate, eternal outcome of Lucifer's revolt. The measureless limits of hell in all its dimensions are symbols of the infinite power of good over evil. Whatever more of horror may lurk in the vast expanses of hell, its grim darkness is pregnant with Satan's stunned and sudden recognition of God's almighty strength, and with his own despairing memories of celestial glory, once known and for ever forfeit.

[1] *Christ and Satan*, 698–707.

THE REBELLION AND FALL
OF LUCIFER

(Genesis 1–91)

It is proper and right   that we praise with our lips
And love with our hearts   the Warden of heaven,
The Lord of hosts.   He is Source of all strength,
Of all high creatures   Almighty King!
Never had He birth   nor any beginning;
Nor ever shall His glory   come to an end;
But always for ever   as Ruler He reigns
O'er angelic thrones.   Righteous and just
He held in high splendour   the courts of heaven
Which far and wide   were stablished and founded
By the might of God   for the sons of glory,
The wardens of souls.   The heavenly hosts
Knew joy and delight,   bright bliss with their Lord.

Great was their glory!   His mighty thanes
Honoured their Prince,   praised Him with gladness
As Lord of life,   had exceeding delight
In their Sovereign's splendour.   They knew no sin
Nor any evil,   but lived in peace
With their Lord for ever.   Naught else they knew
In the heavenly realms   save right and truth,
Till an angel prince   misled through pride
Fell into error.   Then they followed no longer
Their eternal welfare   but turned them away
From love of the Lord.   Loudly they boasted
In their banded strength   they would share with God
His glorious dwelling   spacious and shining.
Evil befell them,   envy and pride
And the angel's presumption,   he first who sought
To perform this folly,   to wake it and weave it.
Thirsting for battle   he boldly declared

(1–32)

He would build a home   and a high seat
In the northern regions   of the heavenly realm.
   Then God was wrathful,   enraged at the band
He formerly honoured   with grandeur and glory.
He built for those traitors   a wretched abode,
The terrors of hell   and fearful afflictions,
To reward their works;   made ready hell's dungeon,
The bottomless, joyless   abode of pain,
For the angel warden,   the exiled host.
He saw hell spread   in eternal darkness
Fraught with torment   and filled with flame,
With freezing cold,   red fire and smoke;
Dire the pain   He ordained in that prison.
Grimly begotten   their sins against God;
Grim in return   the reward He gave them!
   Savage-hearted   they said they willed
To seize the kingdom,   as they easily could.
But that hope failed them   when Heaven's High-King,
He the Most High   and Monarch of all,
Lifted His hand   against their host.
The fallen angels   foolish and false
Might not prevail   with force against God;
But He bowed their courage   and broke their pride;
In His anger deprived them   of triumph and power,
Of glory and splendour;   despoiled His foes
Of peace and blessing,   of honour and bliss.
By His sovereign strength   on His adversaries
With crushing ruin   He wreaked His wrath.
   His heart was hardened.   Grimly incensed
He grasped the rebels   with hostile grip;
Angry-hearted   He held them and broke them
And took from those traitors   their heavenly thrones.
Our Maker banished   and hurled from heaven
The insolent angels,   the faithless horde.
That hostile host,   those hateful spirits,

(32–68)

The Lord sent forth   on a long, long journey.
Their boasting failed;   their vaunt was broken,
Their force defeated,   their form defiled.
Thereafter those dark souls   dwelt in exile;
They had little cause   to delight in their lot,
But abased in hell-torment   wretched abode
Enduring woe   in the depths of darkness,
Suffering sorely   in sorrow and pain
A gruesome requital,   a grim reward,
Because they began   a strife against God.
    Then was peace once more   and repose in heaven,
Fair customs of concord,   a Leader beloved
By all His thanes,   and a glory growing
For the blissful band   that abode with God.
The citizens of heaven,   the home of glory,
Were once more united.   Dissension ceased,
Struggle and strife   between angel legions,
When the rebel spirits   bereft of light
Were hurled from heaven.   Behind them lay
In God's fair kingdom   far-stretching seats
Filled with abundance   of growing gifts,
Verdant and sunny,   vacant of dwellers,
After the evil angels   were cast into hell
And imprisoned deep   under locks of pain.

(68–91)

D

LAMENTATIONS OF THE
FALLEN ANGELS

(Christ and Satan 1—364)

It was manifest   that the Maker had power,
Virtue and strength,   when He stablished the world!
Himself, He created   the sun and moon,
Stones and earth   and the streams of ocean,
Water and clouds   by His wondrous might;
In His sway the Measurer   wide encircles
The deep expanse   and mid-earth's space.
He Himself,   God's own Son,
May search out the sea,   the depths of ocean,
And fully reckon   the showers of rain,
Every drop.   The number of days
Himself He ordained   by His single might.
In six days the Shaper   in heaven on high
In the glory of majesty   made and established
The dales of earth   and the deep sea.
Who hath perception   to fully discern
His great design   save Eternal God?

Joys He appointed,   manhood and peoples,
Adam first   and the famous race,
The angel princes   who later perished.
It seemed to their minds   it so might be
That they themselves   were the lords of heaven,
Wielders of glory.   But worse befell
When in hell's depths   they found a home,
One after one   in that woeful pit
Where they needs must abide   the burning fires
And searing pain,   no more possessing
The light of heaven   or her high-built halls;
But must needs plunge down   to the depths of flame,
Far under ground   to the bottomless abyss

(1–31)

Ungorged and greedy.   God only knows
How He had sentenced   that sinful host.
   There out of hell   the Old One bellows
With bitter outcry   and baleful voice
Bewailing his woe: "Whither is fled
The wealth of bliss   we should have in heaven?
This is the home of darkness   dreadfully bound
With fettering bonds of fire.   The floor of hell
Is a blaze of flame   burning with poison.
Not far is the end   when we all together
Must suffer torment,   torture and pain,
No longer possessing   the splendour of glory
In heaven above,   or joy in her high halls.
   "Lo! once of old   before the face of God
In happier hours   we knew heavenly bliss
Singing in glory,   where now round Eternal God
The righteous dwell   in heaven's high hall
Adoring the Lord   with words and works,
While I in this torment   must abide in bonds,
Nor hope for a better home,   because of my pride."
   Then unto him made answer   the foul fiends
Bemoaning their misery,   sinful and black:
"By your lies you taught us   not to serve the Lord.
To you alone it seemed   you had power over all,
Over earth and heaven;   that you were Holy God,
The Shaper Himself.   But now you are one of the fiends
Fettered fast   in this bondage of fire!
In your glory you weened   that you owned the world,
Had power over all things,   and we angels with you.
Foul is your aspect!   The worse have we fared
Through your lying words.   You told us as truth
That your son was the Shaper,   the Maker of man.
Now is your torment   and torture the greater!"
   So the sinful spirits   spoke to their leader
With taunting words   in their bitter woe.

(32–67)

Christ had banished them,   stripped them of bliss.
They had lost in heaven   the light of God
Through their haughty pride.   They had for their hope
The floors of hell   and burning affliction.
Swart of hue,   misshapen monsters,
Those wretched spirits   roamed through hell,
Through the loathsome pit,   because of the pride
They formerly flaunted.   The lord of the fiends
Cried out again   as groaning in terror
He felt the weight   of his heavy woe.
He spat out sparks   beginning his speech,
Fire and poison.   No pleasant delight
Was the anguish he uttered   out of his pain:
     "I was a holy angel   in heaven of old
Dear unto God;   knew delight with the Lord,
Great joy with our Maker;   this multitude likewise.
But I planned in my heart   to hurl from His throne
The Splendour of glory,   the Son of God;
To rule over all things   with this wretched band
Which I have brought home to hell.   Clear was the token
When I was cast down to perdition,   deep under earth
To the bottomless pit.   I have brought you all
From your native home   to a house of bondage.
     "Here is no glory of wealth,   no wine-hall of the proud,
No worldly joys or angelic,   no hope of heaven.
This foul home flames with fire.   I am God's foe!
Ever at the doors of hell   dragons stand guard
Fierce and flaming.   Hope not for help from them!
This terrible home   is filled full with horror.
We have nowhere to hide our heads   in the gloom of hell,
Or cover ourselves in the depths   with shadows of darkness.
Here is the adder's hiss!   Here serpents dwell!
Firmly the bonds of pain   are fastened upon us.
Fierce are the fiends of hell,   dusky and dark.
Day never lightens this gloom   nor the glory of God.

(67–105)

"Once of old I had might   and dominion of glory;
But now in this foul abode   I must needs abide
What sentence the Lord may assign   in hell for my sin.
I have led a host of fiends   to this dismal home.
And yet at times   I shall take my flight
And wing my way   over homes of men,
And many of you who had part   in our arrogant pride.
We can not now have hope   that the King of glory
Will grant us a dwelling and home   as He did of old,
Or everlasting sway,   for the Son of God
Has power to rule over all   with blessing and bane.
Therefore, o'erwhelmed and accursed,   I must wander in exile
Shorn of glory   and stripped of strength,
Nor ever again know joy   with the angels in heaven
Because of old I declared   I was King of glory
And Lord of all.   But my lot was the worse!"
    So the miserable spirit   bemoaned his plight
Sentenced in hell;   and a surge of fire
Mingled with poison   filled the foul pit.
    "I am so large of limb   I may not lie hid
In this wide hall,   wounded with my sins.
At times cold and heat   in hell are mingled;
At times I can hear   the hell-slaves howl,
A wretched race   bewailing this realm of pain
Deep under the nesses   where naked men
Strive with serpents.   All this windy hall
Is filled with horror.   Never shall I know
A happier home,   city or stronghold,
Nor ever mine eyes have sight   of the gleaming world again.
    "Worse is it now for me   that ever I knew
The gleaming light of glory   with angels on high,
And the harmonies of heaven   where hosts of the blessed
Encircle the Son of God   with sweetest song.
No evil can I bring   on any soul
Except those only   whom God casts out.

(106–146)

These I may have in thrall   in the bondage of hell,
Bring to their long abode   in the bitter abyss.
    "How unlike are we all   to those earlier days
When once we had beauty in heaven,   honour and bliss.
Often the sons of God   sang hymns of glory
When as thanes about our Beloved   we praised the Lord,
Sang glory to God.   But now I am stained with my sins,
Branded with evil;   now burning with fire
I must bear on my back   the bondage of torment,
Hot in hell,   without hope of good."
    And still the Foul Fiend,   shepherd of sins,
Cried out of hell   in torment accursed.
The words he spoke   flew forth in sparks,
Most like to poison   as he poured them out:
    "Farewell to the glory of God!   Farewell to the Helm of hosts!
Farewell to the might of the Maker!   Farewell to the world!
Farewell to the light of day   and the grace of God!
Farewell to the angel host!   Farewell to heaven!
Alas! that I have lost   those lasting joys!
Alas! that I may not reach with my hands   to heaven above,
Nor thither lift up mine eyes,   nor hear with my ears
The pealing trumpet sound,   because from His seat
I would have driven God's Son   and seized for myself
Dominion of glory and grace.   Worse fate befell
Than I could foresee.   From the shining host I am severed,
Cast down out of light   to this loathsome home.
    "I cannot now conceive   how I sank thus low
Into this steep abyss,   stained with my sins,
Cast out from the world.   But well I know
That he shall for ever be banished   from eternal bliss
Who planneth not to obey   the Prince of heaven
And to please the Lord.   Now must I suffer pain,
Torment and misery   and mortal woe,
Stripped of all good,   stained by my former deeds,
Because I thought to o'erthrow   the Lord from His throne,

(147–186)

The Ruler of hosts.   Now wretched and ruined
My ways shall be exile,   my wanderings wide."
　　Then abased and humbled   he plunged into hell,
The Foe of God   and his followers with him
Rapacious and greedy;   God drove them down
Into that house of fire   whose name is Hell.
　　Therefore let every man   ever be mindful
That he stir not to anger   the Son of God;
Let him mark the fate   of the black fiends
Who for arrogant pride   utterly perished.
Let us take delight   in the Lord of hosts
And celestial joys   with the Lord of angels.
He showed His strength   and fullness of might
When He drove out of heaven   those captives to hell.
Let us be mindful   of the Mighty Lord,
The God of all creatures,   and dwell in glory
With the King of all kings   whose name is Christ.
Let us bear in our bosoms   kindly thoughts,
Meekness and wisdom,   remembering right and truth
When before His high throne   we bow our heads
Beseeching Almighty God   for mercy and grace.
　　Well it behoveth him   who dwelleth here
In worldly bliss   that he shine in beauty
When he seeks at the last   that other life,
That land more beauteous   than this world can be.
There it is fair and lovely   with fruits that shine
Bright o'er earth's cities,   a spacious realm,
The home of the happy in heaven   chosen of Christ.
Let us turn thither   where He sits Himself
The Saviour God,   Giver of triumph.
Round His high throne   stand angel hosts
Shining and bright,   the band of the blessed,
Heaven's holy legions   praising the Lord
With words and works.   World without end
They shall shine in grace   with the King of glory.

(187–223)

Then further still   the fiends confessed,
As I have heard tell.   Heavy upon them
Lay the soil of their sin   and the weight of their woe.
They had forsaken   in stubborn pride
The King of glory.   Again they spoke:
  "Now is it seen   that we sinned in heaven,
In our home on high.   Therefore for ever
We must wage vain war   on the might of God.
We could have lived   in the light of glory
If we only had hearkened   to Holy God
And around His throne   served Him in thousands,
Singing His praises.   There we abode in bliss
Hearing the heavenly strains   and the trumpet's sound.
Sublime of speech   rose the Shaper of angels
Before Whose splendour   the saints bowed down.
Triumphant arose   the Eternal Lord
High over us standing   with His dear Son,
The Shaper of souls,   showering blessing
Each day on the sinless.   And God Himself
Showed mercy on all   those mounting souls
Who believed on Him   in their lives on earth.
  "But to me it seemed   that the Prince was stern
And bitter-minded.   Then I went about
Among the angels   telling them all:
  'Lo! I can teach you   eternal good
If you trust my strength.   Let us spurn this Prince,
The Lord of hosts;   gain the light of glory
All for our own.   This is idle boasting
That we once endured   all this while.'
  "And so it came   that we strove together
To drive the Lord   from His dear home,
The King from His city.   Now is it seen
We must dwell in exile   in the depths of hell!
It is God Himself   Who holds the sway!
He only is King   Whose wrath overcame us,

(224–260)

The Everlasting,   the Lord of might.
And now this array   must rest in their sins,
Some winging through air   in flight over earth,
Each mantled in fire   though he mount on high;
Yet he may not lay hand   on those happy souls
Who from earth seek heaven.   But the heathen hordes,
God's foes, I may hold   and drag into hell.
Some shall roam   through the realms of earth
And sow dissension   in the tribes of men.
But here I must suffer   heart-sick and sad
Every sorrow,   bewailing the woe
Of the bitter war   that I waged in heaven.
Will Eternal God   ever grant us again
To have a home   in the heavenly kingdom,
A realm to rule,   as He did of old?"
So grieved God's foes   in the heat of hell;
God's wrath had been roused   by their impious evil.

   Therefore let every man   of living men
Whose heart is good   take thought to guard him
From sinful thoughts   and shameful vices.
Let us be mindful   of the might of God
And prepare green paths   up to the angels,
Where sits the Almighty.   God's own Son
In His arms will enfold us   if only on earth
We early take thought   and trust His help.

   Then will God not forsake us,   but will grant us life
And blessed joy   above with the angels.
There He will show us   a steadfast home,
Bright city-walls,   where blessed souls
Shall gleam in glory   sundered from sorrow,
Thenceforth for ever   possessing a city,
A noble seat.   Let us make it known!
Let us determine   in this earthly time
To unlock with skill   the secrets of God,
And grasp their meaning   by spiritual grace.

(260–300)

Then a thousand angels   shall throng to meet us
If we may heavenward   make our way,
And have earned this bliss   in our lives on earth.
    He shall be blessed   who despises sin,
Who is pleasing to God,   putting down evil.
Our Ruler hath told us: "The righteous shall shine
Apparelled in splendour,   most like to the sun,
In their Father's realm,   in the City of Refuge."
Then the King Himself,   the Lord of mankind,
In His peace shall enfold them,   lovingly lift them
To the light of heaven   where they may live
For ever with God,   knowing joy of joys
With the Lord for ever,   world without end.
    Alas! how rashly   the wretched Fiend
Resolved not to hearken   to heaven's King,
The Comforting Father!   The floor of hell
Flamed with poison   under the captives' feet.
The fiends went howling   through that windy hall
Bewailing their evil,   their sin and woe;
Lo! all that band   were burning with fire.
Fearful their fate   when he who led them,
Their prince, was fast   in fire and flame,
A torture unending!   And all his thanes
Must dwell for ever   in that dreadful home,
Never hearing the holy joy   in heaven above
Where long they had service so sweet   with angels on high.
For their transgression   they had lost all good,
And might have no dwelling   save the deep abyss
And the fires of hell,   the cursed hall
Where the noise of wailing   is known afar,
A gnashing of teeth   and the moaning of men.
    They have no hope   but frost and fire,
Pain and sorrow   and swarming serpents,
Dragons and adders,   and a home of darkness.
He might hear, who stood   as far from hell

(300–337)

As twelve miles distant,   a gnashing of teeth
Loud and grievous.   The foes of God
Wandered through hell   flaming with fire
Below and above;   all about them was woe.
Racked with torment,   bereft of joy,
Shorn of glory,   they bitterly grieved
That ever they dreamed   while they dwelt in heaven
They could wrest from the Saviour   His celestial realm;
But He rightfully held   the household of heaven,
Those courts on high   and His holy throne.
    There is none so sage,   so shrewd of heart,
So understanding,   save God Himself
Who can truly tell   of the light of heaven,
How a splendour shines   by the might of God
On that glorious host   in radiance gleaming;
Where angel legions   know lasting joy
And the saints sing hymns   unto God Himself.
Then are they blessed   who come from earth
And bear in their bosoms   fragrant blooms
And winsome herbs   (which are words of God).
The Father of men   in His arms shall enfold them,
With His right hand bless them,   lead them to light
Where they may have life   for ever and ever,
A bright city-dwelling,   a home on high;
He shall know bliss   who obeys his Saviour.
It is well with him   who may win that reward!

(338–364)

THE FALL OF MAN

(Genesis 92—964)

Then our Lord pondered   how to people again
With a better host   His ample creation,
The native settlements   and sun-bright seats
High in heaven   whence the insolent angels
Had been driven out.   Holy God ordained
By His sovereign strength   that earth and sky
And the stretching sea   should be established
Under compass of heaven;   earth-creatures in stead
Of the rebel host   that He hurled from on high.

   As yet was naught   save shadows of darkness,
But the wide abyss   stood deep and dim,
Alien to God,   empty and idle.
The Steadfast King   beheld and saw
The vast expanse   devoid of joy;
Saw black mist brooding   in eternal night
Dark under heaven,   wan and waste,
Till the world was made   by the word of the Maker.

   There in His might   the King of all creatures,
Almighty Monarch,   Eternal Lord,
Shaped heaven and earth;   stretched out the sky;
Laid out the limits   of the spacious land.
Not yet was the wide earth   green with grass
But the black seas bathed it;   dusky floods
Covered it over   with endless dark.
Then shining in glory   the spirit of God
Moved on the waters   with wondrous might;
The Lord of angels,   Giver of life,
Bade light shine out   o'er the bounds of space.
Swift was fulfilled   the command of the Maker;
At His word holy light   broke over the waste.

   The Victor-Lord   divided asunder

Light from darkness   over the deep,
Shadow from shining.   The Lord of life
Gave each a name;   by the word of God
Was light called Day,   a dazzling birth.
In this first of days,   in Creation's dawn,
Was God well pleased   as He saw the shadows
Dissolve and vanish   o'er the spacious ground.

  Then day went flying   o'er the frame of earth;
And after the light   our Lord thrust on
The first of evenings.   On the feet of day
Pressed darkling gloom;   God named it Night.
Our Saviour sundered them;   ever thereafter
They worked God's will   over earth for ever.

  The second day dawned,   light after darkness;
In the midst of the waters   the Lord of life
Formed the fair firmament;   with mighty power
Raised up the heavens   high above earth.
By His holy word   the waves were divided,
Water from water,   under the sky.

  Then a third bright morning   broke over earth.
Not yet were the wide land   and the far ways
Useful to God;   but the spacious ground
Lay fast enshrouded   in enfolding floods.
Then the word of the Lord   commanded the waters
To come together,   where, gathered and joined,
They kept their course   and their place appointed.
Suddenly, wide-stretching   lay the sea
Outspread under heaven   as the Holy One bade
When the Lord set asunder   water and land.
The Warden of life,   the Lord of hosts,
Beheld the dry land's   ample limits,
The King of glory,   and called it earth.
For the waves of the flood,   the far-flung seas,
He appointed a path   and fettered their flowing. . .[1]

---

[1] Because of a break in the MS. at this point, narrative is missing for part
of the third, all of the fourth and fifth, and part of the sixth, days of Creation.

To the Ruler of heaven   it seemed not right
That Adam longer   should be alone
As watcher and warder   of Paradise,
His new creation.   The Almighty King
Wrought him an helpmeet;   the Lord of life
Created woman   and shaped her as stay
To His dear man;   dismembered the substance
Of Adam's body;   cunningly borrowed
A rib from his side.   He was fast in slumber,
Softly sleeping;   he knew no pain
Nor any pangs.   There welled from the wound
No whit of blood,   but the Warden of angels
Drew from his body   a living bone
And the man was unhurt.   From it God fashioned
A lovely woman;   breathed in her life,
Everlasting spirit.   They were like to the angels
When Eve, bride of Adam,   was blessed with soul.

By God's might both   were born upon earth
In the splendour of youth.   They knew no sin
Nor any evil,   but love of the Lord
Burned in their breasts.   The Kind-hearted King,
Creator of all,   blessed the first of mankind,
Father and mother,   the woman and man.

Our Maker decreed: "Bring forth and increase,
Fill earth with your offspring,   with daughters and sons.
Ye shall have sway   o'er the salt sea-floods,
Over all Creation.   Enjoy earth's wealth,
The fish of ocean,   the fowls of the air.
The herds I have hallowed,   the beasts of the wild,
All living creatures   that move on land,
All living things   that the floods bring forth
Throughout the sea,   to you shall be subject."

Then God saw the wonder   and grace of His works,
The numberless fruits   of His new Creation.
Inviting and pleasant   Paradise lay

(169–209)

Filled with good gifts   and abundant blessings.
Welling fountains   and flowing springs
Bountifully watered   the winsome land.
No driving clouds   dark with wind
Till then bore rains   o'er the roomy earth,
Yet the land lay enriched   and laden with increase.
    From this new Paradise   four fair rivers
Flowed in their courses,   sundered and shaped
From one fair stream   and sent over earth
By the might of God   when He made the world.
One is called Pison   which compasses round
Havilah's soil   with its shining waters.
In that fair country   from far and near
The children of men   find gold and gems
All of the best,   as the books tell us.
The second river   lieth around
The Ethiopians'   wide domain,
A goodly kingdom.   Its name is Gihon.
The third is Tigris   whose teeming floods
Limit and bound   the Assyrian land.
Likewise the fourth,   which many a folk
Call the Euphrates. . . .[1]
"Enjoy every other,   from this one tree refrain;
Beware of its fruit!   Nor shall ye know want,
Or dearth of good things."   Then they bowed them down
Before heaven's Lord   and with grateful hearts
Gave thanks for His counsels.   The Steadfast King
Let them live in that land;   the Holy Lord
Returned into heaven.   His handiwork
Dwelt together on earth,   knew naught of grief
Nor any care,   but only to cleave
To the will of the Lord.   They were God's beloved

[1] Another break in the MS. cuts off the account of the Creation at this point.
The narrative is resumed with a portion of God's speech to Adam and Eve
warning them against the fruit of the forbidden tree.

(209–244)

As long as they heeded   His holy word.
    With mighty hand   the Holy Lord,
All-Ruling God,   had stablished and strengthened
Ten angel orders   in whom He trusted
That they would serve Him   and work His will,
Since the Holy Lord   with His hands had shaped them,
Had given them reason   and granted them bliss.
    He made one so strong,   so mighty of mind;
Gave him such power   next unto God
In the heavenly kingdom;   shaped him so shining;
So fair the form   God fashioned for him;
That his beauty was like   to the blazing stars.
He should have said praises   and prayers unto God,
Prizing his bliss   and blessing in heaven;
Should have thanked his Lord   for His gifts in light
Which God would have let him   long enjoy.
But he turned it all   to a terrible outcome;
Began to stir up   strife against God,
Heaven's Highest Ruler   on His holy throne.
    He was dear to our Lord,   nor long was it hid
That His angel was growing   ungrateful and bold.
He rebelled against God   with scoffing and boasting,
Refusing to serve Him;   said his form was fair,
Bright and shining   and brilliant of hue.
He found it not   in his heart to be faithful,
To serve his Lord   or be subject to Him.
It seemed to his mind   that he had more might
And a greater following   than Holy God.
Many words of presumption   the angel spoke;
By his own strength only   he thought to construct
A mightier throne   and a higher in heaven.
He said that his mind   moved him to fashion
And establish a stronghold   in the north and west.
He said that he doubted   he would still serve God.
    "Why must I slave?   What need (quoth he)

(245–278)

That I serve a master?   My hands have might
To work many wonders.   I have strength to rear
A goodlier throne,   a higher in heaven.
Why must I yield   or fawn for His favour
Or bow in submission?   I may be God
As well as He.   Brave comrades stand by me,
Stout-hearted heroes   unfailing in strife.
These fighters fierce   have made me their leader;
With such may one plan   and muster support.
They are loyal friends   and faithful of heart;
I may be their lord   and rule this realm.
So it seems not good   that I grovel before God
For any boon.   I will obey Him no longer."
   Now when the Almighty   had heard these words,
How the arrogant angel   was rousing revolt
From his Lord and Leader   in insolent folly,
Needs must he pay   for that deed of pride,
Know the pain of that struggle,   and suffer his punishment,
Most dreadful of deaths.   So every man shall,
Whoever wickedly   wars against God,
The Lord of might!   Heaven's Ruler was roused
And hurled him in wrath   from his heavenly throne.
He had gained God's hate,   forfeited His favour;
The heart of his Lord   was hardened against him.
Needs must he plunge   to the pit of torment
For his prideful strife   against heaven's Prince.
God cast him from favour   and flung him to hell,
To the deep abyss   where he was changed to a devil,
The Fiend and his followers.   They fell from heaven,
Three days and three nights   from heaven to hell;
And God changed them all   from angels to fiends.
   Because they dishonoured   His words and His works
God sent them from light,   set them defeated
Deep under earth   in the darkness of hell.
There through the endless   hours of night

(279-313)

E

The fiends must suffer   relentless flame;
Then, when dawn breaks,   blows from the east
Biting wind   and bitter-cold frost.
Ever in anguish   they suffer the pain
Of fire or spear-point   set for their penance.
Woefully, swiftly   their world was changed;
God filled with His foes   the fires of hell.

　　The angels thereafter   held the heavenly heights,
Who had won God's favour.   The others, the fiends,
Lay in the fire;   they had waged fierce war
Against their Prince.   They suffer pain,
A blaze of heat   in the bosom of hell,
Broad flames of fire   and bitter smoke,
Black darkness and gloom.   They revolted from God;
The folly they planned,   and their pride, betrayed them.
Because they would not   honour God's word,
Great was their punishment!   Into the pit,
To the burning bosom   of hell's abyss
They fell through folly,   presumption and pride;
Found another land,   that was void of light
And filled with fire,   a flaming death.
The fiends soon found,   to punish their pride
And their arrogant insolence   most of all,
They had met through God's might   a measureless woe.

　　Then spoke the proud prince,   once fairest of angels,
Most shining in heaven,   beloved of his lord,
Dear to his leader,   till error misled him
And Almighty God   was roused to wrath.
He cast him down   to the depths of torment,
The couch of corpses,   and named him anew;
Said his name thenceforth   should be known as Satan;
He bade him reign over   Hell's black abyss
And never again   contend with God!

　　Then spoke Satan   in sorrow of spirit,
Who must henceforth rule   o'er the depths of hell.

(314–349)

Once he was white,   God's angel in heaven,
Till his heart betrayed him,   his haughty pride,
And he would not obey   or honour the word
Of the Lord of hosts.   Hell's heat was around him,
His heart surged within him;   he spoke these words:
    "Unlike indeed   is this narrow land
To that other home   that of old we held
In heaven's high realm,   though we could not keep
What our Lord had granted,   or govern our kingdom
Against God's will.   He has wrought us wrong,
In hurling us down   to the fiery depths of hell,
Deprived of heaven.   He has marked those heights
For man to settle.   'Tis my greatest sorrow
That Adam, fashioned   and formed of earth,
Should hold my high seat   and abide in bliss
While we suffer this torture,   this torment in hell.
    "Woe! Alas!   Could I lift my hands
And feel their strength,   be free for an hour,
One winter hour,   with this host I would—
But bands of iron   bind me about,
Sorely the rings   of my bondage ride me!
I am stripped of my kingdom.   Firmly hell's fetters
Are fastened upon me;   the fires burn
Above and below.   A loathlier landscape
I never have seen,   flame unassuaged
Surging through hell.   These clasping shackles,
These cruel-hard chains,   hinder my going.
Hell's doors are bolted,   the ways are barred,
My hands are fastened,   my feet are bound,
I can no way get free   of these fettering chains.
Gratings huge   of heavy iron,
Hammered hot,   press hard upon me,
Wherewith God has fastened me   firm by the neck.
I know full well   that He knew my purpose
Of evil for Adam   and all his hopes

(349–387)

Of the heavenly realm,   had I power of my hands.
    "But now we endure   the darkness of hell,
Its bottomless fires   blazing and grim.
God has banished us   into the black mists!
Though He may not charge us   with any evil
Or any wrong   that we wrought in that realm,
He has cut us off from light   and cast us down
To the worst of all woes.   Nor may we requite it,
Or repay Him with harm   Who deprived us of light.
    "He has marked out the margins   of middle-earth
And created man   in His own image
By whom to re-people   the plains of heaven
With pure souls.   We must earnestly ponder
How we on Adam   and on his offspring,
If ever we can,   may avenge this wrong
And pervert His will   by any device.
    "No longer have I any   hope of that light
That He thinks long to enjoy   in bliss with His angels,
Nor may we in any way   soften the mood
Of Almighty God.   Since we may not regain it
Let us wrest heaven's realm   from the sons of men,
Make them forfeit His favour,   break His command.
Then His rage will be kindled.   He will cast them from grace;
They shall be banished   to hell's grim abyss.
We shall have them to serve us,   the sons of men,
As slaves fast-bound   in these fettering bonds.
    "Begin now to plan   and plot this assault!
If to any thane ever   in days of old
When we dwelt in that good kingdom   and happily held our thrones
I dealt out princely treasure,   at no dearer time
Could he give me requital,   repayment for gifts,
If some thane would be my helper   and outward hence
Break through these bolted gates,   with strength to wing
On feathered pinions   circling in the sky
To where new-shaped on earth   Adam and Eve

(388–419)

Abide in bliss   surrounded with abundance,
While we are cast out hither   to this deep hell.
    "They now indeed   are dearer unto God
And have the wealth   that we should have in heaven,
Our rightful realm.   The advantage lies with man!
My soul is sorrowful,   my heart is sore
That they should hold   the heavenly realms for ever.
If one of you can win them   in any way
To forsake God's law,   they will lose His love;
If they break His commandment   His mood will be roused
And all their wealth   will be changed for the worse,
Their punishment made ready,   some penalty grim.
Take thought how you may ensnare them.   More softly then
Shall I lie in these chains   if they lose the heavenly kingdom.
Whoever shall bring that to pass   shall have portion for ever
In all we may win of advantage   in these wide flames.
I will let him sit next myself   who returns to tell,
In this hot hell,   that the will of the King of heaven
Unworthily they forswore   by their words and works . . ."[1]
    Then God's enemy   began to arm,
To put on his war-gear.   He had a wily heart.
He placed on his head   the helmet of darkness,
Fastened the buckles   and bound it firm.
He had craft of speech   and cunning of word.
He circled upward   and darted out
Through the portals of hell.   (He had a pitiless heart.)
Fell of purpose   he soared in flight
Cleaving the fire   with fiendish craft.
He wished to ensnare   God's servants in sin,
Seduce and beguile them   until they had gained God's hate.
    With fiendish cunning   he found his way

[1] At this point in the MS. a leaf or two is missing. The lost text must have dealt in some detail with the response to this *comitatus* appeal of the chained and shackled Satan. Evidently one of his followers came forward and was accepted as his agent in evil. As the text continues after the break, this deputy of Satan is pictured as "God's enemy" arming himself for the work of revenge.

(420–453)

To where on earth   he came upon Adam,
God's own handiwork   wisely fashioned
And Eve beside him,   fairest of women,
Serving God well   in all good works
For the Maker of man   had made them His stewards.

  By them two trees stood   filled with fruit
And clothed with increase.   Heaven's High King,
The Almighty, had set them   that the sons of men
Might choose of good or evil,   weal or woe.

  Unlike was their fruit.   One tree was fair,
Lovely and shining   pleasant and sweet.
That was the tree of life!   He might live for ever,
Who ate of that fruit.   Nor would age thereafter
Or woeful sickness   work him a hurt;
But long might he live   in happiness for ever,
Have here on earth   the favour of heaven's King
And the glory ordained on high   when he went hence.

  The other tree was in shadow,   sunless and dark;
That was the tree of death!   Deadly its fruit!
Disgraced in this world,   knowing good and evil,
He needs must suffer   in sorrow and sweat
Who ate of the fruit   that formed on that tree.
Old age would despoil him   of deeds of strength,
Of bliss and lordship,   with death for his lot.
A little time only   he might joy in this life,
Then seek in the flames   the most loathsome of lands,
Be subject to fiends   where most fearful horrors
Afflict men for ever.   That the fiend knew well,
The devil's dark steward   who strove against God.

  Then the fiend put on   the form of the serpent
In twining coils   round the tree of death;
Took of the fruit   and turned him thence
To where he saw Adam,   God's handiwork.
With wily falsehood   from the first word
The devil began   to ask of Adam:

(454–496)

"Have you any longing, Adam,   that looks to God?
I come in His service,   faring from afar;
Nor has the time been long   since I sat at His side.
On this errand He sent me,   bade you eat of this fruit;
Said your power and might   and your mind will be greater,
Your body brighter,   your form more fair,
And you shall lack naught   of the world's wealth.
Because you have done His will   and won His favour,
And served Him with gladness,   you are dear unto God.
In His heavenly light   I have heard Him speak
Of your way of life,   praising your words and works.
So must you also   obey the bidding
His heralds bring you   hither to this land.
Wide reaching   are the green realms of the world
And God, the All-Ruler,   reigns in the highest heavens.
He does not wish   to have the hardship
Of making this journey   but sends His servants
To tell His commandments,   bidding us teach
Wisdom by precept.   Now do His will,
Take this fruit in your hand,   taste it and eat.
Your heart will grow roomy,   your form more fair.
The Lord, your God,   sent this help from heaven."
   Then Adam answered   where he stood on earth,
The first of men: "When I heard the Almighty,
The Victor Lord speaking   with solemn voice,
And He bade me dwell here   and do His will,
Gave me the woman,   this glowing bride,
And bade me guard   that I be not beguiled
Or ever tempted   to the tree of death,
He said that blackest hell   shall hold him fast
Who harbours in his heart   aught of evil.
Though you come with lies   and with cunning guile
I do not know   that you come from God,
An angel from heaven.   I can understand nothing
Of the bidding you bring,   of your errand or sayings,

(496–534)

Of your words or ways.   But well I know
What our Saviour said   when last I saw Him:
To honour His word   and keep it well,
To fulfil His law.   You are not like
Any of His angels   that ever I saw,
Nor do I find in you   any token of faith
That God has sent me   as sign of His favour.
Therefore I can not hearken.   Get you hence!
I fix my faith   on Almighty God
Whose hands created me.   From His high Kingdom
He can give us all good things,   though He send no servant."

    Then the tempter in anger   turned unto Eve
Where he saw her standing,   the lovely woman.
He said that thereafter   her offspring would suffer
The worst of all evils: "I know well that God
Will be much displeased   with the message I bring,
When I come from my weary journey   over this long way
To tell Him you will not heed   the new behest
He sends you out of the east.   He only, forsooth,
Must come to instruct you;   His messengers may not
Tell you His bidding!   Truly I know
The Almighty's wrath   will be roused against you.

    "But if willingly, O woman,   you hear my words
Your mind will be freer,   your wit more firm
To ponder good counsel.   Plan in your heart
That you both may avert   the vengeance to come,
As I shall show you.   Eat of this fruit!
Then your eyes shall have light   to look afar
Over all the world,   even unto the throne
Of your Lord in heaven,   and have His favour.
Over Adam thereafter   you shall have sway
If you have the will   and he trusts your words.
If you tell him truly   the precepts you heed
To work God's will   and keep His commandments,
He will cease this strife,   these evil answers,

(535–574)

As we both shall urge him   to his own good.
Entreat him earnestly   to follow your teaching
Lest you grow displeasing   to the Lord, your God.
    "If you can perfect this attempt,   O fairest of women,
I will conceal from your Lord   Adam's insolent speech,
His churlish words.   He charges me with falsehood,
Says I am eager in evil,   no angel of God
But a servant of fiends!   Yet I know full well
All the angel orders   and heaven's high span,
So long was the time   I served my Lord
With loyal heart.   I am not like a devil."
    And so with lies   and with luring wiles
He urged the woman   to that deed of evil,
Till the serpent's words   began to work within her
(For God had fashioned for her   a feebler mind),
And her heart inclined   according to his counsel.
Defying God's bidding   she took from the fiend
The fatal fruit   of the tree of death.
Never was worse deed   ordained for men!
Great is the wonder   that Eternal God
Would ever permit   so many of His servants
To be tricked with lies   that came as good counsel.
    She ate of the apple   and set at naught
The word and the will   of Almighty God.
Then she saw afar   by gift of the fiend
Who misled her with lies   and shrewdly deceived her
So that earth and heaven   and all this world,
The mighty and wondrous   work of God,
Seemed to her fairer   and filled with light.
She beheld it not   by human vision
But the devil slyly   deceived her soul
And gave her sight   to see afar
O'er the heavenly kingdom.   With hostile heart
The cursed one spake: (No boon was his counsel!)
    "O worthy Eve!   You may see for yourself

(574–611)

How you now have altered,   nor need I tell
How bright your beauty   or your form how fair,
Since you trusted my words   and followed my teaching.
All round about you   shines radiant light
Which I brought from God,   blazing from heaven.
Lo! You may touch it!   Tell Adam in truth
What vision you have,   what virtue, through my coming.
Even yet, if humbly   he will hear my words
I will give him abundance   of this good light
Wherewith I have blessed you.   Nor will I upbraid
Or charge against him   his graceless speech
Though he does not deserve   to have it condoned,
So great the ill will   he uttered against me."
    So must their offspring   live thereafter:
When they do evil   they must earn God's grace,
Make amends to God   for their grievous wrong
And have His help   and eternal favour.
    Then went unto Adam   the fairest of women,
The winsomest maid   that ever came into this world,
For she was the handiwork   of the King of heaven,
Though so slyly ensnared   and misled with lies
That through fiendish craft   and the devil's cunning
She grew hateful to God,   forfeited His favour,
And lost her glory   and her heavenly home
For many a while.   Woe to the man
Who departs not from evil   when he has the power!
    Some she bore in her hands,   some on her breast,
Of the fatal apples,   the fruit of the tree
Which God forbade her,   the Giver of glory,
Saying His servants   need not suffer death.
Holy God gave all men   a heavenly home
And abundant blessings   if they would but forgo
The fearful harvest,   the bitter fruit,
Which that baleful tree   bore on its branches.
Those were the boughs of death   which the Lord forbade!

(611–646)

But the loathed of the Lord,   the tempter, betrayed her
Into God's hatred,   misled with lies;
Deceived Eve's soul,   the woman's weak will,
Till she trusted his words   and followed his teaching.
She believed that his counsel   came from God
As he cunningly said   and showed her a token,
A pledge of good faith   and of friendly heart.
Then she said to her liege:
                  "Adam, my lord,
This fruit is so sweet   and blithe in the breast;
This shining envoy   is God's good angel;
I see by his garb   he is sent by our Lord,
The Warden of heaven.   Better that we
Should win his favour   than have his ill will;
If today you made answer   with aught of evil
He will still forgive   if we do his service.
Of what avail   is this venomous strife
With the angel of God?   We need his good will.
He can plead our cause   with the Almighty Prince,
The King of heaven.   I can see from here
Where He sits in splendour   in the south and east,
Who shaped this world.   I can see His angels
Wheeling about Him   in winged flight,
Unnumbered legions,   most lovely of hosts.
Who could bestow   such virtue and vision
Unless it came   from the heavenly King?
Far can I hear,   far can I see
Through all the world   and the wide Creation;
I can hear the hymns   of rapture in heaven.
My heart is illumined   from without and within
Since I ate of the apple.   Here in my hands
I bring this fruit   and give of it freely.
O good my lord,   I do believe
It is come from God   and brought by His bidding,
As in truthful words   this herald has told me.

(647–681)

It is like naught else   in all the earth
Except, as he says,   it is sent by God."
   Over and over she urged him,   all the long day
Driving Adam   to that dark deed,
That they disobey   the bidding of God.
The fiend stood near   inflaming desire,
Boldly enticed him,   cunningly tempted.
Full close stood the fiend   who came from afar
On that fatal mission.   He planned that men
Should be driven down   unto utter death,
Deceived and misled   so that they would lose
The Almighty's gift,   the grace of God
And their heavenly home.   The hell-fiend knew
They must bear God's wrath   and bitter affliction,
Sore bondage in hell,   because they forsook
The will of God   when with lying words
He misled to that folly   the lovely maid,
The fairest of women,   till she spoke as he willed
And helped to seduce   the work of God's hand.
   Over and over   the most winsome of women
Pled with Adam   until Adam's mind
Began to change,   and he trusted the token
The woman offered.   Yet she did it all
With a loyal heart   and knew not the harm,
The fearful afflictions   that would follow for men,
When she hearkened to the counsel   of the hateful herald.
She thought by her words   to win God's favour
When she offered Adam   that token of truth
And the heart of the man   was moved in his breast,
And his soul was turned   unto Eve's desire.
   From the woman's hand   he took death and hell,
Though it bore not these names   but the name of fruit.
Yet the sleep of death   and the devil's seduction,
Death and damnation,   perdition of men,
Were the fatal fruit   whereon they had feasted.

(681–723)

When the apple within him   touched at his heart,
Then laughed aloud   the fierce-hearted fiend,
Capered about,   thanked his lord for both:
  "Now have I won your favour   and done your will.
For many a day   is man undone,
Adam and Eve.   They shall know God's anger
Because they neglected   His word and His will.
No longer may they hold   their heavenly kingdom
But must go the dark journey   deep into hell.
So you need not languish   lying in bondage,
Or mourn in spirit   that men shall dwell
In heaven on high   while we must suffer torment,
Deadliest pain   in the darkest of lands,
And because of your proud mind   many have lost
Their goodly dwellings,   their heavenly homes.
God was bitter   when we would not bow
In submission before Him.   But it was not meet
That we should serve Him   or be subject to Him.
Then God was angered;   He hardened His heart
And hurled us to hell,   the greatest of hosts
Into hell-fire;   and with His hands
He restored in heaven   celestial seats
And gave that kingdom   unto mankind.
  "Blithe may your heart be   in your breast!
For here today   are two things done:
The sons of men   shall lose their heavenly mansions
And come to your kingdom   to the fiery flames;
Also, heart-sorrow and grief   are ordained for God.
Whatsoever of evil   we suffer here
Is now repaid to Adam   in the anger of God,
In man's perdition   and the pangs of death.
Therefore my mind is healed,   my heart made roomy,
For all our harms are avenged,   and the hurt we suffered.
Now I return to the flames   and seek out Satan
Where he lies in the darkness of hell   loaded with chains."

(723–762)

Then downward plunged   that most dreadful of heralds
To the pitiless fires   and the portals of hell
Where his lord lay bound.   But Adam and Eve
Were sick at heart.   Sorrowful words
Passed between them.   They were in terror of God;
They feared the hate   of their heavenly king.
They knew they had made of naught   the commandment of God.
   The woman mourned   wretchedly weeping,
(She had forfeited God's favour,   broken His word)
When she saw the light fade   which the faithless herald
Who advised that evil   had falsely revealed
That they might endure   hell's dreadful affliction,
Suffering infinite.   Therefore heart-sorrow
Burned in their breasts.   They bowed them in prayer,
Man and woman together,   and called upon God
Imploring their Lord,   the Prince of heaven,
To punish their sin,   let them suffer their penance,
Because they had broken   the bidding of God.
   Then they saw their bodies   that they were bare.
They had in that land   no settled home,
Knew naught of trouble   or the pain of toil,
But might have lived well   and long in the land
If they only had worked   the will of their Lord.
Many a sorrowful word   each spoke to the other,
The man and the woman.   Adam said unto Eve:
   "Bitter the fate, O Eve,   you have brought upon us!
Behold now the blackness of hell   unglutted and greedy.
You can hear it raging.   Unlike is the heavenly realm
To that blaze of fire.   But this is the best of lands,
Which we might have held   through the grace of God
Had you hearkened not to him   who advised this evil
So that we disregarded   the word of God,
The King of heaven.   In sorrow of soul
Well may we mourn   that evil mission.
For He Himself bade us   beware of sin

(762–801)

And the greatest of harms.   Now hunger and thirst
Are bitter in my breast,   whereof we both
From the first beginning   have been always free.
How shall we live now   or dwell in this land
If wind blows on us   from west or east,
From south or north?   Clouds assemble,
Storms of hail   beat down from heaven,
And sharp frost cometh   wondrous cold.
At times from heaven   with burning heat
Shines this bright sun   and we stand bare,
Naked of raiment.   We have no refuge
From the storms of weather,   nor any store
Allotted for food.   But the Almighty Lord
No longer cares for us.   What shall become of us?
Now I repent   that ever I prayed
To our gracious Ruler,   the God of heaven,
And He fashioned you for me   of mine own flesh,
For you have misled me   to the hate of my Lord.
Well may I rue it   to all ages
That ever mine eyes   had sight of you."

    Then answered Eve,   that loveliest maid,
The fairest of women,   the work of God,
Though sadly seduced   by the devil's cunning:

    "Well may you blame me   with these words,
Beloved Adam.   But no bit worse
Can you rue it in your heart   than my heart rues it."

    And Adam answered: "If I but knew
The will of God,   the penance I must pay,
You could see no one more swift,   though the Lord of heaven
Should bid me fare   through the ocean-flood;
It could never be so deep   or the sea so wide
That my heart would falter,   but I would follow
Even unto ocean's   deepest depths
If I might work   the will of God.
There is none I would serve   in all this world

(802–836)

Since I have lost   my Lord's good will,
Forfeited His favour.   But we may not be thus bare,
We two together.   Let us go into this grove
And under the shelter of this wood."

                                                 Then they turned away
And with grieving hearts   entered the green wood,
Sat there apart   to await the portion
Heaven's Lord would allot them,   for they had lost
The former estate   which God had given.
They covered their bodies   and clothed them with leaves
With the foliage of the grove,   for they had no garments.
Both together   they bowed in prayer,
Each morning beseeching   Almighty God
That He would not forget them,   that the gracious Lord
Would teach them how to live   thenceforth in the light.

    Then His heart was moved   and after the mid-day
Almighty God,   the glorious Prince,
Came walking in the garden.   Our gracious Saviour,
The merciful Father,   would fain discern
What His children did.   He knew they were undone
And the glory gone   which He formerly gave them.
Sad of spirit   they stole away
In the shade of the trees,   shorn of their splendour,
And hid in the shadows   shaking with fear
When they heard the voice   of the holy Lord.

    Then swift to His presence   the Prince of glory
Called Adam, the keeper   of Paradise;
God summoned His son   to come quickly to Him.
Wretched, lacking raiment,   Adam replied:

    "I will cover my nakedness,   clothe it with leaves,
O Lord of life,   for my guilt is grievous,
Dreadful to think of.   I dare not now
Be in Your presence,   for I am bare."

    And God made answer: "Tell Me, My son,
Why seek you the shadows,   covered with shame?

                    (836–874)

From Me you received   no cause for shame,
But delight in all things.   Wherefore with loathing,
Knowing sorrow   and sore distressed,
Do you cover your body,   cloak it with leaves,
And ruefully say   you have need of raiment,
Except you tasted the fruit   of the tree I forbade?"
    And Adam answered: "The woman, my Lord,
This goodly maiden,   gave me the fruit
And I ate of the apple   and broke Your command.
Now I bear the mark   imprinted upon me,
And my grief is the greater."   God said unto Eve:
    "To what end, My daughter,   were My ample gifts,
All the new creations   of Paradise,
Its growing riches,   when you reached to the tree
Your covetous hand   and broke from its branches
The fatal fruit;   ate of the apple
In trespass against Me,   and gave to Adam
The fruit that I firmly   forbade you both?"
    The beauteous woman   made answer, abashed:
"The foul worm deceived me   with fair words,
Urged me to sin   and to guilty greed,
Till I wickedly did   that deed of evil,
Wrought the wrong   and against the right
Filched from the tree   and ate the fruit."
    Then the Saviour of man,   the Lord Almighty,
Decreed for the serpent,   the guilty snake,
Wanderings wide;   and spoke these words:
    "Accursed forever   on your belly shall you crawl
Faring without feet   over earth's wide fields,
While life endures   and the breath you draw.
Dust shall you eat   all the days of your life.
Because you have done   this loathsome deed
The woman shall hate you,   abhor under heaven.
She shall crush with her foot   your unclean head;
You shall lurk in hiding   to strike at her heel.

(874–914)

F

Between your seed   shall be strife for ever
As long as the world stands   under the sky.
Now you have learned,   now you know,
Loathsome Tempter,   how you shall live."

   And moved to anger   God said unto Eve:
"Turn now from joy!   Under man's dominion,
With fear of your master   sorely distressed
You shall suffer in sorrow   the sin of your deed,
Waiting for death,   bearing sons and daughters
Into the world   with weeping and pain."

   Upon Adam also   the Author of life,
The Eternal Lord,   passed terrible sentence:
"To another home,   an unhappier dwelling,
You shall wander in exile   naked and needy,
Deprived of the blessings   of Paradise.
Your body and soul   shall be shorn asunder.

   "Lo! you have wrought   a grievous wrong.
Therefore you shall labour,   living by toil,
Eating your bread   in the sweat of your brow
As long as you dwell here,   till hard at your heart
Grips the grim disease   which you ate in the apple.
So shall you die."   Lo! now we have learned
How our many sorrows,   our mortal woe,
Befell us all.

               Then our Creator,
The Lord of Glory,   robed them with raiment,
With their first clothes   bade cover their shame.
Then He drove them out   to a drearier life.
Behind them there   by the Lord's behest
A holy angel   with flaming sword
Locked up that land   of joy and delight.
Therein no sinful   or evil man
May ever enter   for the warder is mighty,
Dear to the Lord,   who guards that life.

   But the Almighty Father   would not withdraw

(914–951)

All His favours   from Adam and Eve,
Though they had transgressed   and fallen from grace.
He left for their solace   the sheltering sky
Bright with stars,   the wide earth's abundance;
Bade the spawning legions   of land and sea
Bring forth and increase   to fill man's need.
But they lived thereafter   in a more sorrowful land,
An abode and a realm   less rich in blessings
Than the former home   where first they dwelt,
Wherefrom they were driven out   after their sin.

(952–964)

CHAPTER II

THE REDEEMER

FOREWORD

THE poems which form the material of this chapter, the *Advent Lyrics*, *Dream of the Cross*, and *Ascension* have two characteristics in common. They all have to do with aspects of the mission of Christ, the Redeemer, and they all, in origin and structure, are closely governed by the liturgy, or religious homily, or elements of ritual in the services of the medieval Church. They offer excellent illustration of the manner in which some of the best of Early English poetry grows directly from the religious impulse, and from the ceremonial and literature of the Christian faith.

The *Advent Lyrics* and *Ascension* have been preserved to us in the pages of the Exeter Book. United with the 798 lines that follow them in the MS.,[1] they are often referred to as the *Christ*. This title derives from a theory that the three sections constitute a single poem on the Nativity, Ascension, and Second Advent.[2] But these three sections deal with separate subjects, and represent different poetic types. The Advent poems are a series of short lyrics of invocation and petition, the *Ascension* is a poetic rendering of a Latin homily on the Ascension by Gregory the Great,[3] and the *Last Judgment* is an apocalyptic poem, descriptive-lyrical in mood. Granting that the inter-relationship of these three themes provides a theological unity, one may still doubt whether we have here unity of literary composition, and unity of authorship. It seems more probable that the three sections constitute three separate poetic compositions: a group of Advent lyrics, the *Ascension*, and a poem on the Last Judgment. The second of these compositions is marked by the runic signature as the work of Cynewulf.

THE ADVENT LYRICS

The *Advent Lyrics* illustrate well the creative influence of the Catholic liturgy in Old English verse, an influence which is equally evident

---

[1] The third section of the so-called *Christ* is translated in the present volume under the title *The Last Judgment*, and is printed with appropriate commentary in Chapter VI.

[2] Dietrich, *Haupt's Zeitschrift*, IX 193–214.

[3] Migne, *Patr. Lat.*, LXXVI 1218–19.

in other Old English poems, notably the *Exodus*.[1] These lyrics are founded on eleven antiphons used during the Advent season, which forms so significant a prelude to the cycle of the Christian year. Of the eleven, seven were the so-called "greater" antiphons appointed for use in the services of the seven days immediately preceding the Vigil of Christmas, and four were the so-called "lesser" antiphons sometimes associated with them. One of the lyrics included in the Old English series was founded, not on Advent antiphons, but on two others designated for the service of Lauds on Trinity Sunday.

The seven "greater" antiphons listed by their invocations were: O Eternal Wisdom; O Lord and Ruler of the House of David; O Root of Jesse; O Key of David; O Rising Brightness; O King and Desire of All Nations; and O Emmanuel. The "lesser" antiphons included for the Advent season: O Virgin of Virgins; O Mistress of the World; O King of Peace; and O Jerusalem.[2]

The phrases of invocation, recital, and petition which the Old English poet borrows from these antiphons are poetically elaborated and expanded, in some instances at great length. In the process of expansion the doctrinal implications of the antiphons are often stressed by the addition of cognate material which the poet draws from Scriptural or patristic sources. His use of this method can be illustrated by comparing the first of the Advent lyrics with the text of the antiphon on which it is based.[3] The antiphon reads: "O King and Desire of All Nations, and chief Corner-Stone, who makest two to be one: come and save man whom Thou didst form of clay."

The Old English lyric adopts the image of the corner-stone,[4] but the

[1] Cf. Kennedy, *The Earliest English Poetry*, pp. 177–80.

[2] The correspondences between the Advent antiphons and the Old English Advent lyrics are as follows: *Christ*, 1–17, O King and Desire of All Nations; *Christ*, 18–49, O Key of David; *Christ*, 50–70, O Jerusalem; *Christ*, 71–103, O Virgin of Virgins; *Christ*, 104–29, O Rising Brightness; *Christ*, 130–63, O Emmanuel; *Christ*, 214–74, O King of Peace; *Christ*, 275–347, O Mistress of the World; *Christ* 348–77, O Root of Jesse and O Eternal Wisdom. For a detailed study see E. Burget, "The Dependence of Part 1 of Cynewulf's *Christ* upon the Antiphonary", Washington, D.C., 1921.

[3] It is to be noted from the grammatically solitary word "cyninge" with which the poem begins that some portion of the Old English lyric, preceding the present seventeen lines, has been lost.

[4] Cf. Psalm cxviii 22–3; Matthew xxi 42; Mark xii 10–11.

phrasing "who makest two to be one" has been considerably elaborated. The Old English poet stresses the "lengthy walls" of "unbroken flint" which are to be united by the corner-stone in such a "firm embrace" that the eyes of all men for ever may marvel at the Lord of glory. This "marvelling of all men for ever" is an addition to the phrasing of the antiphon, and suggests a knowledge of the statement which follows the corner-stone image in the cognate passages in the Psalms, Matthew, and Mark: "This is the Lord's doing, and it is marvellous in our eyes." It is also possible that the phrase may reflect the poet's acceptance of Gregory's interpretation of the two walls bound into one as mystically representing a union (1) of the Jews with the Gentiles, and (2) of the Church on earth with the angelic hosts in heaven.

Another expansion of the antiphon grows from the petition "save man whom Thou didst form of clay". In the poet's mind the "corner-stone" suggests the Builder; and "man formed of clay", either individually or as incorporated into the body of the Church, is the work of the Builder. But this structure has become decayed "under its roof", or ruined by sin. There is great need that the Craftsman Himself come to rebuild "what now is broken".

In a lyric dependent on one of the "lesser" antiphons the poet's interpretative elaborations of material are even more notable. This is the lyric shaped from the antiphon: "O Jerusalem, City of the Great God: lift up thine eyes round about and see thy Lord, for He comes to loose thee from thy chains." In his use of this material the poet develops three parallel themes: the earthly city of Jerusalem, the Heavenly Jerusalem, and the Virgin Mary. These themes run through the lyric, sometimes expressed separately, sometimes fused or interwoven. Lines 57–8, for example, can appropriately refer either to the Heavenly Jerusalem or to the Virgin; lines 59–66 to the Virgin or to the earthly Jerusalem.

The Old English poet is equally skilful in his handling of the antiphon: "O King of Peace born before all ages: come through the golden gate, visit those whom Thou has redeemed, and lead them back to the place whence they fell through sin." In his reference to man's need of redemption the poet introduces two images not found in the antiphon but supplemental to it. These intensifying additions are the reference to the "Accursed Wolf that has scattered and widely dispersed the sheep", and the descriptive epithet which the poet coins for this Wolf:

the dark Death-Shadow. The Wolf image, borrowed from John x 12, and the poet's description of it as the personified shadow of death, are dramatic symbols of the devouring power of evil.

One of the finest examples of the poet's reshaping skill is found in his development of the antiphon: "O Mistress of the World sprung of royal seed: from Thy womb Christ went forth as a bridegroom from his chamber; here in a manger lies He who rules the stars." In the Old English lyric this is expanded to seventy-two lines. Mary is not only Mistress of the World, but of the heavenly hosts, and the dwellers in hell. She is Bride of the Lord of glory. There is reference to the Annunciation. But most elaborate of all expansions is the interpretation of her perpetual virginity in terms of Ezekiel's[1] prophetic vision of the closed gate looking toward the East: "This gate shall be shut, it shall not be opened, and no man shall enter in by it; because the Lord, the God of Israel, hath entered in by it, therefore it shall be shut."[2] The gate is described by the Old English poet as a "peerless portal compassed about with treasure and with cunning bands", and as a "golden gateway firm-locked and bolted". Through this "wall-door" the Lord shall come to earth, and shall lock it after Him with a key, and never shall any unlock it save God, the Saviour.

Except for a remarkable passage of dialogue between Joseph and Mary,[3] possibly the earliest dramatic scene in English literature, these Old English Advent poems, lyric in mood, are often memorable in their expression of that mood. They combine a poet's skill and a Churchman's religious feeling. They clothe with lyric grace the meditations of a devout Christian deeply moved by the spirit of Advent, and trained in the significance of its mysteries.

A DREAM OF THE CROSS

There are three Old English poems in which veneration of the Cross is feelingly expressed: the *Elene*,[4] a narrative of St Helena's finding of the True Cross; the *Last Judgment*,[5] in which a narrative of the Crucifixion is a prominent feature; and the *Dream of the Rood*.

---

[1] Mistakenly Esaias in the Old English text, *Christ*, 303.
[2] Ezekiel xliv 1–2.   [3] *Christ*, 164–214.   [4] See Chapter IV.
[5] See Chapter VI.

This last, a sensitively written lyric expressing passionate adoration of the Cross, is found in the Vercelli MS. with the *Elene*. Thus the two poems in the corpus of Old English poetry which are specifically concerned with the Cross are contained in the same manuscript.

Brief passages from the *Dream of the Rood* are carved in runic letters on the well-known Cross at Ruthwell in Dumfriesshire near the Scottish border.[1] This is a beautiful Latin Cross of red sandstone about seventeen feet tall and elaborately ornamented with carvings of figures, flowers, and foliage in addition to the runic inscriptions. In 1642 it was overthrown and broken, and the transverse arms were lost. After many years, the broken pieces were reassembled in 1802, the arms added in restoration, and the Cross set up in Ruthwell churchyard. Later it was moved into the church where it now stands.

It was at one time believed that partially obliterated letters on the Cross could be interpreted to mean: "Caedmon made me,"[2] and on this slight basis the authorship of the incised lines, and of the *Dream of the Rood* itself, was attributed to the poet-herdsman of Whitby. But more recent examinations of the Cross have failed to corroborate this claim, and detailed studies of the carvings suggest that the Ruthwell Cross was later in workmanship than was first believed, and should be dated, perhaps, not far from the middle of the eighth century.[3]

It is possible that the runic inscriptions on the Cross are from an earlier poem, of which the *Dream of the Rood* is a later, revised version. In any case, scholarly judgment tends to regard the *Dream* as Cynewulfian in style, and as written either by that poet, or by an imitator. Though there is no runic signature, it should be noted that the poem concludes with a passage of personal reference that reflects the sadness and loneliness of old age, in which respect it resembles the personal passage that forms a part of Cynewulf's signature of the *Elene*. But there is little firm evidence with which to establish authorship of the poem, Cynewulfian or otherwise. At most we know that we have here a lyric

---

[1] The runic inscriptions on the Cross correspond to parts of the following passages of the *Dream*: 39–41; 44–5; 48–9; 56–9; 62–4.

[2] Haigh, *Archaeologia Aeliana*, Nov. 1856, p. 173; and Stephens, *Old Northern Runic Monument*), 1 419–20.

[3] See Dobbie, *The Anglo-Saxon Minor Poems*, Introd., cxx–cxxii.

of religious faith and adoration somewhat in the Cynewulfian manner, and as fine as anything we know to be Cynewulf's, or finer.

Not only the subject matter of the *Dream*, but the sensitive lyric emotion with which it was written, make it appropriate that this lovely poem should be read in the same chapter with the *Advent Lyrics* with which, as with the *Ascension*, it shares in a triadic setting forth of the great theme of man's Redemption. The author has employed the literary convention of the dream-vision for the shaping of the poem. In his dream the Cross is personified, with endowment of human speech. It narrates the story of the Crucifixion, and the tale told by the unwilling instrument of Christ's Passion takes on an extraordinary intimacy of tragic implication.

At the beginning of his dream the poet beholds the vision in the form of some richly ornamented, familiar Cross, gilded with goldwork and inset with gems. But the vision expands. The wondrous Tree is lifted high in air, and the jewels at its foot and on the shoulderbeam gleam in the light that shines upon it. Angels and men and all the great Creation gaze in awe. In the first moments of the vision the image wavers, at one moment revealing the Cross in jewelled splendour, at another wet with the blood of the Crucified Saviour. But as an image is gradually focused to sharpness by a lens, the vision finally takes, and keeps, the form of the Cross of the Crucifixion. The element of personification in the dream-vision permits a dramatic rehearsal of its story. Long years before, it had grown as a tree on the edge of a wood. Men came and hewed it down, shaping it to a gallows. They bore it to a hilltop and fastened it there. In horror the Tree beheld the Lord of the World hastening in heroic mood to mount upon it for the redemption of mankind. Shrinking in terror from that embrace the Cross yet knew its destiny was to stand fast. "I dared not bow nor bend." The words of the vision evoke and personalize the ordeal of Christ's Passion with startling vividness.

The scenes of the Deposition and Burial are etched with pathos, and the description of the Cross standing alone with a few lingering mourners, sorrowfully weeping after the crowd had dispersed and the wailing died away, is a memorable passage of imaginative realism. There follows the hewing down of the Tree and its burial in the earth. But in

later days, it tells the dreamer, friends and thanes of God recovered it
and graced it with adornments of silver and gold. As the Prince of
glory had honoured His mother, Mary, above all women, so He had
honoured the Cross above the wood of any forest-tree. Let the "beloved man" to whom the Cross has spoken reveal the vision to all men
so that, when the Saviour shall come again to judge mankind, "every
soul through the Cross may come to heavenly glory, whoso wishes to
dwell with God." So ends the vision.

In the final lines of the lyric the poet speaks of himself, of his burden
of years and his longing for death. He is companionless and lonely; no
longer has he in this world many powerful friends. Each day he dreams
of the hour when the Cross, whereof he had vision, may fetch him
from this fleeting life to the home of God's people where he may abide
in bliss with the saints. It is interesting to note that even in this final
passage the Cross is still personified in the dreamer's memory, as it
had been in his vision. It is his heart's desire, and all his hope, that the
Cross may come and conduct him to the Kingdom where he fain would
be. In its reflection of a spirit of religious adoration that finds in the
Cross its appropriate symbol, and in the mood of lyric grace with
which the vision is told, the *Dream of the Rood* is one of the most beautiful of Old English poems.

THE ASCENSION

The *Ascension*, like the *Advent Lyrics*, shows us the Old English poet
composing under direct and continuous control of Latin source
material which his Churchman's office, and theological studies, have
made familiar. In the *Ascension* Cynewulf is reshaping the material of a
Latin homily by Gregory the Great.[1] This chief source furnishes, as it
were, the skeleton upon which by extensive enrichment and elaboration he has fashioned the artful substance of his poem.[2] In addition to

[1] Number 29 of the *Homilies on the Gospels* (Migne, *Patr. Lat.*, LXXVI 1218–19).

[2] At one point in the text of the *Ascension* a passage of twenty-seven lines
is apparently out of place (see Cook's *Christ of Cynewulf*, p. 131, note). Lines
558–85 are certainly a continuation of the speech of the angels to the Galileans
who stand gazing after their Ascended Lord. In the present translation these
lines have been placed immediately after line 527, where they seem to belong.
The usual line numbering, however, has been retained on the appropaiate
pages to avoid any confusion.

this principal source the poet apparently drew upon other subsidiary sources. The Ascension hymn, *Hymnum canamus gloriae*, attributed to Bede, is certainly an important analogue to Cynewulf's poem, and in lines 683–5, for an important point of doctrine regarding the diversity of God's gifts to men, he is indebted to another homily of Gregory, in this instance the *Homily on Ezekiel*.[1]

In its beginning the *Ascension* poses a question for which we have no answer. Could we answer it, we should know more than we do about Cynewulf, and about the circumstances attending the composition of this particular poem. Who was the "illustrious" man that Cynewulf addresses in the second line, urging him to strive earnestly "by meditation" to understand a point of Scriptural exegesis that bears directly on the theological significance of the Ascension? Was he noble patron, or protégé? Was he layman or cleric? All that we can surmise is that it seems unlikely this shadowy unknown was a man high in the Church, or learned in theological matters, for to such a man the point of exegesis posed by Cynewulf should have been familiar doctrine.

The question asked is no triviality. It is borrowed from the opening lines of Gregory's homily, where it receives immediate answer. But in Cynewulf's poem, since his "illustrious" reader is asked to meditate upon the question, the answer is never explicitly given, though repeatedly hinted.[2] Gregory writes: "We ought first to inquire why it is that the angels who appeared at the Nativity are not said to have been robed in white, whereas the angels who appeared at the Ascension are said to have worn white raiment."[3] His explanation of this point of difference in the Biblical account of the two events springs from a double root: first, the concept of Christ as Son of God and Son of Man, and second, Gregory's assertion that white is the appropriate colour for the observance of joyous festivals. Since the Nativity represented Divinity humbled into human flesh, and the Ascension represented humanity exalted into heaven, white robes are inappropriate to the first event, but appropriate to the second. This is Gregory's answer to his own question. With this beginning there follows a description of

---

[1] Migne, *Patr. Lat.*, LXXVI 899.

[2] For example, lines 550–4, and the phrase *with our body* in line 755.

[3] *Homilies on the Gospels*, XXIX 9.

the Ascension scene wide-spread upon the heavens, and the recital of the songs of the angel hosts who attend their risen Lord rejoicing in the light that shines from the Saviour.

Cynewulf passes on to a rehearsal of God's goodness to men in providing them with food, kindly weather, the light of sun, moon, and stars, and the fall of dew and rain which enlarge the abundance of earth. For all these should men give thanks but "more especially for the salvation which He has granted us in His Ascension" by dispelling the primal curse upon mankind.

Cynewulf follows Gregory's homily in adopting Job's image of the flight of a bird[1] as a symbol of the Nativity and the Ascension. He also follows Gregory, and Psalm lxviii 18, in linking the Ascension to the giving of gifts. In the list of gifts conferred upon mankind through the manifestation of the Spirit Cynewulf draws both on Gregory and on the familiar passage in 1 Corinthians xii 8–11. To these lists he adds contemporary skills such as harp-playing, expertness in armoury, and seamanship.

The most unusual bit of symbolism in the *Ascension* is taken directly from Gregory who had it in turn from other patristic writings. Cook finds the ultimate source of the image in two passages of Ambrose.[2] By this symbolism the important phases of Christ's ministry are mystically conceived as "leaps". The image derives ultimately from the Song of Solomon ii 8: "Behold He cometh leaping upon the mountains, skipping upon the hills." In Gregory's homily the "leaps" are five in number: the Incarnation, Nativity, Crucifixion, the Deposition and Burial, and the Resurrection and Ascension. In Cynewulf's poem the Harrowing of Hell is an added "leap", and in some other lists the baptism in the Jordan is also a "leap".

Near the end of the *Ascension*[3] we have the runic signature of Cynewulf imbedded in an extended description of the judgment which shall come to men at Doomsday, a customary juxtaposition of material in the Cynewulfian signatures. As in many other depictions of the Second Advent, the poet enforces sharply on his readers the contrast between

[1] Job xxviii 7.
[2] Cook, *The Christ of Cynewulf*, p. 143, note on line 720.
[3] *Christ*, 797–814.

the meekness in which the Redeemer "humbled Himself to be born of a Virgin" and the stern and righteous mood in which He shall come in the latter Day to reward every man according to his record of words and works.

The *Ascension* ends with a beautiful sea-picture of sixteen lines which Cynewulf elaborated from a brief suggestion of Gregory. There is reference in the Latin homily to the mind "tossed by the fluctuations" of life, and to the need of fixing the "anchor of hope" in an eternal Fatherland. From these brief phrases Cynewulf has developed an extended symbolic description of the stormy voyage of earthly life toward that haven which the Lord of Heaven made ready for us "by His Ascension", where at last, over the ship's side, we may moor our old sea-steeds fast at anchor.

ADVENT LYRICS

(Selected from *Christ 1*)

Thou art the wall-stone   the workers rejected
Of old from the work.   It befits Thee well
That Thou shouldst be Head   of the glorious hall
Locking together   the lengthy walls,
The flint unbroken,   in a firm embrace,
That ever on earth   the eyes of all
May look with wonder   on the Lord of glory.
    With cunning skill   display Thy craft
Triumphant, Righteous;   and quickly raise
Wall against wall.   The work hath need
That the Craftsman come,   the King Himself;
That He then rebuild   what now is broken,
The house under its roof.   He wrought the body,
The limbs, of clay;   now the Lord of life
Must rescue from devils   the droves of the wretched,
The damned from their terrors   as He oft hath done.

O Thou Ruler   and Righteous King,
Keeping the keys,   unlocking life,
Grant us salvation   and the joyous journey
Denied to others   if their works be weak.
In great necessity   we speak these words
Asking of Him   Who created man
That in anger He utter not   doom on the wretched,
Who in this dark dungeon   sit here sad
Through all the sweet journey   of the sun,
Till the Lord of life   vouchsafe us light,
Become a safeguard   unto our souls,
And mantle in glory   our weak minds.
Make us worthy   whom He marked for honour
When wretched in spirit,   bereft of home,

(1–32)

We had need to journey   to this narrow land.
    Wherefore one may say,   who speaketh truth,
That He saved mankind   when they went astray.
The Maid was young,   the Immaculate Virgin,
Whom He chose as Mother;   without man's love
The Bride grew great   with the Son's conception.
Never in all the world   early or late
Was woman's conceiving   such as this.
It was a marvellous mystery   of God!
    Then ghostly grace   spread over the earth;
And much was illumined   by the Lord of life
That once was secret   and concealed in dark,
Ancient lays   and lore of the prophets,
When the Wielder came,   fulfilling each word
Of those who wisely   with warm hearts
Praise and exalt   the Creator's name.

    O holy Jerusalem,   Vision of peace,
Fairest of royal seats,   City of Christ,
Homeland of angels,   in thee for ever
Rest the souls   of the righteous alone
In glory exulting.   No sign of sin
In that city-dwelling   shall ever be seen,
But from thee all evil   shall flee afar,
All trouble and toil.   Thou art wondrously filled
With holy hope,   as thy name is named.
    Lift up thine eyes   on the wide creation,
The dome of heaven,   on every hand;
Behold His coming;   the King of glory
Himself approaches   to seek thee out,
To abide in thee,   as the blessed prophets
In their books foretold   the birth of the Christ,
To thy comfort spoke,   thou fairest of cities!
Now is the Babe come   born to transform

(32–67)

The works of the Hebrews.   He brings thee bliss,
Looses thy bondage,   draws nigh unto men,
For He only knows   their harrowing need,
How man in his wretchedness   waits upon mercy.

   O Rising Sun!   Most radiant angel
Over the middle-earth   sent unto men!
Thou steadfast glow   and gleaming of the sun
Bright beyond stars!   Thou from Thyself
Dost illumine with light   the time of every season.
   As Thou wast once begotten   God of God,
True Son of the Father,   before all ages
For ever Lord   in celestial light,
So now in need   Thy work doth beseech Thee
Send the bright sun   and come Thyself
To illumine those   who have long been sitting
Attired with darkness   in eternal night,
Where clothed with sin   and covered with shadows
They needs must endure   Death's dark shade.
   Hopefully now   we trust in Thy healing
To the hosts of men   heralded by the Word,
Which in the beginning   with God coeternal
Was One with the Father,   the Warden of might;
And then was made flesh   faultless of evil
Which the Virgin bore   to succour the sad.
God was seen with us   without sin!
Then dwelt together   God's Mighty Son
And the Son of man   in union among us.
And for this for all ages   thank we the Lord,
By our deeds, for sending   Himself to save us!

   O Righteous Ruler   and Prince of peace!
King of all kings!   Christ Almighty!
Before all worlds   Thou wast one with the Father,

        (67–70; 104–129; 214–217)

Begotten Son   by His strength and might!
Nor is there any eorl[1]   under the heavens,
Or man of counsel,   so cunning of wit
That unto the sea-dwellers   he may recite,
Or rightly rehearse,   how heaven's Lord
Took Thee in the beginning   to be God's Son.
Of all that mortals   have heard under heaven
In the Creation   it first befell
That All-Wise God,   Author of life,
Cleft light from darkness   with lordly might.
With dominion of power   God made this decree:
"Let there be light   henceforth and for ever,
A gleaming delight   for every living thing
That shall be born   of all earth's breeds."

    Then swift it ensued,   as well it should,
That radiance shone   for the sons of men,
Bright with stars,   through the rolling seasons.
He ordained, Himself,   that Thou, His Son,
Shouldest live co-eval   with Thy Sole Lord
Ere aught of Creation   had come to be.
Thou art the Wisdom   that, with the All-Wielder,
This wide Creation   fashioned of old.
Therefore none is so quick   or cunning of mind
Who can tell Thy beginning   to the tribes of men.
Come, Lord of triumph,   Maker of man,
And mercifully show   Thy compassion upon us!
Great is our wish   to know the wonder
Of Thy mother-kinship,   for we may not know
Thy Father-kinship   further a whit.

    Bless earth with Thine advent,   O Saviour Christ,
And the golden gates   which in days gone by

---

[1] As the O.E. word, *eorl*, occurs frequently in the original texts, often inwoven in the alliterative structure, it is sometimes taken over into these translations in an occasional passage where the context makes its meaning clear in the general sense: *man*, *leader*, *hero*.

(218–251)

Full long stood locked,   High Lord of heaven,
Bid Thou swing open   and seek us out
Humbly descending   to the hordes of earth.
   We have need of Thy mercy.   The dark Death-Shadow,
The Accursed Wolf,   hath scattered Thy sheep
And widely dispersed them;   what Thou, the Wielder,
Bought with Thy blood,   that doth the Wicked One
Take into bondage,   and smiteth sore
Against our desire.   O Saviour Lord
In our inmost thoughts   we eagerly beg:
Hasten to help us,   miserable sinners,
That the Prince of torture   may plunge to hell
And Thy handiwork   mount up on high,
Creator of men,   and come to righteousness,
To the beauteous realms   in the land above
From which the Dark Spirit   led us astray,
Beguiled and seduced us   through grievous sin
So that, empty of all glory,   unto all ages
We must suffer affliction,   except Thou first
O Living God,   Eternal Lord,
Shield of all,   may will to save us
Out of the clutch   of the Foe of mankind.

   Hail, O most worthy   in all the world!
Thou purest Maiden   that ever on earth
Through the long ages   lived among men!
Rightly all mortals   in blithe mood
Name thee blessed   and hail thee Bride
Of the King of glory.   The thanes of Christ,
In heaven the highest,   carol and sing
Proclaiming thee Lady   of the heavenly legions,
Of earthly orders,   and the hosts of hell.
   Thou only of women   didst purpose of old
To bring thy maidhood   unto thy Maker
Presenting it there   unspotted of sin.

(252–290)

Of all mankind   there came no other,
No bride with linked jewels,   like unto thee
With pure heart sending   thy glorious gift
To its heavenly home.   The Lord of triumph
Sent forth His herald   from the hosts on high
To bring thee knowledge   of abundant grace:
That in pure birth   thou shouldst bear God's Son
In mercy to men;   and thou thyself, Mary,
Remain for ever   Immaculate Maid.
    We have also learned   that long ago
In ages past   Isaiah the prophet
Sang of thee;   said he was carried
To where he looked   on life's dwelling-place
In its lasting home.   The learned prophet
Surveyed that region   round about
Till he fixed his gaze   where firmly set
Was a peerless portal.   With precious treasure
The measureless door   was bound about,
All encompassed   with cunning bands.
Full well he weened   no hand could heave
The firm-fixed bars,   or loose the bolts
Through endless ages   of that city-gate;
Until God's angel   with gracious heart
Unriddled the secret,   and spoke this word:
    "I say for sooth   that God Himself,
The Father Almighty,   one day shall fare
In power descending   to the peoples of earth
Through these bolted bars,   these golden gates.
And after that advent   to all ages
They shall stand to eternity   closed so tight
That never another,   save God the Saviour,
Shall ever again   those gates unlock."
    Now is fulfilled   what the prophet foresaw.
Thou art the wall-door   through which the dear Lord
Once fared unto earth.   Just so Christ found thee

(290–330)

Adorned with power,   pure and elect;
The King of angels,   the Lord of life,
After Him left thee   locked with a key,
An Immaculate Maiden.   Make manifest now
The honour God's angel,   Gabriel, brought thee.
All we mortals   beseech thee show us
Thy Son Who came   for a comfort to men.
With one accord   we may all win hope
As we gaze on the Babe   upon thy breast.
Intercede thou for us   with fervent prayer
That no longer he leave us   subject to sin
In this Vale of Death;   but conduct us forth
To the Father's kingdom,   where freed of sorrow
We may live in glory   with the Lord of hosts.

   Hail, Thou Holy   Lord of heaven,
With the Father co-eval   in that exalted home!
Of the angel legions,   the limitless hosts,
Who in heaven on high   keep watch o'er Thy kingdom,
The glorious courts,   and the service of God,
Not one had being   when first with the Father
Thou didst stablish the base   of this spacious work,
These boundless lands.   For You Both is union
With the Blessed Spirit,   the Comforter!
   Hear, O Saviour,   O Healing Christ,
We humbly pray Thee,   the prayers of captives,
Thy pitiful thralls.   How are we harassed
Of our own self-will!   The evil outcasts,
The cursed spirits,   the hostile scathers,
Have harried us hard   and bound us with bonds.
Our hope is in Thee alone,   Eternal Lord.
Help Thou the hopeless   that Thine advent hither
May comfort the sorrowful,   though lust of sin
Has set us against Thee   in grievous feud.
Pity Thy servants   and remember our sorrows,

(330–370)

How with weak minds we stumble,   go sadly astray.
Come, King of men,   delay not too long.
We have need of Thy favour,   that Thou set us free,
And truly grant us   Thy saving grace,
That we may henceforth   here among men
Perform the better things,   fulfil Thy will.

　　Lo! that is a marvellous change   in the life of men
Since the Mild Creator   of all mankind
From the Virgin received   flesh undefiled;
Never had she known   the love of man,
Nor came the Saviour   by any seed
Of man on earth.   That was greater marvel
Than men may know,   in its mystery:
How the Splendour of heaven,   High Lord of the skies,
Brought help to man   through His Mother's womb.
　　By this forth-coming   the King of all nations
Every day granteth   forgiveness to men,
The Lord of hosts.   So should we lovingly
Serve Him well   by our words and works.
Wise is it for all men   who have remembrance
Most often, and most sincerely,   and with most zeal
To glorify God.   He granteth them grace,
Even the Hallowed One,   the Healer Himself,
In a country whereto   they came not before,
The land of the living,   of angels' delight,
Where their home shall be   henceforth for ever
In bliss to all ages,   world without end.   Amen.

(371–377; 416–439)

A DREAM OF THE CROSS

(Dream of the Rood)

Lo! I will tell the dearest of dreams
That I dreamed in the midnight when mortal men
Were sunk in slumber. Me-seemed I saw
A wondrous Tree towering in air,
Most shining of crosses compassed with light.
Brightly that beacon was gilded with gold;
Jewels adorned it fair at the foot,
Five on the shoulder-beam, blazing in splendour.
Through all creation the angels of God
Beheld it shining— no cross of shame!
Holy spirits gazed on its gleaming,
Men upon earth and all this great creation.
 Wondrous that Tree, that Token of triumph,
And I a transgressor soiled with my sins!
I gazed on the Rood arrayed in glory,
Shining in beauty and gilded with gold,
The Cross of the Saviour beset with gems.
But through the gold-work outgleamed a token
Of the ancient evil of sinful men
Where the Rood on its right side once sweat blood.
Saddened and rueful, smitten with terror
At the wondrous Vision, I saw the Cross
Swiftly varying vesture and hue,
Now wet and stained with the Blood outwelling,
Now fairly jewelled with gold and gems.
 Then, as I lay there, long I gazed
In rue and sadness on my Saviour's Tree,
Till I heard in dream how the Cross addressed me,
Of all woods worthiest, speaking these words:
 "Long years ago (well yet I remember)
They hewed me down on the edge of the holt,

(1–29)

Severed my trunk;　strong foemen took me,
For a spectacle wrought me,　a gallows for rogues.
High on their shoulders　they bore me to hilltop,
Fastened me firmly,　an army of foes!
　　"Then I saw the King　of all mankind
In brave mood hasting　to mount upon me.
Refuse I dared not,　nor bow nor break,
Though I felt earth's confines　shudder in fear;
All foes I might fell,　yet still I stood fast.
　　"Then the young Warrior,　God, the All-Wielder,
Put off His raiment,　steadfast and strong;
With lordly mood　in the sight of many
He mounted the Cross　to redeem mankind.
When the Hero clasped me　I trembled in terror,
But I dared not bow me　nor bend to earth;
I must needs stand fast.　Upraised as the Rood
I held the High King,　the Lord of heaven.
I dared not bow!　With black nails driven
Those sinners pierced me;　the prints are clear,
The open wounds.　I dared injure none.
They mocked us both.　I was wet with blood
From the Hero's side　when He sent forth His spirit.
　　"Many a bale　I bore on that hill-side
Seeing the Lord　in agony outstretched.
Black darkness covered　with clouds God's body,
That radiant splendour.　Shadow went forth
Wan under heaven;　all creation wept
Bewailing the King's death.　Christ was on the Cross.
　　"Then many came quickly,　faring from far,
Hurrying to the Prince.　I beheld it all.
Sorely smitten with sorrow　in meekness I bowed
To the hands of men.　From His heavy and bitter pain
They lifted Almighty God.　Those warriors left me
Standing bespattered with blood;　I was wounded with spears.
Limb-weary they laid Him down;　they stood at His head,

(30–63)

Looked on the Lord of heaven   as He lay there at rest
From His bitter ordeal all forspent.   In sight of His slayers
They made Him a sepulchre   carved from the shining stone;
Therein laid the Lord of triumph.   At evening tide
Sadly they sang their dirges   and wearily turned away
From their lordly Prince;   there He lay all still and alone.

   "There at our station   a long time we stood
Sorrowfully weeping   after the wailing of men
Had died away.   The corpse grew cold,
The fair life-dwelling.   Down to earth
Men hacked and felled us,   a grievous fate!
They dug a pit   and buried us deep.
But there God's friends   and followers found me
And graced me with treasure   of silver and gold.

   "Now may you learn,   O man beloved,
The bitter sorrows   that I have borne,
The work of caitiffs.   But the time is come
That men upon earth   and through all creation
Show me honour   and bow to this sign.
On me a while   God's Son once suffered;
Now I tower under heaven   in glory attired
With healing for all   that hold me in awe.
Of old I was once   the most woeful of tortures,
Most hateful to all men,   till I opened for them
The true Way of life.   Lo! the Lord of glory,
The Warden of heaven,   above all wood
Has glorified me   as Almighty God
Has honoured His Mother,   even Mary herself,
Over all womankind   in the eyes of men.

   "Now I give you bidding,   O man beloved,
Reveal this Vision   to the sons of men,
And clearly tell   of the Tree of glory
Whereon God suffered   for man's many sins
And the evil that Adam   once wrought of old.

   "Death He suffered,   but our Saviour rose

(64–101)

By virtue of His great might   as a help to men.
He ascended to heaven.   But hither again
He shall come unto earth   to seek mankind,
The Lord Himself   on the Day of Doom,
Almighty God   with His angel hosts.
And then will He judge,   Who has power of judgment,
To each man according   as here on earth
In this fleeting life   he shall win reward.

   "Nor there may any   be free from fear
Hearing the words   which the Wielder shall utter.
He shall ask before many: Where is the man
Who would taste bitter death   as He did on the Tree?
And all shall be fearful   and few shall know
What to say unto Christ.   But none at His Coming
Shall need to fear   if he bears in his breast
This best of symbols;   and every soul
From the ways of earth   through the Cross shall come
To heavenly glory,   who would dwell with God."

   Then with ardent spirit   and earnest zeal,
Companionless, lonely,   I prayed to the Cross.
My soul was fain of death.   I had endured
Many an hour of longing.   It is my life's hope
That I may turn   to this Token of triumph,
I above all men,   and revere it well.

   This is my heart's desire,   and all my hope
Waits on the Cross.   In this world now
I have few powerful friends;   they have fared hence
Away from these earthly gauds   seeking the King of glory,
Dwelling now with the High Father   in heaven above,
Abiding in rapture.   Each day I dream
Of the hour when the Cross of my Lord,   whereof here on earth
I once had vision,   from this fleeting life may fetch me
And bring me where is great gladness   and heavenly bliss,
Where the people of God   are planted and stablished for ever
In joy everlasting.   There may it lodge me

(102–142)

Where I may abide in glory   knowing bliss with the saints.
   May the Lord befriend me   who on earth of old
Once suffered on the Cross   for the sins of men.
He redeemed us, endowed us with life   and a heavenly home.
Therein was hope renewed   with blessing and bliss
For those who endured the burning.   In that great deed
God's Son was triumphant,   possessing power and strength!
Almighty, Sole-Ruling   He came to the kingdom of God
Bringing a host of souls   to angelic bliss,
To join the saints   who abode in the splendour of glory,
When the Lord, Almighty God,   came again to His throne.

(142–156)

THE ASCENSION

(Christ 440—866)

By the spirit of wisdom,   Illustrious One,
With meditation   and discerning mind,
Strive now earnestly   to understand,
To comprehend,   how it came to pass
When the Saviour was born   in purest birth
(Who had sought a shelter   in Mary's womb,
The Flower of virgins,   the Fairest of maids)
That angels came not   clothed in white
When the Lord was born,   a Babe in Bethlehem.
Angels were seen there   who sang to the shepherds
Songs of great gladness: that the Son of God
Was born upon earth   in Bethlehem.
But the Scriptures tell not   in that glorious time
That they came arrayed   in robes of white,
As they later did   when the Mighty Lord,
The Prince of splendour,   summoned His thanes,
The well-loved band,   to Bethany.

Not long they delayed   their Master's bidding,
Their Lord's behest,   on that happy day;
But swift set forth   to the Holy City
Where the Lord of glory,   the Giver of grace,
Made many things plain   which the prophets had sung
Ere the Only-Begotten,   One with the Father,
Forty days after   He rose from the dead
Out of the earth,   ascended on high.

He had fulfilled   what was formerly spoken,
The words of the prophets   through all the world,
By His Cross and Passion.   His followers praised Him
Gratefully loving   the Lord of life,
The God of Creation.   He graciously gave
Fit reward   to His well-loved thanes,

(440–473)

And ready to fare   to His Father's kingdom
The Lord of angels   uttered this word:
  "Be of stout heart;   I will never forsake you
But will grant you favour   and give you might
And remain with you ever,   that you never may know
Any lack of good   within My gift.
Go now through all   the regions of earth
Over wide-running ways.   Make known to the nations,
Preach and publish,   radiant faith;
Baptizing the people   turn them to heaven.
Destroy their idols,   break and abolish;
Snuff out enmity,   sow seeds of peace
In the minds of men   with abundant might;
And I will be with you   and bring you blessing
And steadfast strength,   wherever you may be."
  Then suddenly in air   came a rush of sound,
A host of heaven's angels,   a beauteous, bright band,
Messengers of glory,   in gathering throngs.
Our King rose up   through the temple's roof,
Where the gazing throng   of His chosen thanes
Remained on earth   in their place of meeting.
They saw their Lord   ascend on high,
Their God from the ground.   Their souls were sad,
Their spirits burning   within their breasts;
They mourned in heart   that they might no longer
See their Beloved   beneath the sky.
Then sang their songs   the heavenly angels,
Adored the Prince,   and praised life's Lord,
Rejoiced in the light   that shone from the Saviour.
  There by the First-Born,   the Flower of kings,
They saw two angels   in shining white.
In wondrous words   clear-voiced they called
From heaven on high   o'er the hosts of men:
  "Why remain ye waiting   ye men of Galilee?
Clearly you see   the Saviour Lord,

(474-512)

The Ruler of triumph,   rising to glory.
The Prince of princes,   Lord of all peoples,
With this angel host   ascends to His home,
His Father's country.   With this great crowd,
This blithesome company,   we will bring our Lord
To the bright City   above the arching sky,
This Best and Strongest   of the sons of triumph
On Whom you gaze,   and see for your solace
Gleaming with glory.   Yet shall He come
With countless train   to the tribes of earth
On a later day,   and will judge each deed
That men have performed,   the folk under heaven.
    "Now has the Holy One   harrowed hell
Of all the tribute   that in days of old
It wrongfully swallowed   in that seat of strife.
Now the fiends' warriors   are overwhelmed,
Laid low and imprisoned   in living pain,
Deprived of blessings   in the pit of hell.
God's adversaries   could not win at war
In the casting of weapons   when the King of glory,
The Defender of heaven,   with His Ancient Foe
Engaged in strife   by His single might;
There He freed from bondage   abundant spoil,
A countless folk   from the City of fiends,
This very host   which you here behold!
    "And now the Saviour   ascends to seek
The throne of grace,   God's Own Son,
After the battle-play.   Plainly you know
Who is the Lord   that leads this band.
Go ye glad-minded   to meet with friends!
Open ye gates!   The Lord of all
Will enter in;   the King will come
Unto His City   with assembled hosts,
The Lord of Creation   leading this folk
That by His triumph   He took from the fiends.

                (513–526; 558–581)

Peace shall prosper   for angels and mortals,
And a covenant common   to God and man;
Holy faith,   and hope of life,
Love for ever,   and joy in all light."
    Then the Lord of glory   was compassed with clouds
O'er the roofs of earth,   High-King of angels,
Helm of the holy.   Hope was renewed,
Bliss in the cities,   through the Saviour's Coming.
He was seated triumphant,   Author of joy,
At the right hand   of His Ruling Father.
    The disciples set forth   to the Holy City,
Unto Jerusalem,   sad of soul,
From the spot where so lately   their eyes had seen
God ascending,   their Giver of good.
There was sound of weeping;   with bitter sorrow
True love was flooded,   hot at heart;
Their souls welled up,   their spirits burned.
There in the great city   those glorious thanes
Awaited the promises   of their Prince
For ten nights' time,   as the Ruler of all,
The Lord of glory,   had given command
Ere He entered in   through the arching heavens.
    Clothed in white   came angels to meet Him,
The Saviour of men;   it is well said,
As the Writings tell,   that radiant angels
In that holy hour   came forth in hosts
From heaven on high   to attend their Lord.
In celestial glory   was the greatest of feasts,
And fitting was it   to that festival
Came angels in white,   a beauteous band,
To the City of Christ.   Most welcome they saw
Heaven's Lord seated   on His High-throne,
Life-Giver of men,   in radiance ruling
Over all this world   and the heavenly hosts.
    Lo! now we have heard   how the Healing Saviour

(581–585; 527–557; 586)

H

Through His hither-coming   has granted us grace,
Has freed and defended   the folk under heaven,
God's Mighty Son,   that every man
In his days on earth   by his deeds may choose:
The shame of hell   or the splendour of heaven,
The shining light   or the loathsome night,
The rush of glory   or the gloom of darkness,
Rapture with God   or riot with fiends,
Glory with angels   or anguish with devils,
Or life or death,   as he may find dearer
While body and spirit   abide in this world.
Glory to the Trinity   and eternal thanks!
    It is meet and right   that the race of men
Bless the Lord   for all the abundance
Which early and late   He prepared for us all
Through the great mystery   of His manifold might.
He assigns us food   and bounty of substance,
Wealth in wide lands,   and kindly weather
Under sheltering skies.   The sun and moon,
Candles of heaven,   most stately of stars,
Shine unto all men   throughout the earth.
Dew falls and rain   bringing forth plenty
To sustain the lives   of the sons of men,
Enlarging abundance.   Praise we the Lord
With manifold thanks,   and most of all
For that Salvation   which by His Ascension
The Only-Begotten   gave for our hope,
Undoing the woe   we endured before,
And with His Sweet Father   settling for men
The greatest of feuds.   He recalled the curse,
In peace to our souls,   which was formerly spoken
In wrathful mood   to the sorrow of men:
    "I wrought thee of earth; on the earth shalt thou live
Enduring exile,   dwelling in woe,
Chanting death-songs   to the joy of devils,

(587–623)

And to the same earth   turning again
Teeming with worms;   from the mould once more
Shalt thou fare to find   the fires of torment."

  Lo! this has the Lord   made easier for us all,
Putting on limbs   and a living body.
When God's Son ascended   to the seat of angels
Came the will to help us   at that holy time.

  Of Him sang Job,   who well could sing,
Adoring the Prince   and praising the Saviour;
He contrived a surname   for the Son of God
In loving-kindness,   and called Him Bird,
Whom the Jews in no wise   had wisdom of spirit
To comprehend.   For the flight of that Fowl
Was concealed and secret   from its foes on earth,
From all who bore   within their bosoms
A darkened spirit   and a stony heart.
Nor would they recognize   those radiant tokens
Which God's Fair Son   performed among them
Many and varied   throughout the earth.

  So the Faithful Fowl   made trial of flight
When Mighty and Strong   it sought out heaven,
The realm of angels,   that radiant home;
And again when it stooped   to seek the earth,
The spacious ground   through the Spirit's grace,
And sank to the world.   Of this Job sang:

  "He was lifted up   in the arms of angels
In all the mastery   of His great might,
High and holy,   o'er the host of heaven."

  Nor could they recognize   the flight of that Fowl,
Dissenters denying   our Lord's Ascension,
Who would not believe   that the Lord of life
Was lifted up,   the Holy One from earth
In man's image,   o'er the heavenly hosts.

  Then the Son of God   Who shaped this world
Showed us honour   and gave us gifts,

(624–660)

Eternal homes   with angels in heaven;
In men's minds also   He sowed and set
Manifold skills.   He sends to one
Wisdom of speech   in word and thought,
Excellent insight;   he may sing and say
All things well   who has wisdom's power
Locked in his heart.   Loud before men
One stirs with fingers   the sounding harp,
Strikes sweetly the glee-wood.   Godly law
One may interpret.   One tells aright
The stars in their courses,   the spacious sky.
One fashions well   the eloquent word.
To one He awards   war-might in battle
When the archers send   a shower of darts,
A flickering arrow-flight   o'er the shield's defence.
One may with boldness   drive his bark
Over the salt wave,   stirring the foam.
One can mount   on the tall steep tree.
One can work weapons,   the tempered sword.
One knows the plains,   and earth's far paths.
    Even so the Ruler,   the Son of God,
Gives His gifts   to us on earth.
But to no one man   will He give all wisdom
Lest in his might   beyond other men
Pride take hold upon him   to his hurt.
Thus God Almighty,   King of all creatures,
Honours earth's offspring   with great gifts.
Likewise to the blessed   He gives bliss in glory
Stablishing peace for ever   for angels and men.
    So He honours His Creation.   Of Him the prophet
Said holy gems   were raised on high,
Bright stars of heaven,   the sun and moon.
What are these gems so glowing   save God Himself?
He is the faithful shining   of the sun,
A radiant light for angels   and men on earth.

                    (661–697)

Over the world the moon gleams,   a ghostly star;
Even so shines the Church of God   where are met together
Right and truth   —as the Scriptures tell—
Since the Son of God,   the Prince of the pure,
Ascended from earth.   Under heathen shepherds
The Church of the faithful   has suffered affliction.
The sinful heathen   heeded not truth
Nor the spirit's need; but destroyed God's temples,
Broke and burned   and poured out blood,
Hated and harried.   Yet by grace of the Spirit
A glory has come   for the thanes of God
Since the Ascension   of the Eternal Son!
    Of Him sang Solomon,   son of David,
Versed in songs   and spiritual grace,
The Ruler of nations,   pronouncing this word:
    "It is widely known   that the King shall come,
The Lord of might,   leaping upon the mountains,
Skipping upon the hills,   and girding with glory
The knolls and high dunes;   He shall redeem the world,
All who live on earth,   by that noble leaping."
    It was the first leap   when our Lord descended
To the spotless Virgin,   and free of sin
Took human flesh.   That came for a comfort
To all the dwellers   over all the earth.
It was the second leap   when the Babe was born
Cradled in a manger   in swaddling clothes,
The Glory of all glories   in the guise of a child.
It was the third leap   when the Lord of heaven,
The Father, the Comforter,   mounted the Cross.
It was the fourth leap   when He left the Tree
And turned to the sepulchre,   fast in the tomb.
It was the fifth leap   when He harrowed hell
With bitter torment   and bound her king,
The fiends' fierce Spokesman,   with bands of fire
Where he still lies fettered,   fast in his sin.

(698–736)

It was the sixth leap   when our Lord in triumph
Ascended on high   to his former home.
In that holy hour   the angel host
Grew blithe with rapture   and blissful joy
Beholding the Lord of glory,   the Leader of princes,
Returning to his native country,   those shining courts.
Then for the citizens of heaven,   for all the saints,
Came eternal joy   from the triumph of their Prince.

As here on earth's soil   God's Son Eternal
Mounted by leaps   above the high hills,
Bold on the mountains,   so we mortal men
In our hearts' musings   must mount by leaps
From strength to strength,   and strive for glory,
That we may ascend   by holy works
To the highest heavens,   where are joy and hope,
A goodly band of thanes.   Great is our need
In our secret souls   that we seek salvation,
If we have in our hearts   a fervent faith
That the Healing Son,   the Living Saviour,
With our own body   ascended from earth.

Wherefore we should ever   despise idle lusts,
The wounds of sin,   finding bliss in the better.
We have for our comfort   our Father on high,
Almighty God.   From heaven the Holy One
Sends His angels   hither to earth,
Who shield us from spoilers   and their deadly darts
Lest the fiends work wounds   when the Author of evil
Against God's people   shoots bitter shafts
From his bended bow.   Therefore fast and firm
We must warily watch   against the sudden shot
Lest poisoned arrow   or pitiless dart,
Or the Foe's swift cunning,   should pierce our frame.
Grievous that hurt,   most ghastly of wounds!

Let us guard against it   while we dwell on earth.
Let us pray the Father   that He grant us peace,

(736–773)

The Son of God,   and the blithe Spirit,
That He who shaped us   with life and limbs,
With body and soul,   may shield us well
From the wiles of the wicked,   the weapons of foes.
To Him be praise   and glory in heaven
For ever and ever,   world without end.

   Nor need any man   of the race of men
Fear darts of devils   or spear-flights of fiends
If the Lord God of hosts   is his defence.
The Judgment is near;   we shall know reward
According as we have won it   by our works
During days of life   dwelling on earth.
The Scriptures tell us   how the Treasure of might,
God's Glorious Son,   in the beginning
Stooped to the world,   to the womb of the Virgin,
Holy from heaven.   Verily I await,
And also dread,   a sterner doom
When the King of angels   shall come again—
· I who obeyed not well   what my Saviour bade me
In the Books.   I shall surely see
The terror of vengeance of sin,   as I count it true,
Where many shall be summoned   to the Assembly
Before the face   of the Eternal Judge.
C   Then even the *bold*   shall tremble in terror
Hearing the King,   the Ruler of heaven,
Speak wrathful words   to those in the world
YN Who obeyed Him feebly   when *affliction* and *need*
Most easily may find comfort.   There many a one
In that place shall wearily   await with fear
What dreadful punishment   God shall ordain
W According to man's works.   *Winsomeness* of earth's treasures
U Shall be departed.   *Our* portion of life's joy
LF Was long washed with *floods*,   all *wealth* on earth.
In that day earth's treasures   shall burn in the blast;
Fiercely shall ravage   the swift, red flame.

               (774–809)

It shall rush in rage   over the wide world;
Plains shall perish,   castles shall crumble;
The fire shall be fleet;   most greedy of spirits
It shall eat up all   the ancient treasure
Men gained of old   when was glory on earth.
    Therefore I urge   each of my beloved
That he never slight   the need of his soul,
Nor engulf it in pride   while God may will
That here in the world   he has his dwelling
While soul fares in body,   that friendly inn.
Let each of men earnestly   in his days on earth
Muse in his heart   how the Lord of might
First came with pity   by the angel's promise.
But He shall be grim   when He comes again,
Just and stern.   Then the heavens shall be shaken,
And the mighty limits   of earth shall be moved.
He shall give their reward   to those who through wickedness
Lived upon earth   soiled with their sin.
Soul-weary and sad   they shall long receive,
In the bath of fire   begirt with flame,
In return for their sin   a terrible requital.
    Then the King of might   shall come to that meeting
With the greatest of hosts;   loud shall be heard
The terror of men   'mid the tumult of heaven,
The wailing of them that weep.   The lost shall lament
Before the face   of the Eternal Judge,
Those who rely but little   on their works.
To many shall be manifest   more of terror
Than ever was known   from the world's creation.
To every sinner   in that sudden hour
It shall be dearer far   than all this fleeting world
That he may have shelter   in that happy band
When the Lord of hosts,   the Prince of princes,
Shall judge unto all,   the loved and the loathed,
Unto every one   a just reward.

(809–847)

Dire is our need   ere that day of terror
That we think of the soul's beauty   in this barren time.
   Now is it most like   as if on ocean
Across cold water   we sail in our keels,
Over the wide sea   in our ocean-steeds,
Faring on in our flood-wood.   Fearful the stream,
The tumult of waters,   whereon we toss
In this feeble world.   Fierce are the surges
On the ocean lanes.   Hard was our life
Before we made harbour   o'er the foaming seas.
Then help was vouchsafed us   when God's Spirit-Son
Guided us to the harbour of salvation   and granted us grace
That we may understand   over the ship's side
Where to moor our sea-steeds,   our ocean-stallions,
Fast at anchor.   Let us fix our hope
Upon that haven   which the Lord of heaven,
In holiness on high,   has opened by His Ascension.

(847–866)

CHAPTER III

ACTS OF THE APOSTLES

FOREWORD

ONE of the most interesting of Old English religious poems is a narrative of the adventures of St Andrew among the cannibals of Mermedonia. This poem, more than half as long as the *Beowulf*, is known as the *Andreas*, and is found in the Vercelli MS. It is immediately followed in the manuscript by the *Fates of the Apostles*, which contains one of the four runic signatures of Cynewulf.

Some critics would have us regard the *Fates* as an epilogue to the *Andreas*, and the runic passage as Cynewulf's signature of the combined poems. But the general weight of evidence does not support this opinion. The *Fates of the Apostles* is a distinct type of literary composition in itself, and the nature and development of the subject matter of the two poems oppose a theory of unity. The *Andreas*, therefore, must be considered a separate and complete poem which, on the evidence available, can hardly be assigned to Cynewulf.

The really striking result of comparative tests of vocabulary and style is to establish a closer relationship of the *Andreas* to the *Beowulf* than to any other Old English poem. Parallelisms of phrasing, and echoes of the language of the *Beowulf*, continually recur throughout the text of the *Andreas*.[1] Apparently its unknown author was definitely attempting to imitate the heroic style and epic mood of the *Heldenepos*.

There are two Old English versions of the story of St Andrew in Mermedonia, one a prose version, the other the *Andreas*. Both versions reach back to an ultimate source in a Greek text of the *Acts of St Andrew and St Matthew*.[2] But the Greek *Acts* can not be regarded as the immediate or direct source. The Old English poet must have found the legend in some intervening text, probably a Latin version. Three fragments of such a Latin text do exist, and comparison of them with the Greek *Acts*, and with the *Andreas*, suggests that it was from such a Latin translation of the Greek *Acts* that the Old English poet drew his material.[3]

[1] See Krapp, *Andreas and the Fates of the Apostles*, Introduction, lvi, note 1.
[2] Tischendorf, *Acta Apostolorum Apocrypha*, 132–6.
[3] See Krapp, *Andreas and the Fates of the Apostles*, Introduction, xxi–xxix.

The legend of St Andrew is part of a body of Apocryphal literature which began to grow up in the second century regarding the missions and acts of the various Apostles. An early pattern for such material was the legend of the *Sortes Apostolorum*, or *Lots of the Apostles*. The legend arose from the mission of the Apostles to teach and baptize all nations,[1] to the uttermost part of the earth,[2] and deals with the casting of lots to determine the land in which each apostle was to preach. There is a reference to this casting of lots in the passage on the Apostles which serves as a brief heroic prologue to the *Andreas*.[3] This story of the "lots" was paralleled by Apocryphal material of various kinds until in course of time there grew up a corpus of popular legend which had to do with the journeys, acts, miracles, and martyrdoms or "fates" of the respective Apostles.

The source from which the Old English poet borrowed for his heroic tale of St Andrew seems to have been a portion of an Eastern body of legend setting forth the saint's adventures among a cannibal tribe in Scythia, a somewhat vaguely bounded territory around the shores of the Black Sea. This early material was obviously popular in tradition, and romantic in mood. It is possible that in its remote beginnings the Greek legend of St Andrew felt some influence of Mediterranean sailor stories of the marvels of distant places, and the dangers and hardships of sea-adventure.

Perhaps the most significant quality of the *Andreas* is the clearly marked intention of the author to use this borrowed material, not in the simple narrative of a saint's legend, but with an imitative shaping to the familiar literary pattern of the epic tale. The poem suggests this by its heroic mood and action, its dramatic dialogue, and by the characteristic descriptive and decorative "set pieces" dealing with war, scenery, and weather. One has only to compare the way in which the poet of *Andreas* tells his story with the style and manner of the conventional saint's legend as illustrated in Cynewulf's *Juliana*, or in the *Death of St Guthlac*, to note how sharply the two methods differ.

The heroic mood is simulated from the first line of *Andreas*. The poem begins with the appeal to oral tradition and the ancient past, the "Lo! we have heard" with which the *Beowulf* also begins, instead of the

[1] Matthew, xxviii 19.   [2] The Acts, i 8.   [3] *Andreas*, 5–6.

references to written tradition which occur early in the *Phoenix*.[1] The brief opening prologue about the twelve Apostles employs the martial imagery and heroic language of the epic tale to describe them. They were famous heroes whose glory was won in the conflict of war; they were "bold in strife" when "hand and buckler defended the helm in battle". In the first ten lines of *Andreas* the heroic pattern is clearly set.

Throughout the *Andreas* this pattern persists, and the heroic mood is maintained by various poetic devices including, as we shall see later, a passage so eloquent of *comitatus* loyalty that it might have come straight out of a Germanic epic. Early in the poem the thronging of savage men about the prison where St Matthew lies bound is pictured as the gathering of an armed host in an Old English battle scene. The martial imagery of the heroic tale is employed in passages where it is even less appropriate. When the divine command comes to Andrew in Achaia to go to Mermedonia, there to free Matthew from bondage, the mission is represented as the sending forth of a warrior prince to battle:

> The path shall lead   to the power of the foe
> Where the crash of battle   shall come upon you,
> The war-might of heroes   and heathen strife.[2]

From time to time the Old English poet attains a striking vividness in descriptive passages. A delineation of weather that is as biting as that of a Northumbrian winter, and for which the poet is in no way indebted to his source, is an excellent example.[3] Frost and cold are personified as "hoary warriors locking fast the homes of men". Elsewhere in the poem, hunger is a "pale table-guest",[4] and a "fierce ravager of the folk";[5] Hatred rising in the heart is a "serpent hostile to happiness" and a "baleful poison".[6] The miraculous flood which St Andrew called forth upon the Mermedonians, carrying many of them to death, was a "bitter beer-drinking".[7]

The *Andreas* is especially notable as a sea poem. The voyage of St Andrew to Mermedonia is the most elaborated sea-voyage in Old English poetry. There are, of course, not a few Old English poetic

[1] *Phoenix*, 29–30.   [2] *Andreas*, 216–19.   [3] *Andreas*, 1253–65.
[4] *Andreas*, 1088.   [5] *Andreas*, 1115–16.   [6] *Andreas*, 768–70.
[7] *Andreas*, 1533.

descriptions of ocean voyaging which are memorable for their realistic sense of the sea. Among these are the two voyages of Beowulf,[1] the Mediterranean voyage of St Helena,[2] the ocean realisms of the *Sea-farer*,[3] and the poetic description of this life and the hereafter in the detail of the metaphorical sea voyage with which Cynewulf concludes his poem on the Ascension.[4] All these sea pictures are well done. But nowhere else in Old English poetry do we have a sea-voyage set forth at the length, and with the realistic detail, which the poet employs in the *Andreas*. Beginning with the passage in which St Andrew and his followers come to the seashore and the waiting ship, the voyage element in the poem extends for 587 lines, a little more than one-third of the entire poem.

Not only the extended narrative, but also the graphic realisms of much of the descriptive detail, mark the poet's account of the voyage as unusual. At first Andrew shrinks from his mission. Fear of the sea, and of the far country to which he has been sent, rises in his heart. He knows no man among that foreign people, and the ocean-ways across the cold water are unfamiliar to him. He suggests instead that God send His angel, who from heaven beholds both land and sea, and knows well the stretching ocean-stream. But Andrew is told that God could, if he wished, bring the Mermedonian city to the land of Achaia. Let Andrew, therefore, obey God's will and set about his mission. At dawn he will find a vessel waiting at the shore of the sea.

The description of daybreak as Andrew and his men tramp along the shingle with the roar of the surf in their ears is vividly done. There at the shore is a ship with three sailors. The Master Mariner, the poet tells us, is the Lord Himself, with two of His angels, all garbed as sailors. St Andrew, hailing them and learning that they are from Mermedonia, asks passage for himself and his companions. The Mariner warns Andrew against the voyage since in Mermedonia foreigners are put to death. When St Andrew still insists, the Mariner agrees to transport him when he has paid the appointed toll. St Andrew explains that he has "no gold, or goodly treasure", nor has he any food. The Shipman then asks how it happens that without money, or food or water for

---

[1] *Beowulf*, 207–24 and 1896–1913.   [2] *Elene*, 225–55.
[3] *The Seafarer*, 1–64.   [4] *Christ*, 850–66.

refreshment, Andrew would undertake a voyage "over the climbing billows, past the cold headlands, to the far sea-limits"? St Andrew's answer is a rehearsal of the mission of the Apostles to preach the Gospel to all peoples of earth.[1] He explains his lack of money and provisions by quoting Christ's command that they take with them neither gold, nor silver, nor brass in their purses, nor scrip for their journey.[2] Hearing that St Andrew and his companions are followers of Christ, the Mariner accepts them on board and the ship sails.

Into his account of the voyage the Old English poet inserts a description of a storm at sea which owes nothing to his source material except a suggestion that the sea was rough. The details of the picture are perhaps the most realistic of any Old English seascape with the one exception of the vigorously wrought depiction of the storm and shipwreck in the "Wind" Riddle.[3] The play of the hornfish in the stormy waters, the grey gulls wheeling overhead against a dark sky, the whining of the ship's rigging, the heavy, sea-drenched sails, the surging billows, these are details the experienced sailor will note with instant recognition.[4]

One addition to the source brings another. It is the inserted description of the storm at sea which leads to the elaborated passage on *comitatus* loyalty. St Andrew's followers are overcome with fear of the storm, and the Shipman suggests that they be put ashore to await the return of Andrew from his mission. Their refusal is couched in the conventional phrasing of such expressions of loyalty to an over-lord. If they desert their leader now, where shall they wander lordless and lonely? How shall they endure the loathing of men when valiant warriors gather to debate who best has aided his battle-lord in the hour of danger? As the voyage continues the storm at length blows itself out, the seas subside, and St Andrew's followers fall asleep, "sea-weary sailors by the mast".

In a long conversation that follows between St Andrew and the Master Shipman while the men slumber, Andrew compliments the Mariner on his seamanship. He himself has sailed sixteen voyages and

---

[1] Matthew, xxviii 19; Mark, xvi 15; Matthew, x 7—11.
[2] These lines have a parallel in a passage in Cynewulf's *Christ*, 481—90.
[3] *Riddle* 3, 17—23. [4] *Andreas*, 369—80.

never met such skill. How has one, apparently so young, gained such experience? The Shipman's reply is that there is no sailor who is not at times hard pressed on stormy seas, even if he survives the danger. But Ocean can never work harm to any man against God's will. In turn, He requests Andrew, since he was a follower of Christ, to tell of His life and work. How had it happened that Christ was crucified by the Jewish people? Was it true that He showed His power by miracles, and were these miracles publicly known?

St Andrew narrates at length the various miracles he had seen performed in the course of Christ's teaching, some publicly, some in secret. All day long he recounts the marvels of Christ's power as shown to His disciples, and to the people. It is a naïve touch that at the end of his tale, unknowingly addressing the Lord of whom he has been telling, Andrew uses words reminiscent of those employed by Christ Himself to His disciples in John xvi 12. St Andrew tells the Mariner, "I still know many a glorious story of the labours He wrought, the Lord of the skies, but you can not bear them now, or fully fathom, wise though you be." As his story ends and the day draws to a close he also at last is overcome with slumber. As he sleeps, Andrew, by the Mariner's command, is born in the arms of angels to the Mermedonian coast. There at daybreak he awakens to find himself lying, with his companions about him, not far from the gates of the city.

The adventures of St Andrew in Mermedonia form a record of torture, of miracles and wonders, and of ultimate triumph. The poet's delight in telling this story of violent and sensational events is evident throughout. Though the shaping of his borrowed material into epic form here and there makes greater demands than the author's skill can supply, the joy and zest of telling the tale never leave him.

After awaking from his slumber St Andrew enters the city and makes his way to the prison where Matthew is held. There the seven gaolers are miraculously slain, and at "one hand-touch" the prison doors are opened. St Matthew and 289 fellow prisoners, men and women, come forth to freedom. God covers the marching company with a cloud lest the savage warriors work them harm.

The poem then recounts the gathering of the cannibals, a description done in terms of the mobilizing of an Old English fighting force. They find the prison empty and the victims, who had been held for food, escaped. Immediately, as the poet naïvely tells the tale, they become tortured with hunger. That terrible foe rides them hard. They cast lots among themselves to decide who shall be taken for food. The lot falls upon an aged warrior, who offers them his stripling son in his place and so purchases his own safety.

Then it seemed to Andrew an appalling evil and bitter to bear that the youth should lose his life. When the armed host attacks the lad, by God's help Andrew causes their weapons to melt in the fray "most like to wax", and the youth escapes. This detail of the "melting" weapons would seem to be a reminiscence of Beowulf's struggle with Grendel's dam when the great sword he had wielded, "eaten with blood of battle", melted in iron icicles "most like to ice".

A characteristic feature of the saints' legend as a literary type survives in the epic pattern of *Andreas* in the appearance before the people of the Devil, the Cripple of hell. This is the scene in which Satan reveals to the Mermedonians that it is Andrew who has done them these great wrongs, and incites them to violence against him. At the Devil's urging Andrew is bound and imprisoned. For four days he is dragged about the countryside, and repeatedly flogged. For the night after the first day's torture the poet introduces a realistic description of winter cold and storm with all the details of the conventional Northern winter scene: frost and snow, bitter wind and hail, ice that "builds a bridge".

On the second day the Devil appears again, urging on the torture, this time accompanied by six other fiends. It is in keeping with the poet's imitation of the epic tale that on both appearances the Devil is portrayed as a warrior prince. His language throughout is the martial idiom. The struggle between Andrew and himself is warfare of "spear-point and poisoned arrow", of "doomed flesh" and "warrior's boast". As the Fiend urges his followers to the attack on Andrew, they behold on his forehead the sign of Christ and are turned to flight. One of them utters a warning to Satan, the "dearest of eorls":

> We can not readily   work him ruin,
> Or devise his death.   Go you against him!
> There you will quickly   find fierce combat,
> Terrible fighting,   if further you dare
> Against that lone one   to risk your life.

For four days St Andrew's torture continues. Again and again he is flogged, dragged through the land, and thrown back into prison. But in the end flowers spring up in his bloody footprints and by God's grace "the fringe of a garment was not loosed from his raiment, nor a lock of hair from his head, nor a bone broken, nor had bloody wounds brought baleful hurt."

At this point in the narrative (1478–89), the author introduces a personal "aside" to those who may read, or hear, his poem. The tone of the passage suggests that he has paused to survey the scope of his poem as a whole. For some time now, he writes, he has been telling the story of the saint and his labours, a well known tale and one "beyond his measure". There is still much to tell but it takes a wiser man than he counts himself to know all the struggles and hardships that St Andrew endured. Nevertheless, he will carry forward the poem a little further. The passage may imply that the poet has found that the work of translating and versifying requires more time than he can devote to the task, or that he feels the poem is becoming unduly long. In any case, he is planning, after a little, to bring it to a conclusion.

There follow two miracles by which the stubborn spirits of the Mermedonians were converted. From a marble column St Andrew strikes out a flood that overflows the land, sweeping the leaders of the folk to death. As the people turn to flee, an angel overspreads their city with surging flame, and flight is cut off. The description of flood and fire is written with the same dramatic stress, and the same delight in violent imagery, that have characterized the poet's descriptive method in other outstanding passages.

The elders of the people call aloud to St Andrew for succour, and at the saint's bidding the flood abates, and a mountain opens to drink into its deep chasm the dark flood. All those who had perished in the waters are restored to life. In joy the people acclaim the power of the new faith, and receive the bath of baptism. St Andrew commands that a church be built on the spot where those who were drowned had been raised up, and over the people he ordained Platan to be Bishop. Then Andrew prepares to return to Achaia.

The poem concludes with a sea-picture which recalls us once more to the heroic spirit of the epic tale. A sorrowing people accompany the beloved saint to his sea-boat under the hill, and there on the shore stand weeping for his departure as long as they can behold his sail upon the sea-line. It is interesting that this same image of the sail that grows smaller and smaller on the horizon to mark the departure of a beloved leader, and end a poem, was used by Tennyson to conclude the *Passing of Arthur*.

So ends the *Andreas*. It is no marvel if here and there the poet's ambitious design for his chosen material was not wholly achieved. He himself tells us that the poem was somewhat "beyond his measure". But, in spite of his humility, his love of the legend and his joy in the telling of the tale have left us a memorable poem. We have in the *Andreas* a vividness of imagery, a vivacity of mood, a sense of design, and a sustained narrative flair that make this tale of St Andrew notable among Old English religious poems.

ST ANDREW'S MISSION TO MERMEDONIA

(Andreas)

Lo! we have heard   of twelve mighty heroes
Honoured under heaven   in days of old,
Thanes of God.   Their glory failed not
In the clash of banners,   the brunt of war,
After they were scattered   and spread abroad
As their lots were cast   by the Lord of heaven.
Famous those heroes,   foremost on earth,
Brave-hearted leaders   and bold in strife
When hand and buckler   defended the helm
On the plain of war,   on the field of fate.

One was Matthew.   Among the Jews
With wondrous wisdom   he first set forth
The words of the Gospel.   And Holy God
Assigned his lot   in a foreign land
Where no one alien   might have his home
Or happy estate.   Sorely he suffered
At hostile hands   in the stress of strife.

All that district   and dwelling of men
Was compassed with death   and the crime of the foe.
No bread for food   was found in that country,
No draught of water.   The dwellers there
Ate blood and skin,   the bodies of any
Who came from afar.   It was their custom
To feed the hungry   with flesh of men
Who fared from outland   to seek their shores.
'Twas a hostile token   of that hateful tribe,
A monstrous violence   of wicked men,
That the savage foe   in hostile fury
With point of spear   put out men's eyes,
The gems of the head.   By craft their magicians

(1–34)

Blended a bitter   and deadly drink
Perverting the reason,   the minds, of men.
Their hearts were altered;   for human joys
They grieved no longer   but fiercely greedy
And plagued with hunger   ate grass and hay.

   To that famous city   within the fortress,
Came Matthew faring.   Mermedonia was filled
With clamour and tumult,   a crowding of men
In savage throngs   when those thanes of Satan
Learned of his coming.   With lance and shield
They rushed against him.   The wrathful foe
Were no wise slow   in the work of war.
Hell-destined men,   they seized on the saint,
Fastened his hands   with fiendish craft,
And with point of sword   destroyed his sight.
Receiving the deadly   and poisoned drink
Still in his heart   he revered heaven's Lord,
Boldly praising   the Prince of glory
With saintly voice   in his prison cell,
The love of Christ   firm locked in his breast.
Weeping there   with weary tears,
In sorrowful voice   and accents sad,
He called on the Lord,   the King of mankind,
The Giver of good,   and spoke this word:

   "Alas! how the heathen   weave their webs
And fashion for me   these fettering snares!
Always and ever   my heart has been eager
In working Thy will.   But now in distress
Needs must I bear me   like the dumb beasts.
Thou alone knowest,   O Maker of men,
All man's thoughts   and his inmost mind!
If it be Thy will,   O God of glory,
That the faithless heathen   slay me with sword,
With weapon's edge,   O Lord of angels,
Prince of warriors,   I am prepared

(34–72)

To suffer the fate   Thou assignest me here,
A homeless man.   Grant me in mercy
Light in this life,   Almighty God,
Lest in this city   after the sword-hate
In blindness I suffer   the scorn of the foe
Through the bitter sentence   of blood-greedy men.
On Thee alone,   O Lord of earth,
Have I set my heart   and my steadfast love,
And Thee I beg,   Bright Giver of bliss,
Father of angels   and Judge of all,
To assign me not   among savage foes,
Vile workers of sin,   to the worst of deaths."
    After these words   holy from heaven
Came a sign of glory   like the gleaming sun
To the dungeon cell.   It was clearly disclosed
That Holy God   wrought help for the saint
When there came the voice   of the King of heaven,
The wondrous words   of the Mighty Prince,
With help and healing   in accents sublime
To his fearless thane   fast in his fetters:
    "Unto you, Matthew,   I grant My grace;
Be not afraid   or fearful of heart.
I will be with you   and free you from bonds,
From all this host   that hedges you round,
In your heavy need.   By My holy might
The radiant Paradise,   brightest of blessings,
Happiest of dwellings   and fairest of homes,
Shall open before you   where you shall exult
In grace and glory   for ever and ever.
Bravely endure   these blows of affliction.
The time is not long   that these treacherous men
May afflict you in malice   with fettering chains.
I will send Andrew   unto you straightway
To comfort and keep you   in this cruel town,
And he shall free you   from the hate of this folk.

(73–112)

Seven nights and twenty   the span shall be
Till weary with sorrow   and spent with woe
But crowned with triumph   you shall come at last
From this grievous torture   to the grace of God."
Then departed the Holy One,   Helm of all creatures,
Creator of angels,   to His home on high.
He is by right   the Steadfast Ruler
In every place,   the Prince of all!
    Then Matthew was heartened   with hope anew.
The gloom of night   glided away;
The shades of darkness   faded fast;
Daylight came   and the stir of dawn.
The host assembled;   the heathen warriors
Gathered in bands.   Their battle-gear rang,
Their war-spears rattled;   their hearts were enraged
Under their bucklers.   They were eager to know
If the prison-lodgers   were still alive
In that dismal dwelling,   fast in their fetters,
And which they might plan   at the time appointed
To deprive of life   and apportion for food.
For those flesh-greedy spirits   had written in runes
And reckoned the day   of every man's death
When each might serve   as food for the famished
Among that folk.   Fiercely they clamoured,
Band followed band;   their brutish chiefs
Recked not of right   or the grace of God.
Often they plunged   to the pit of darkness
Through the Devil's teaching   when they put their trust
In the power of fiends.   In the prison gloom
They found the holy man   wise of heart
Awaiting bravely   what fate the Bright King,
The Lord of angels,   might allot to him.
    The time appointed   was over and past
Save for three nights,   as those wretches had reckoned,
When they thought to sever   his frame asunder,

(113–150)

Soul from body,   and serve to all,
To old and young,   for their food and feasting
The flesh of the hero   fated and dead.
For his life they grieved not,   those greedy war-wolves,
Nor how his soul's journey   might be assigned
After his death-pangs.   Each thirty days
They gathered together   and great was their craving
With bloody jaws   to feed on man's flesh.
     Then was He mindful   Who with potent might
Established mid-earth   how Matthew lay
In pain and misery   among alien men
Fast in his fetters,   he who had often
Before Hebrews and Israelites   worked God's will
Withstanding the evil   arts of the Jews.
A voice from heaven   was heard on earth
In the land of Achaia   where Andrew lodged
Leading the people   in the way of Life.
To the great-hearted hero   the Glory of kings,
Lord of hosts   and Maker of men,
Opened His mind-hoard,   uttered this word:
     "Go forth straightway   faring afar
To seek the coasts   where the Cannibals dwell
With murderous fury   defending their land.
Such is their custom   that in that country
No foreign man   is allowed to live;
If it be that they find one   defenceless there
Deadly torture   and death is his lot.
In bondage of chains   your brother lies
Among that people.   Three nights from now
Through heathen hatred,   smitten with spears,
He shall send forth his soul   on a far journey
Except ere that hour   you haste to help."
     Unto Him promptly   Andrew replied:
"O God of heaven   and Lord of glory
How can I fare   on so far a course

(151–191)

Over the deep ocean   so soon as Thou sayest?
But this Thine angel   may easily do.
From heaven he sees   the ocean-stretches,
All the swan-road   and the salt sea-streams,
The tumult of waves,   the water-terror,
The ways that lengthen   across wide lands.
I have no friends   in that foreign folk,
I know not the mind   of any man there,
And the ocean-ways   across the cold water
To me are unknown."
                        Then God made answer:
"Alas! Andrew!   that ever your heart
Should be slow to this journey!   Slight were the task
For God Almighty   to command on earth,
Under the sun,   that this city be moved
Unto this country,   the stately seat
And all who live there,   if the Lord of glory
Decreed it by His word.   You may not weary
In this wayfaring,   nor waver in heart
If you think to keep covenant,   compact with God.
At the hour be ready.   In performing this errand
Can be no delay.   You shall risk your life;
The path shall lead   to the power of the foe
Where the crash of battle   shall come upon you,
The war-might of heroes   and heathen strife.
In the early dawn   with the coming of day
At the ocean's margin   straightway take ship
And drive through the surges   on the cold sea.
My blessing go with you   where you go."
    Then returned Holy God,   Protector and Ruler,
Prince of angels   and Lord of earth,
To His native land,   the lovely home
Where the souls of the righteous   after death's ruin
Long may rejoice   in eternal life.
    So the charge was given   to the glorious hero

(192–230)

Within the city.   His heart was not slow.
He was well resolved   on this work of valour,
Firm and steadfast,   not laggard in strife
But willing and bold   in the warfare of God.
      Then in the dawn   at the break of day
Over the sand dunes   he strode to the shore
Keen of courage,   his comrades beside him
Tramping the shingle.   The ocean resounded,
The combers crashed.   The hero rejoiced
When he saw at the sea's edge   a broad-beamed boat.
Morning sun came,   the brightest of beacons,
Heaven's candle flaming   over the flood,
Holy light dawning   out of the dark.
He saw there waiting   three stately sailors
Geared for the voyage,   great-hearted men
In their wave-boat sitting   as if come from over sea.
'Twas the Lord Himself,   the Leader of men,
Almighty, Eternal,   with His angels twain.
They were garbed like mariners,   seafaring men,
When they plunge in their keels   over cold water
On a far journey   o'er the flood's expanse.
      Ready for sea   as he stood on the shingle
Andrew bespoke them   with hearty hail:
"Sea-crafty men,   whence come you sailing
In your ocean-plunger,   your peerless bark?
Whence have the sea-streams   brought your ship
O'er the tossing main?"
                              The Almighty made answer
As if He wist not   what man it was
Of mortal men   who awaited His word,
With whom He held speech   on the sandy shore:
"From the Mermedonian folk   we have come faring
On a far journey.   Over the flood
Dowered with speed   our swift sea-stallion,
Our high-prowed courser,   carried us on

(231–267)

Along the whale-path   until at last
We came to this country   urged by the waves
As the wind drove us."
                    Humble of heart
Andrew made answer: "A boon I would beg
Though I've little to give   of treasure or gold,
That you take us along   in your tall-sided ship,
Your high-prowed floater,   o'er the home of the whale
To the place of that people.   And God will reward
Your kindness to us   in this ocean-crossing."
    The Creator of angels   again made answer,
The Warden of heroes,   from the wave-ship's side:
"No one who comes   from a far country,
No alien man,   may live in that land;
But in that city   they suffer death
Who venture thither   faring from afar.
And do you now wish   beyond the wide ocean
In savage warfare   to lose your life?"
    Then to Him Andrew   answered and said:
"Unto that folkland,   that famous city,
Desire spurs us   and eager zeal,
Dearest of princes,   if you will do us
This act of kindness   on the ocean-flood."
    The Prince of angels   made reply,
The Saviour of men,   from the ship's prow:
"Gladly will we bear you   o'er the fishes' bath
To the land that your longing   leads you to seek
When you have paid toll,   the appointed tribute,
Even as sailors   over the ship's side
Are willing to agree."
                Then Andrew gave answer
Friendless, penniless,   making reply:
"I have no gold   or goodly treasure,
No food or riches   or woven rings,
No land or linked jewels,   to spur your desire

(268–303)

Or whet your willingness   as your words suggest."
  The Sovereign of men   where He sat on the gangway
Said unto Andrew   o'er the breaking seas:
"How does it happen,   dearest friend,
That lacking money   you would make a voyage
O'er the climbing billows,   past the cold cliffs,
To the far sea-limits?   Have you no food
To bring you comfort,   or clear water
For your refreshment,   on the ocean-flood?
Hard is the life   for one who long
Tries ocean-voyaging."
                       Andrew in answer,
Wise of wit,   his word-hoard unlocked:
"Ill befits it   since God has given you
Food and fortune   and worldly wealth
That you question me thus   with cruel pride
And bitter word.   Better a man
Hail the wayfarer   with humble heart
And kindly spirit,   as Christ once bade,
Our glorious Warden.   We are His thanes,
His chosen champions.   He is True King,
God and Ruler   of celestial glory,
One Lord Eternal   of every created thing,
In His sole power   comprising all,
The earth and the heavens,   by His holy might,
The best of triumphs.   It was He who bade,
The Father of all,   that we go forth
Through the spacious world   to win men's souls:
'Go now to every   region of earth
As far as the seas spread,   the paths o'er the plains.
In every city   over earth's expanse
Preach true faith   and I will defend you.
Nor need you on that journey   take precious gems,
Or gold or silver,   but of all good things
I will grant you store   to your heart's desire.'

               (304–339)

Now have you heard   in your wise heart
The news of our mission.   And now I must know
What aid you will give us."
                     Eternal God answered:
"If, as you say,   you are His servants
Who raised up heaven   high above earth,
And have kept the law   of the Holy Lord,
Gladly will I sail you   over the sea-flood
As you have begged."   Then the heroes brave,
Bold of spirit,   embarked in the ship
And their hearts rejoiced   in the ocean-journey.

    Then Andrew began   o'er the ocean surges
To pray for the mariner   mercy and grace
From the God of glory,   speaking this word:
"May the Lord of all,   the Maker of men,
Grant you honour,   your wish in the world
And glory in heaven,   because you accorded me
Friendly good will   on our ocean-way."

    There the saint took seat   near to the Shipman,
Noble beside noble.   Never did I hear
Of fairer vessel   more richly freighted
With stately treasure.   Within it sat
Glorious princes,   and goodly thanes.
And the Powerful Prince,   Eternal and Mighty,
Bade His angel,   His honoured thane,
Bring food to nourish   those needy men
On the thronging billows,   that they might the better
Endure their lot   on the surging deep.

    Then the depths were troubled.   The horn-fish darted
Gliding through ocean;   the gray gull wheeled
Searching for carrion.   The sun grew dark.
A gale arose   and great waves broke;
The sea-streams were stirred.   Halyards were humming,
Sails were drenched.   Sea-terror grew
In the welter of waves.   The thanes were adread

(340–377)

Who sailed with Andrew   on the ocean-stream,
Nor hoped with life   ever to come to land.
Not yet was it known   Who steered their ship
Through the breaking seas.

                        Then again the saint
As a loyal thane   thanked his Great Leader
On the ocean-highway,   the oar-stirred sea,
Because his strength   had been stayed with food.
   "For this repast   may the Righteous Ruler
Author of life,   and Lord of hosts,
Grant you reward,   and give you for food
The bread of heaven   because you accorded me
Love and good will   on the mountainous waves.
My youthful warriors,   willing thanes,
Are sorely troubled.   The sea resounds,
The surging ocean;   the depths are stirred,
Terribly shaken.   My troop are aghast,
My force of brave followers   deeply dismayed."
   Then from the helm   spoke the Maker of men:
"Let us steer the ship,   our floater, to shore
O'er the ocean-main   and there let your men
Tarry on land   until you return."
   But straightway the eorls,   strong to endure,
Gave Him answer;   they would not agree
That they should forsake   at the vessel's stem
Their beloved leader   and choose the land:
"If we desert you   whither shall we wander
Lordless and lonely,   lacking all good?
We shall be loathed   in every land,
Hated of all men   where valiant heroes
Sit in assembly   holding debate
Who best has bolstered   his lord in battle
When hand and buckler   were bearing the brunt,
Hacked with swords,   on the field of fate."
   Straightway the Great Prince   gave reply,

                (377–415)

The Faithful Sovereign   spoke this word:
"If you are His servant   Who sits in splendour,
The King of glory,   as you proclaim,
Recount the marvels   how He taught mankind
In His life on earth.   Long is the journey
O'er the heaving billows;   hearten your men!
Far is the way   o'er the ocean waves
And land far to seek.   The deep is stirred,
Surf against sand.   But God may easily
Bring help to those   who sail the sea."
     Then Andrew began   with words of wisdom
To hearten the spirits   of his splendid thanes:
"You all had purposed   when you put to sea
To lead your life   mid a hostile folk
And suffering death   for love of the Lord
To lay down your lives   in the Ethiopian land.
Full well I know   the Creator of angels,
The Lord of hosts,   will shield us from harm.
The water-terror   shall be curbed and quelled
By the King of might   and the mountainous seas
Grow peaceful and placid.   So it happened of old
When over the billows   in our ocean-boat
We made trial of the waters,   riding the waves.
Terrible seemed   the perilous sea-paths;
Over the rigging   broke the roaring waves.
The sea cried out   one wave to another,
And ocean-terror   towered from the deep
Over our sea-boat   into the hold.
There God Almighty,   Bright Maker of men,
Sat in the ship.   The sailors were fearful;
They besought the Master   for safety and help.
All the ship's company   cried in terror.
     "Then the King arose,   the Ruler of angels,
And stilled the waters,   the surging waves,
Subdued the winds.   The seas subsided;

(416–453)

K

Calm were the stretches   of the ocean-stream.
Our hearts rejoiced   when we saw under heaven
The water-terror,   the winds and waves,
Cower in fright   for fear of the Lord.
Wherefore I tell you   in very truth
That the Living Lord   will never forsake
Eorl on earth   if his courage holds."
    So spoke the holy man   thoughtful-hearted;
The happy warrior   heartened his thanes,
Teaching his comrades   till sleep overcame them,
Sea-weary sailors   lying by the mast.
Then the waves subsided,   the sea's fierce tumult;
The rush of the waters   was turned away.
The saint's heart was happy   that the terror was past.
Sage of counsel   he began to speak,
Wise of wit   he unlocked his word-hoard:
    "Never have I met   more skilful mariner
Or more sea-crafty   than you seem to me;
No stouter sailor,   none sager in counsel
Or wiser in word.   A boon I would beg
Illustrious eorl,   though it's little I have
Of goodly treasure   or gifts of gold.
Gladly would I gain,   O glorious Prince,
Your welcome friendship   if I may win it,
And you shall have grace   and holy hope
In heavenly glory   if you'll graciously share
Your wise counsels   with sea-weary men.
O noble hero,   since the Maker of men,
Our King, has granted you   glory and might,
One art from you   I am eager to learn:
If you will teach me   how you sail your ship,
Your spray-drenched floater,   across the sea.
    "Sixteen voyages   early and late
It has been my lot   to sail in my sea-boat
With freezing hands   as I smote the sea,

(453–491)

The ocean-stream.   This now is another.
Never have I known   one like to you
Of the sons of men   steering over stem.
The roaring billows   beat on the strand;
Full swift is this bark   and most like a bird
Foamy-necked faring   over the waves.
Full well I know   I never have seen
In any sailor   more wondrous sea-craft.
Most like it is   as if on land
The boat stood still   where wind and storm
Could stir it not,   nor breaking billows
Shatter the high prow;   yet it speeds over ocean
Swift under sail.   You yourself are young,
O warden of warriors,   man of the sea;
Not many your winters!   Yet in your mind
You have an eorl's answers;   in any assembly
You have wise understanding   of every word."
    God the Eternal   made answer to Andrew:
"Oft it befalls   on the watery way
That storms arise   as we break through the billows
In ships with sailors,   in our ocean-steeds.
At times it goes hard with us   on the high seas
Even though we survive   the perilous voyage.
But never may Ocean   work ill to any
Against God's will.   He governs life
Who binds the seas,   Who bridles and fetters
The dark flood.   Over every folk
He rules by right   Who raised up the heavens,
With His hands fastened   and fixed their support.
That bright habitation   He filled with bliss,
By His sole might blessed   the abode of angels.
    "Now is it known   and clearly disclosed
That you are His servant   Who sits in glory,
For the sea perceived,   the circle of ocean,
That you had the gift   of the Holy Ghost.

(492–531)

The billows abated,   the tumult of breakers;
The terror was stilled   and the wide-stretching waves.
The seas subsided   when the waters saw
That He Whose might   shaped heavenly glory
In His safe-keeping   held you close."
   Then with holy voice   spoke the valiant hero
Revering his Leader,   the Lord of bliss,
And thus he said: "O Lord and Saviour,
King of all kindreds,   blessed art Thou!
Thy glory lives   unto everlasting,
Thy name is hallowed   near and far,
Clothed with splendour   among mankind,
For mercies magnified.   O Lord of men,
Saviour of souls,   there is none on earth
Of mortal men   under dome of heaven
Who can truly rehearse   or fully tell
In what glorious manner   Thou dost grant Thy grace.
Truly is it seen,   O Saviour of souls,
That unto this young man,   wise of wit
And sage in council,   Thou hast been kind
Honouring his youth   with gracious gifts.
Never in one   of equal age
Have I met more wisdom   or prudence of mind."
   Then from the keel   spoke the Glory of kings,
End and Beginning,   boldly asking:
"O thane sage-hearted   say if you can
How it came to pass   among mankind
That the impious Jews   with evil thoughts
Reviled God's Son.   Unhappy sinners,
False and cruel,   they had no faith
In the Lord of life   that He was God.
Though He did many miracles   open and manifest
They could not recognize,   sunk in their sins,
The Child of God   Who was begotten
As a help and comfort   to all mankind,

(531–567)

All peoples of earth.   The Prince prospered
In word and wisdom   but of His wonders
Revealed no part   to that folk perverse."
    And unto Him Andrew   answering said:
"How could it happen,   dearest of men,
That you have not heard   of the Healer's might,
How the Son of God   showed forth His grace
Through the spacious earth?   To the dumb He gave speech,
To the deaf hearing.   He gladdened the hearts
Of the lame and lepers,   limb-sick men
Long weary and wretched   and racked with pain.
Throughout the cities   the blind received sight;
Many He wakened   by His word from death.
Such were the wonders   the Noble One worked
By the power of His might.   Before men He hallowed
Wine from water   bidding it turn
For man's blessing   to the better kind.
Likewise He fed   with two fishes
And five loaves   five thousand men.
The host was seated   sad at heart,
Weary from their journey,   joying in rest;
On the ground reclining   they fed on that food
As they found most pleasing.   Now may you know,
Beloved youth,   how the Lord of glory
Showed us favour   by His words and works,
By His teaching led us   to that lovelier joy
Where in freedom abide   in bliss with angels
Those who after death   dwell with the Lord."
    Then the Warden of the wave   unlocked His word-hoard,
Across the gangway   the Stout-hearted spoke:
"Can you now tell me,   that I may know truth,
When your Lord did His miracles   often on earth
To the comfort of men,   were they openly manifest
Where bishops and bookmen   and magistrates met
Sitting in council?   To me it seems

(568–609)

In dissension and error   they plotted evil.
All too eagerly   those death-doomed men
Obeyed false foes   and the Fiend's teaching.
Fate deceived them,   tricked and ensnared,
And now in misery,   damned with the damned,
They shall suffer vengeance   and a bitter burning
In the Devil's embrace."

                  Andrew answered:
"I tell you for truth   that wonder on wonder
Before the folk's rulers   He openly wrought
In sight of the people.   Likewise in secret
The Lord of men   gave assistance to many
According as He regarded it   for their good."

    The Helm of princes   to him replied:
"O wise hero,   stout of heart,
Can you tell me plainly   the power He showed,
The Hero in secret,   when often you sat
Counselling with your Leader,   the Lord of heaven?"

    Unto Him Andrew   answering said:
"Why do you question me,   dearest man,
With troubling words   when you know the truth
Of every issue   through your wisdom's art?"

    The Warden of the wave   uttered this word:
"I do not ask   with ill intent
Upon the whale-path,   or in reproach;
But my heart is blissful,   blossoms with joy,
Hearing your discourse   endued with worth.
Nor I alone,   but every man's mind
Leaps with delight   and his spirit is stirred
Whoever fervently   far or near
Is mindful of the marvels   God's Mighty Son
Wrought upon earth.   Souls were made ready
By His saving power   and turned to seek
The angels' homeland,   the joys of heaven."

    Unto Him straightway   Andrew made answer:

(610–643)

"Now in yourself   I can see the truth,
Availing insight   and wisdom's wit
Wondrously granted;   your breast within
Blossoms with knowledge   and radiant bliss.
I will tell you truly   end and beginning
As I heard from the lips   of the Lord Himself
Word and wisdom   in the meetings of men.
Often great hosts   were gathered together,
Unnumbered legions   at the Lord's decree,
Who hearkened there   to the Holy One's lore.
Then departed again   the Helm of princes,
Bright Giver of bliss,   to another abode
And to that assembly   came many to meet Him,
Prudent counsellors   praising God,
With blithe hearts acclaiming   the Prince's coming.
    "So of old it befell   that the Judge Triumphant,
The Lord Almighty,   went on His way.
At that faring-forth   were no more folk
But only eleven   loyal thanes
Graced with glory;   our Lord was the twelfth.
    "And so we arrived   at the royal city
Where stood God's temple   horn-gabled and high,
Renowned among men   and gleaming in glory.
There the High Priest   with evil heart
Mocked us with malice   and sneering scorn,
Unlocked his word-hoard   and wove reproach.
Full well he knew   we followed the footsteps
Of the Righteous Lord   obeying His law.
Unfriendly of heart,   infected with evil
He raised his voice: 'Lo! wretched beyond all
Are you who wander   in this wide roaming,
Travelling over many   a toilsome way.
Against the folk-law   you follow the teaching
Of a roving stranger.   Bereft of bliss
You proclaim him Prince,   and tell for a truth

(644–681)

That daily you forgather   with God's own Son.
But it's known to all people   whence this Prince is sprung!
He was born in this folkland,   bred among kinsmen;
The names of his parents,   props of the home,
Are Joseph and Mary   as men know well.
Two brothers were his   born of that blood,
Simon and Jacob,   Joseph's sons.'
So the rulers harangued them,   an arrogant group
Who thought to disguise   the power of God.
Crime was come again,   endless evil,
In the place where offence   arose before.
    "Then the Prince went forth   from that place of meeting,
The Lord of men   made strong in might,
And sought with His thanes   a secret spot.
By many wonders   in the wilderness
He displayed His power,   that He was True Prince
Over all the earth,   potent in strength,
Author and Lord   of celestial glory,
One God Eternal   of every created thing!
Of other wonders   an untold number
He showed forth there   in the sight of men.
    "Then again departed   the Prince of glory
And came to the Temple   with all His train.
His voice was lifted   in the lofty hall.
Yet the sinful received not   the Holy One's teaching
Though He showed forth many   a faithful sign
While the host looked on.   The Lord beheld there
A lovely likeness   of angel forms,
A wonder graven   on the Temple wall
On either hand,   brightly embellished
And winsomely fashioned.   He spoke this word:
    'This is an image   of the angel-order
That is highest of all   in the heavenly realm.
Cherubim and Seraphim,   so are they named
In the bliss of heaven   where firm of heart

(681–720)

They stand in the presence   of the Eternal Prince,
With holy anthems   exalting the glory
Of the Heavenly King   and the grace of God.
Here skilfully fashioned   the forms of those holy ones,
Thanes of glory,   are engraved on the wall.'
   "Then the Lord of hosts,   the Heaven-holy Spirit,
Said before all: 'Let a sign appear,
A marvel unfold   in the sight of men;
Let this wondrous image   step down from the wall
To the ground, and tell   in truthful words
What My lineage is,   that men may believe.'
   "Then before men's eyes   the wondrous image,
The hoary hand-work,   dared not delay
The Saviour's bidding   but sprang from the wall,
Stone from stone,   and stood upon earth.
A voice came forth   through the hard flint
Uttering speech   in resounding tones.
(To the stubborn, strange   seemed the stone's behaviour.)
By a manifest token   it taught the priests,
Wisely constrained them   and spoke this word:
   'You are evil men   enmeshed in the toils
Of base thoughts;   you know not the better.
Distracted in mind   you proclaim as man
The Eternal Son   of the Living Lord
Who shaped with His hands   the earth and the heavens,
Land and ocean,   the angry waves,
The salt sea-streams   and the sky above.
This is the same   All-Governing God
Known to your fathers   in former days.
Of old to Abraham,   Isaac and Jacob
He gave His grace   and granted them wealth.
First to Abraham   He foretold honour,
That of his kindred   should come to birth
The Lord of splendour.   That fate is fulfilled,
Apparent and open;   your eyes may look

(721-759)

Upon God Triumphant,   the Lord of glory.'
    "After these sayings   the host hearkened
And all were silent   through the spacious hall.
But the sinful elders   not seeing the truth
Began to say   it was sorcery's craft
And wrought by magic   that the radiant stone
Spoke to the assembly.   Sin blossomed
In the bosoms of men.   Burning hatred
Rose in their breasts,   that baleful worm,
That bitter venom.   By abuse they showed
The doubting minds   and mischievous thoughts
Of men encompassed   by the coils of death.
    "Then the Lord commanded   the great stone marvel
Over the foot-paths   to fare from that place
Walking the earth-ways,   the green ground,
To bring God's message   to the men of Canaan;
Bidding Abraham   at the King's decree
With his sons rise up   from the sepulchre,
Leave their graves   and gather their limbs,
Receive their souls   and their youth again,
Those ancient sages,   and straightway appear
To give men knowledge   Who is God.
    "The image departed   as the Mighty Prince,
The Maker of men,   had given command,
Over the march-paths   making his way
Mantled in light   till he came to Mamre
As the Lord gave bidding.   There were the bodies
Of the patriarchs of old   long buried in earth.
Soon he bade Abraham,   Isaac and Jacob
To God's assembly   rise from the ground,
Stand up straightway   from their deep sleep,
At God's bidding   gird for the task
And inform the folk   Who fashioned the world,
The all-green earth   and the heavens above,
And where He abides   Who builded that work.

                (760–799)

Nor dared they longer   one whit delay
To work the will   of the King of glory.
    "Then the three wise men   went their way
Treading the border-lands   bold of heart;
They left their earth-house,   their open graves;
They would fain proclaim   the King of creation;
And all the people   were filled with fear
When those patriarchs honoured   the Prince of glory.
The Lord of the kingdom   bade them quickly
In peace and glory   return again
To the joys of heaven   and have them for ever.
    "Now may you know,   O dearest man,
How many wonders   He wrought by His word,
Though mind-darkened men   believed not His lore.
I still know many   a glorious story
Of the labours He wrought,   the Lord of the skies,
But you cannot bear them   or fully fathom,
Wise though you be."   So all the day Andrew
Praised the teaching   of the Holy Prince
Until all suddenly   sleep came upon him
On the whale-path, close   to the Heavenly King.
    Then the Lord of life   bade His angels bear him,
Carry the dear one   across the sea
With tender kindness   o'er the crowding waves,
Safe in God's keeping.   The sea-weary slept.
Borne through the air   he came to the country,
The city appointed   by the angels' Prince. . .
    Upward soaring   those heralds ascended
To their native homeland,   leaving the saint
Sleeping in peace   'neath the sheltering sky,
By the roadside resting   the night-long time
Near the city wall   and the savage foe
Till God let the day-candle   brightly gleam.
Dark under heaven   the shadows withdrew
And a blaze of sunlight   shone from the sky

(800–838)

O'er the homes of men.   The valiant hero
Awoke from slumber   and scanned the plain.
Before the town-gates   rose towering mountains
And lofty hills.   Round the hoary rock
Stood buildings and towers   adorned with tiles,
Windy walls.   Then the wise one knew
His travels had brought him   to the Mermedonian tribe
As the Father of men   had given command.
  He saw on the sand   his comrades reclining,
Battle-brave heroes   beside him asleep;
He straightway began   to waken his warriors
Speaking this word: "I can tell you for truth
That the Lord Himself   on the ocean-stream
Yesterday sailed us   over the sea.
The Glory of kings   was in our keel,
The Ruler of nations.   I knew His sayings
Although He concealed   His face from our sight."
  Then with wisdom of spirit   his young men spoke:
"Verily, Andrew,   we'll tell our adventure
That you may weigh it   in your wise mind.
Sleep fell upon us   weary with the sea;
O'er the surging waves   came eagles winging,
Fairly exulting   in their feathered flight.
As we lay in slumber   they released our souls,
Happily bore them   upward in air
With joyous clamour,   gentle and shining;
Kindly cherished them,   constant in worship
Where song was unceasing,   heavenly strains,
Fellowships fair,   and the hosts of glory.
About the Noble One   bands of angels,
Thanes in thousands,   encircled their Prince
Praising in heaven   with holy voices
The Lord of lords.   There was joy and delight.
There we beheld   the holy patriarchs
And the martyrs beside them,   no small band.

(838–876)

Those glorious hosts   sang heartfelt praise
To their Lord Triumphant.   There also was David,
That blessed champion,   Jesse's son,
Come before Christ,   Israel's King.
Before God's Son   we saw you standing,
The glorious Twelve   with virtue graced,
And holy archangels   living in light
Were in waiting upon you.   Well is it with them
Who may joy in that bliss!   There was grace of glory,
Renown of warriors,   noble demeanour,
Nor was any sorrow there   for any soul.
But there shall be misery,   punishment meted
To all who are banished   from that bliss
Wandering heart-sick   when they go hence."
    When he heard the tale   his young men told
The soul of the saint   was blithe in his breast
That God should so honour them   over all men.
The warden of warriors   spoke this word:
    "O Lord God,   Glory of kings,
Now I know   you were not far from me
When I entered the ship   on the ocean-road
Though I knew it not then   on the way o'er the waves,
Prince of angels,   Saviour of souls!
Be kindly to me   and gracious, Bright King,
God Almighty.   Many a word
I spoke on the sea-stream;   now later I know
Who it was ferried me   over the floods
With wealth of honour   in that wooden boat.
He is Spirit of comfort   for all mankind!
At His mighty hand   there is mercy and help
And abundant blessing   for all who ask."
    Then before his eyes   in that very hour
The King of all creatures,   the Lord, was revealed
In the guise of a youth.   The Prince of glory
Uttered this greeting: "Hail, Andrew,

(877-914)

With this faithful band   so blithe of heart!
I will hold you safe   that savage foemen,
Fierce workers of sin,   may not harm your soul."
    The doughty hero   bowed down to earth
Pleading for favour,   imploring his Lord:
"O Ruler of men,   Saviour of souls,
How did I ever   so greatly err
That sinning against you   I knew you not
On that sea-journey   when I spoke more words
Before God's face   than I rightly should?"
    Almighty God said: "You sinned not so greatly
As when in Achaia   you withstood My will,
Said you could not fare   over far ways,
Or come to this city,   or accomplish this mission
In three nights' time,   when I told you to sail
O'er the climbing waves.   Now more clearly you know
I can easily aid   and further My friends,
Every one of them   in every land,
As pleases Me best.   Now promptly arise
And heed My behest,   O blessed man;
So shall the Bright Father   with glorious gifts
Exalt you for ever   with power and might.
    "Through the city-gates   go into the city
Where your brother abides.   I know that Matthew
At the hands of the wicked   is smitten with wounds,
Your closest kinsman   beset with snares.
Seek out the dear one,   save and deliver
From the hate of the hostile   and all the host
That abide with him there,   bound with evil
And the wicked wiles   of alien men.
He shall have help   and healing in the world,
And reward in glory,   as I gave him pledge.
    "Verily, Andrew,   you must quickly venture
In the grasp of the foe;   the fray is at hand.
Bitter sword-strokes   shall wound your body;

(914–953)

Most like to water   your blood shall well.
Yet may they not doom   your life to death
Though you suffer the stripes   and scourging of sinners.
Endure that pain;   let not the power
Of heathen men   and their savage might
Lead you to turn   from the Lord, your God.
Be heedful of glory   holding in mind
•What men have known   in many a land:
How evil men flouted Me   fast in fetters,
Scornfully taunted   and scourged Me with stripes;
With abuse those sinners   concealed the truth.
In the sight of the Jews   I was stretched on the gallows,
The Rood was upreared;   from My riven side
A warrior let blood,   My gore, to the ground.
Many a woe   I endured in the world
That with gracious heart   I might give you a pattern
As shall soon be seen   on this foreign soil.
Many there are   in this mighty city
Whom you shall lead   unto heavenly light
In My name,   though much of evil
They formerly did   in days that are past."
    Then departed the Holy One   upward to heaven,
The King of all kings,   with kindly joy
To His pure home   where blessing abounds
For every man   who may earlier earn it.
    The patient saint   heeded His sayings.
The battle-strong hero   strode to the town,
A warrior unflinching,   in courage made firm,
Gallant-hearted   and loyal to God;
He walked the road   as the way led him,
And none of those sinners   might see him or know.
The Prince of triumph   on the stretching plain
Kept the loved leader   with kindly care
And gracious favour.   So Christ's defender,
The noble prince   to the prison drew near.

(953–991)

There he beheld   a band of the heathen,
Seven gaolers   who stood in a group
At the prison door.   Death seized all;
Hapless they died;   the death-rush gripped
The blood-stained men.   Then the saint worshipped
The Merciful Father,   praised in his mind
God's glory on high,   the might of heaven's King.
The prison portals   straightway stood open
At one hand-touch   of that saintly soul,
And heedful of valour   the battle-bold hero
Entered the dungeon.   Drunk with blood
The heathen lay sleeping   the sleep of death;
Their gore had reddened   the fatal ground.

   He beheld Matthew   in the house of torture
Constrained in darkness   but stout of heart
Praising the Lord,   the Prince of angels.
Heavy with sadness   he sat alone
In the prison cell.   He saw his beloved;
Saint looked on saint   and hope was renewed.
He arose to go to him   giving God thanks
They might see each other   whole and sound
Under the sun.   Between the two brothers
Was genial affection   and joy anew.
Each clasped the other,   embraced and kissed.
They were loved of Christ.   A light shone about them
Holy, heaven-bright.   Their hearts within
Were filled with happiness.   Andrew first
Graciously greeted   his noble comrade,
The God-fearing saint   in his prison cell,
And told of conflict,   fierce fighting to come. . .

   After his greeting   those thanes of glory,
Both the brothers,   bowed them in prayer,
Made supplication   to the Son of God.
The holy saint   pent in the prison
Called upon God   and asked His aid,

(992–1030)

The Healer's help,   ere his body be broken
By the savage might   of heathen men.
Then he led from prison   to the peace of God
Two hundred forty   from bonds set free,
Saved from affliction.   Fast in the dungeon
He left not one.   Of women likewise
One less than fifty   he loosed from fear.
Fain of their freedom   they soon went forth,
Nor longer awaited   in that house of woe
The impending battle.   Matthew departed
In the Lord's keeping   leading that band
As the Holy One bade.   God covered with cloud
The host as it journeyed   on its joyous way
Lest with flight of arrows   the ancient foe,
Those wicked warriors,   should work them harm.

    The valiant comrades,   faithful friends,
Held counsel together   ere they went their ways;
Each cheered the other   with hope of heaven
Defending their souls   from the fiends of hell.
And so God's soldiers   with saintly voices,
Hardy warriors   and valiant of heart,
Worshipped the King,   the Wielder of fate,
Whose glory ends not   in all the ages.

    So Andrew proceeded   into the city
Going glad-hearted   to where he had heard
Was a massing of foes,   a host of the hostile,
And came at last   to a column of bronze
Near the highway standing.   Beside it he sat;
His heart was filled   with a holy love
And thoughts turned upward   to angels' bliss.
There he awaited   what fate of war-deeds
Within the town-limits   might be his lot.

    Then legions assembled   and leaders of men;
Heathen fighters,   the horde of the faithless,
Rushed with weapons   to the prison walls

(1031–1070)

L

Where the captives in darkness   had endured their woe.
Hostile-hearted   they hoped and desired
To take them as food,   their accustomed fare.
But their hope failed them   when the fierce spearmen
And their following found   the portals wide,
The hammers' work unlocked,   the warders lifeless.
Balked in their wish   they turned away
To spread the ill tidings.   They said to the folk
That of foreign travellers   of alien tongue
They found none left   alive in the prison;
But badged with blood   the warders lay
Dead on the ground,   their doomed bodies
Bereft of life.   Then many a leader
Was shaken with terror   at the shocking news.
They were downcast and doleful,   in dread of hunger,
Pale guest at the banquet.   No better plan
Did they know for their nurture   than that they should feed
On the lifeless corpses.   For the prison-keepers,
For them all at once   in the one hour,
The bed of death had been spread   in the bitter strife.
    Soon, as I learned,   the city-dwellers,
The folk, were gathered.   Fighting men came,
A rout of warriors   riding their steeds,
Heroes on horses   stately with spears,
To attend the meeting.   The tribe was gathered
Crowding together   to the council-place.
Casting lots   they let them decree
Which should die first   as food for the others.
With hellish arts   and heathen rites
They cast the lots   and counted them out.
    Then the lot came   to an aged comrade
Wise in council,   foremost in war.
Hopeless of life   and fastened with fetters
He wailed fierce-hearted   with woeful voice:
Into their power   he promised to give

(1070–1110)

His stripling son   as a stay of life.
Swiftly with thanks   they accepted the gift;
The folk were wretched,   hungry for food.
In treasure they joyed not   nor trusted in wealth;
They were tortured with hunger;   that terrible foe
Rode them fiercely.   Many a fighter,
Battle-bold heroes,   were goaded in heart
By greedy longing   for the young man's life.
The signal for slaughter   was sounded afar,
Spread through the city   to many men
Who cruelly sought   in a great crowd
The young man's death,   that old and youthful
Might share his flesh   to sustain their strength.
There quickly assembled   the hordes of the city,
The heathen temple-guards.   Tumult arose!
    The youth in fetters   before the folk
In woeful accents   bewailed his fate,
Barren of friends   and begging for pity.
But the wretched man   could obtain no mercy
Or favour from the folk   to deliver his life;
The savage warriors   had resolved on slaughter.
The sharp sword-edge   tempered hard
And flecked with fire-marks,   in a hostile hand,
Must seek his death.
                        Then it seemed to Andrew
An appalling evil   and bitter to bear
That one so guiltless   should lose his life;
Great and grievous   was the hate of that folk.
The band rushed forward,   the bold retainers,
Intent on murder.   Those monstrous men
Would fain strike hard   at the young man's head,
Destroy him with spears.   But God defended him,
Holy in heaven,   from the heathen folk.
He bade their weapons   most like to wax
Melt in the fray   lest the merciless foe,

                    (1110–1147)

The wicked warriors,   should work him harm
With press of swords.   So the youth was set free
From the harm and the hate   of that hostile people.
Thanks be to God,   the Lord of lords,
For all His goodness: that He gives His grace
To every man   who with wisdom asks
For help at His hand,   where Eternal love
May always be had   by him who can earn it.

   Then mourning was heard   in the cities of men,
The loud lament   of a mighty host.
Heralds cried   proclaiming a famine;
Haggard they stood   with hunger constrained.
The horn-gabled houses,   the wine-halls, stood waste:
Men lacked abundance   in that bitter time.
In secret council   their sages sat,
Mused on their misery.   Joy was fled!
Often one warrior   asked of another;
"Let him that has wisdom   and prudence of heart
Keep it not hid,   for occasion has come
Of measureless misery.   Now is there need
That we hear such words   as wise men speak."

   Then before the people   the Devil appeared
Hideous and dark   with the hue of the damned.
The King of death,   the Cripple of hell,
Hostile-hearted   began to tell
Who the saint was   and spoke this word:
   "Hither has fared   over far ways
Into your city   an alien whose name,
I have heard, is Andrew.   He did you great evil
When he freed from the fastness   more of mankind
Than was any way meet.   But now may you easily
Punish by deeds   the wrong he has wrought.
Let blow of weapon,   the hard-edged blade,
Cleave through the frame,   the flesh, of the doomed.
Go boldly to battle   and humble the foe!"

(1147–1183)

Unto him there   Andrew made answer:
"Lo! how rashly   you prompt this people,
Inflaming to battle.   The fires of death
You have known in hell;   yet you counsel this crowd,
This horde, to the fray!   You are fighting with God,
The King of warriors.   You'll increase your woe,
You Devil's Dart!   You the Almighty
Humbled deeply   and hurled to the dark
Where the King of Kings   bound you with fetters,
And they call you Satan   ever since then,
All who acknowledge   the law of the Lord."
  But still the Foe   with fiendish craft
Urged them to war: "You hear the words
Of a bitter foe   who wrought this folk
The greatest of injuries.   This is Andrew
Who mocks me strangely   in the sight of men."
  Then the signal was sounded   to the city-dwellers;
The dauntless sprang up   with the din of a host.
To the gates in the wall   the warriors crowded
Bold under banners,   in a mighty band
Pressing to battle   with bucklers and spears.
Then the Lord of hosts,   the Maker Almighty,
Spoke this word   to His worthy thane:
  "Now must you, Andrew,   show forth strength!
Shun not this rabble   but steel your heart
Against their terrors.   The time is not long
Till murderous men   shall try you with torture
And icy bonds.   Now show yourself bold!
Harden your spirit,   make steadfast your heart
That men may perceive   My strength in you.
Nor can they, nor may they,   against My will,
Deep in sin,   deal death to your body
Although you endure   the dreadful lash,
Black deeds of wickedness.   I shall be with you."
  After these words   came a host of warriors,

(1184–1219)

Evil counsellors   with a crowd in arms,
Fierce of heart.   When they found the saint
And beheld with their eyes   the hero before them,
They bore him out quickly   and bound his hands.
Then many a man   of that mustered host
On the field of fate   was eager for battle;
Little they grieved   what their guerdon might be!
Brutal men bade   he be led through the land,
Dragged along cruelly   time after time
As they might contrive   the most terrible pangs.
They haled the bold-hearted   through hill ravines,
Over rocky slopes   and throughout the cities,
As far and wide   as the ways extended,
The stone-paved streets,   old giants' work.
    Then a storm arose   in the city dwellings,
No little uproar   of the heathen host.
The body of the saint   was sodden with wounds,
Wet with blood,   his bone-frame broken;
The hot gore welled   in bloody waves.
Yet he had within him   unwavering valour;
His noble spirit   was sundered from sin
Though he needs must endure   such dreadful pangs
Through wounding blows.   The saint was beaten
All the long day   until evening came.
Pain pierced his heart   till the heaven-bright sun
Shining in radiance   sank to its setting.
Then the people haled   their hated foe
Back to the dungeon.   But dear unto Christ
His heart was light   and holy within him,
And deep in his bosom   a soul that was strong.
    Then was the saint   in the shades of darkness,
The noble hero   through the live-long night,
Bitterly beset.   Snow bound earth
With winter storms.   The winds grew chill
With fierce hail-showers.   Frost and rime,

(1220–1257)

Those hoary warriors,   locked the land,
The homes of men.   The earth was hung
With wintry icicles;   water's might
Shrank in the sea-streams.   Ice made a bridge
Over the black ocean.   Blithe-hearted abode
The virtuous man,   mindful of valour,
Bold and enduring   in his bitter need
Through the winter-cold night.   His soul ceased not,
For fear of the terror,   to glorify God
As was his wont   and worthily praise Him
Till the gem of glory   glowed in the sky.
      Then men came crowding   to the dark dungeon,
No little gathering   greedy for death,
Hastening on   with the din of a host.
They bade that the prince   be led from the prison,
The faithful hero   in the power of the foe;
And again as before   the saint was scourged
All the long day   with deadly blows.
Blood welled in waves,   burst from his body;
His scars were swallowed   in the hot gore.
His flesh knew no respite,   wretched with wounds.
      The sound of sobbing   broke from his bosom,
Tears streamed in waves   and he spoke this word:
"Behold, Lord God,   Joy-Giver of men,
My grievous need;   it is Thou Who knowest
Every man's troubles.   My trust is in Thee,
Lord of my life,   that with loving heart
And ample strength   Thou wilt never forsake me,
Eternal, Almighty,   Saviour of men.
So may I live   while my life endures
That I fail not to follow   Thy pleasant laws.
For all Thy people,   Author of bliss,
Thou art Defence   from darts of the Foe.
Let not man's Slayer,   the Lord of sin,
With fiendish craft   profane with evil

(1258–1295)

Or scoff at those　who sing Thy praise."

　　Then appeared the Foul Spirit,　faithless and fierce,
The Devil from hell,　before the host,
The Accursed in torment,　and counselled the warriors
Before the assembly,　speaking this word:
"Smite now this sinner,　this foe of the folk,
Upon the mouth,　for he talks too much."

　　Once more the struggle　was stirred anew;
Hate held sway　till the sun departed,
Sank to its setting　below the steep cliff,
And dark night covered　and cloaked the hills
As the saintly spirit　noble and brave
Was dragged to the dungeon,　his dark abode.
Fast in the prison,　the foul dwelling,
The faithful man tarried　the night-long time.

　　Then the odious Foe　with six other fiends
Intent on evil　returned to the hall,
The Lord of death　shrouded in darkness,
The ruthless Devil　bereft of might.
With words of insult　he spoke to the saint:

　　"How was it, Andrew,　you ever resolved
On hither-coming　into hostile hands?
Where now is your honour,　so rashly exalted
When you humbled the glory　of all our gods?
For yourself only　you claimed all,
Land and people,　as your Leader did
Whose name was Christ;　over all the earth
He asserted dominion　while so he might.
But Herod slew Him,　despoiled of His kingdom
And conquered in battle　the King of the Jews,
Upraised His body　upon the Rood,
And there on the gallows　He gave up the ghost.
Even so I command　my mighty thanes,
Loyal in battle,　that they abase you!
Let point of spear　and poisoned arrow

(1295–1331)

Drive home deep   in the doomed flesh.
Go boldly now;   break the warrior's boast."
    They were ruthless-hearted   and rushed upon him
With greedy grasp.   But God defended him,
The Steadfast Pilot   with His potent might.
When they saw on his forehead   the cross of Christ,
That glorious sign,   they were filled with fear,
Dismayed with terror   and turned to flight.
    Again as before   the Ancient Foe
The Captive of hell,   howled his lament:
"What befell you,   O warriors mine,
Battle-comrades   so bold in strife,
That you prospered so little?"
                              Then a loathsome spirit,
A hostile fiend,   replied to his Father:
"We can not readily   work his ruin
Or contrive his death.   Go you against him!
There you will quickly   find fierce combat,
Terrible fighting,   if further you dare
Against that lone one   to risk your life.
Now may we easily,   dearest of eorls,
Instruct you better   in the battle-play
Before you rush   to join in the fighting,
The tumult of war,   whatever betide
In the trading of blows.   Let us try again
That we may flout him   fast in his fetters,
Deriding his wretchedness.   Have words ready
And fully pondered   for this foul rogue."
    With bellowing voice   the Vile One shouted,
Wounded with torment,   and spoke this word:
"A long time, Andrew,   you've trafficked with magic!
Many a man   you've deluded with lies!
But now no longer   may your vaunts avail you.
A grim requital   is ordained for your deeds.
Weary of heart,   humbled and hopeless,

(1331–1367)

You shall suffer pain,   sore pangs of death.
My warriors are ready   for the work of battle
And speedily now   in a little span
By deeds of courage   they shall quell your life.
Of men on earth   who is so mighty
That out of these fetters   can set you free
Against my will?"
                 But Andrew answered:
"God Almighty,   the Saviour of men,
May easily do it   Who bound you of old
In sore distress   with fetters of flame.
And from that time   fastened in torment
You abode in misery   shorn of bliss,
For you spurned the behest   of the Heavenly King.
Thus evil began   nor shall ever be end
Of this crushing vengeance.   Your woe shall increase
For ever and ever;   from day to day
More bitter shall be   your way of life!"
Then he turned in flight   who once had fought
Grimly of old   that feud with God.
    Then came in the dawn   at the break of day
A troop of the heathen   attacking the saint
In a great gathering.   They gave command
To lead out a third time   God's patient thane:
Fain would they break   the brave one's spirit,
But it might not be.   Once more anew
Hate was aroused,   savage and ruthless.
The saint was beaten,   cunningly bound,
Pierced with wounds   while the long day passed.
Heavy-hearted   with holy voice,
Brave in his bondage,   he called upon God;
Wearily weeping   he spoke this word:
    "Under heaven's dome   I have never endured
By the will of God   more grievous lot
Whereby I must honour   the law of the Lord.

(1367–1403)

My limbs are loosened,   my body broken,
My bone-house bloody,   my wounds well forth,
My gashes are gory.   O God of triumph,
Saviour Lord,   in one day's span
At the hands of the Jews   Thou didst grow heavy-hearted
Crying from the gallows,   O Living God,
Lord of creation,   unto the Father,
Splendour of kings,   and spoke this word:
'Why hast Thou forsaken me,   Father of angels,
Author of life   and Lord of light?'
    "For three days now   I needs must endure
This grievous torture.   O God of hosts,
I beseech Thee grant me   to give my spirit
Into Thy keeping,   Preserver of souls.
When of old with hope   Thou didst hearten the Twelve
By Thy gracious word   Thou didst give us pledge
That the hate of the hostile   should harm us not,
Nor ever the body   be broken in twain,
Or bone or sinew   be brought to earth,
Or lock of hair   be lost from the head
If we heeded well   Thy holy behest.
Now my sinews are slackened,   my blood is shed,
The hairs of my head   lie strewn through the land,
My locks in the dust.   Death is dearer,
Better far,   than this bitter woe."
    Then came the voice   of the King of glory
Speaking this word   to the warrior-saint:
"Bewail not this misery,   dearest of men;
It is not too hard for you.   I will uphold you
And compass you round   with My sheltering care.
Unto Me is given   might over all things,
Power and triumph.   The truth shall be clear
When many are gathered   on the Great Day
That this fair creation,   heaven and earth,
Shall pass away   ere a word shall pass

(1404–1439)

That My mouth has spoken.   See now your track,
How the blood has gushed   in a gory path
From your wounded body   and broken frame!
No more may they harm you   with hurling of spears
Who have wrought this greatest   of grievous hurts."
    Then looked behind him   the beloved saint
According to the words   of the King of glory;
He saw there standing   budding bowers
Decked with blossoms   where he shed his blood.
The warden of warriors   spoke this word:
"Thanks be and praise,   O Ruler of peoples,
And glory for ever   in heaven on high,
My Saviour Lord,   that Thou hast not forsaken me,
A homeless stranger,   in my sore need."
So with saintly voice   the valiant hero
Glorified God   till the shining sun
Gleaming in glory   sank under the waves.
    For the fourth time then   the folk-leaders,
The dreadful foemen,   dragged the prince
Back to the dungeon.   In the dark night
They would fain destroy   his secret strength,
The counsellor's courage.   But the Lord God came,
The Glory of men,   to the grated dwelling
The Guide of life,   the Lord of mankind,
Greeting His friend   and giving him comfort.
He bade that his body   be healed of its hurts:
"No longer now   in bitter abasement
Shall you suffer pain   in the power of the foe."
    Then he rose in might,   gave thanks to his Maker
Freed from the bondage   of his bitter pangs.
Nor was his beauty defiled,   nor the fringe of a garment
Loosed from his raiment,   nor a lock from his head;
Nor was bone broken,   nor had bloody wound
Brought baleful hurt;   no bit of his body
Was wet with blood   from his wounding blows.

(1440–1475)

But again as before   through His glorious power
He was sound in body,   singing God's praise.
   Lo! now for some time   I have told the tale
Of this saintly man   in words of song,
The praise of his work,   a well-known story
Beyond my measure.   There is much to tell,
A lengthy study,   how he suffered in life
All from the beginning.   Of men on earth
It's a cleverer man   than I count myself
Who must find it in mind   to know from the first
All the affliction   and fierce strife
He bravely endured.   Yet briefly a little
We will carry further   the course of this lay.
   It is old tradition   how the saint endured
Countless tortures   and cruel strife
In the heathen city.   He saw by the wall
Towering pillars   fast in their place,
Old works of giants   worn by the storms.
Bold and stalwart   and wondrous wise
He spoke a word   to one of the columns:
   "Hearken, O marble,   to God's command
Before Whose face   all creatures shall fear
Beholding the Father   of earth and heaven
With His host descending   to seek mankind.
From out your base   let torrents boil
In a gushing river;   the God of heaven
Bids you send forth   on this stubborn folk
Far-flowing waters,   a rushing flood
For the death of men.   Lo! you are dearer
Than gold or treasure!   The God of glory
Wrote on you once,   made known in words
In ten commandments,   His moral laws,
His stern decrees;   and Strong in might
Gave them to Moses   whose glorious kinsmen,
Tobias and Joshua,   just men and bold,

(1476–1516)

Thereafter followed them   fearing the Lord.
Now may you know   that the King of angels
Adorned you more dearly   in days of old
With gifts of grace   than all jewels and gems.
By His holy command   you shall now make known
If you have understanding   and knowledge of Him."
    Nor was any stay   till the stone was split;
A stream welled forth   overflowing the ground.
The foaming waves   in the first dawn
Enfolded earth;   the sea-flood swelled.
The serving of mead was cut off   after the feasting!
Men started from sleep;   sea covered land;
The depths were troubled.   The troop was shaken
With fear of the flood.   Doomed men died;
The rush of waters   with the salt wave
Swept off the young   in the ocean surges.
    That was a burden of sorrow,   a bitter beer-feast!
The cup-bearers did not tarry,   the attendant thanes;
There was drink for all   from the break of day!
Water's might waxed   and warriors wailed,
Aged bearers   of ashen spears.
Fain would they flee   from the dark flood
And save their lives,   seek out shelter
And find a housing   in the hill ravines.
But an angel withstood,   overspreading the city
With gleaming fire,   hot surge of flame.
Fierce through the town   the flood-tide swept.
Nor might the multitude   in any manner
Out of their fortress   find way of flight.
    Waves waxed great,   the sea resounded;
Fire-sparks flew;   the flood flowed on.
A lamentation   was lifted up
Throughout the city.   Smitten with fear
Men wailed their woe,   chanted their death-song.
The fearful flames   were seen afar,

(1516–1550)

Grim devastation,   terrible din!
Ascending in air   the fiery surges
Enveloped the walls.   The waters rose.
Widely was heard   the sound of weeping,
Men's pitiful plaints.   One in his wretchedness
Began to gather   the people together;
Humbled and heartsick   he said in his grief:

   "Now for yourselves   you can see the truth,
How wrongly we punished   with prison and pain
This stranger-guest.   Bitter and grim
Fate is our scourge,   as is now full clear.
It is better far,   as I count the facts,
That with one accord   we break his bonds
(Haste is best),   and beseech the saint
For help and succour.   Peace after pain
May be had by all   if we ask of him."

   Then was clear to Andrew   in his inmost heart
The people's bearing,   that the might of the bold,
The warriors' strength,   was brought to destruction.
The eager waters,   the welling waves,
Spread far and wide;   the flood flowed on
Till it mantled the breasts,   the shoulders, of men.

   Then the prince gave bidding   that the streams be still,
And the storms cease   round the stony cliffs.
Stout of heart   the valiant hero
Departed straightway   from his prison cell
Endowed with wisdom,   dear to God.
Quickly a road   was roomy before him
Through the flooding waters.   Fair was the plain!
The ground was dried   after the deluge
Where his foot trod.

                          Then all the townsmen
Were blithe of spirit,   happy of heart.
Comfort was come to them   after their woe.
At the saint's bidding   the waters abated,

(1551–1586)

The waves hearkened,   the sea lay still.
The mountain was cleft;   a terrible chasm
Drank the deep waters,   the dark flood;
The wide pit swallowed   the swirling mass.
Nor did it engulf   the great waves only
But also the worst   of the heathen host.
Fourteen wicked   workers of evil,
Swept to destruction,   went with the waves
To the vast abyss.   Of those who survived
Many were frightened   and fearful of heart.
They awaited the ruin   of women and men,
A frightful fate,   a more terrible time
After guilty sinners   soiled with evil
Had hurtled headlong   under the earth.
With one accord   all cried aloud:
"Now is it seen   that the Lord in sooth,
King of all creatures,   rules with might
Who sent this herald   for a help to men.
Great is the need   that we bravely obey."
    Then the saint began   to console their spirits
And to comfort the hearts   of the warrior host:
"Be not afraid   though this band of sinners
Has gone to destruction,   suffering death
And vengeance for evil.   To you is revealed
The radiance of glory   if you think aright."
    He sent his prayer   before God's Son,
Prayed that the Holy One   grant His grace
To all the youth   who had lost their lives
In the flowing waters,   the grip of the flood,
That their souls be not carried   to the clutch of fiends,
The anguish of torment,   empty of good
And deprived of glory.   When the plea was spoken
The prayer of the saint   found favour with God,
The Ruler of nations.   Uninjured from earth
He bade the youths rise   whom the sea had slain.

(1586–1624)

There in the assembly   speedily rose
Many a stripling,   as I have heard say.
They had both together,   body and soul,
Though a little before   in the flood's embrace
They had lost their lives.   They received baptism
And a promise of peace;   made rich through their pangs
They had pledge of glory   and favour of God.
   Then the King's craftsman,   the heroic saint,
Bade rear God's temple,   erect a church
On the spot where it happened   by the Father's help
That the youth rose up,   and the flood burst forth.
In the festal city   men gathered from far,
Resolute eorls   and their women with them.
They said they would faithfully   follow his teaching,
Accomplish God's will   and quickly receive
The bath of baptism,   abandon their idols,
Their ancient altars.   Honoured of the folk
Baptism was observed   and the service of God,
His law exalted,   and loyally kept
Throughout the land   among the many.
The church was hallowed.   The herald of God
Established a wise man   sage of word
To rule as Bishop   in the radiant city.
Through his power as Apostle   he hallowed him there
Before the assembly   to serve their need.
His name was Platan.   And Andrew earnestly
Urged the folk   to follow his teaching
And seek salvation.
                    Then he said that his heart
Longed to be gone,   to leave the city,
The hall-joy of heroes,   the giving of gold,
The radiant ring-hall.   His heart was eager
To seek a ship   at the shore of the sea.
   For all the host   it was hard to bear
That their leader no longer   would tarry among them.

(1625–1661)

M

But as he journeyed   the God of glory,
Lord of all peoples,   to Andrew appeared
And spoke this word: . . .   "the folk from their sins.
Their hearts are sad,   they walk in sorrow
Mourning their wretchedness,   man and maid.
The sound of their weeping,   the woe of their hearts . . .
Came swiftly before Me.   Forsake not this flock
In their joy so new,   but stablish My name
Firm in their hearts.   O helm of warriors
Tarry in the city,   the treasure-decked halls,
For seven nights' time.   So shall you go
And have My blessing."
                                        The brave-hearted saint
Mighty in strength,   once more set out
To return to the city,   the Mermedonian town.
The word and wisdom   of those Christian men
Were greatly heartened   when their eyes beheld
The thane of glory,   the herald of God.
He taught the folk   in the way of faith,
Splendidly strengthened them,   guided to glory
A countless band   of blessed souls
To their holy home   in the heavenly realms
Where Father and Son   and Spirit of comfort,
Reigning in Trinity,   rule in glory
Over heavenly mansions   for evermore.
    And so the saint   destroyed their shrines,
Dispelled idolatry   and ended error.
That was for Satan   bitter to bear,
Great sorrow of mind,   when he saw the host
Turning blithe-hearted   from their heathen idols
Through Andrew's urging   to that fairer joy,
That land where never   shall foot of fiend
Or fearsome spirit   find approach.
    Then the days were passed   as the Lord appointed
When He bade that Andrew   abide in the town.

(1661–1697)

The saint began   to make ready for sea,
Blissful-hearted   to sail in his boat
Back to Achaia,   there to abide
The pangs of death   and his soul's departure.
But it was for Satan   no sweet exchange
When he journeyed back   to the jaws of hell
Where never thereafter,   friendless and foul,
Has he found relief.   Then, as I learned,
Sad-hearted men   in a mighty multitude
Brought their loved leader   to the bow of his ship.
For many a man   his spirit was moved,
Welling within him.   The warrior brave
They brought to his sea-boat   under the hill.
Behind him, weeping,   they stood on the shingle
While they still had sight   o'er the tossing sea,
O'er the path of the seal,   of that best of princes.
Then they worshipped together   the Lord of glory,
Chanting in chorus   and crying aloud:
    "There is One Eternal Lord   of all things living!
His might and power   upon all the earth
Are famous and blessed.   His bliss over all
In heavenly splendour   shines on the saints,
Gleaming in glory   for ever and ever,
With angels eternal.   He is True King!"

(1698–1722)

CHAPTER IV

THE HOLY ROOD

FOREWORD

THE *Elene* is a poem of 1,321 lines describing the vision of the Cross that came to Constantine the Great, and the subsequent finding of the true Cross by his mother, Helena Augusta. The text of the poem is preserved in the Vercelli Book. Near the end of the *Elene* is a runic signature by Cynewulf similar to that already noted in the *Ascension*, except that in the *Elene* the name is spelled with an *e* and in the *Ascension* without it.

The source on which Cynewulf drew for the material of his poem must have closely resembled a *Vita Quiriaci* now in the Bollandist collection of *Acta Sanctorum* for the date of 4 May. This particular *Vita* may not have been the actual text which the poet had before him, but in all probability he was working from a generally similar Latin original.[1] This Latin text would seem to have been known in Ireland also, for there is an Irish version of the *Invention* quite similar to the *Elene*.

The story of Constantine's vision and the finding of the true Cross belong to a stream of tradition which grew up during the early Christian centuries. This body of material was concerned with two general themes: the origin of the wood from which the Cross was made, and the disposition of the wood of the Cross after St Helena's recovery of it. This latter strain of tradition included many accounts of miracles wrought by the Cross wood.

Some legends traced the wood of the Cross back to the Tree of Knowledge in the Garden of Eden.[2] A full development of this tradition is found in the *Inventio Crucis* in the *Legenda Aurea*. It is probable that this linking of the Cross wood to the Garden of Eden may have had its source in the Apocryphal Gospel of Nicodemus. According to the accounts there given in Chapter xiv, Adam, falling ill, sent his son Seth back to Eden to beg from the Archangel Michael the healing oil of the Tree of Mercy. Michael refused, but prophesied the redemption of mankind after 5,000 and 500 years, when Christ would be born to anoint with the oil of mercy all those who believe in Him.

[1] Cf. Cook, *The Old English Elene, Phoenix, and Physiologus*, pp. xiv–xxiv.
[2] See *Legend of the Holy Rood*, ed. R. Morris, E.E.T.S. 46.

The *Legenda Aurea* account is a more extended version of this theme. In that account, instead of refusing, Michael gives Seth a branch of the Tree from which Adam had eaten, accompanying the gift with a prophecy that when the branch bore fruit Adam would be healed. Returning to find his father dead, Seth planted the branch on Adam's grave where it grew until Solomon's day. The Queen of Sheba, on her visit to Solomon, saw the Tree and worshipped it, predicting that it would be the instrument of Christ's Passion. Solomon therefore had it hewn down and buried deep in the ground. But the waters of the Pool of Bethesda welled forth on that spot, receiving virtue from the buried wood. When the time of the Crucifixion drew near the wood rose, floating on the surface of the pool, and from it was shaped the Cross.

Our earliest account of Constantine's vision of the Cross is found in the *Life of Constantine* by Eusebius,[1] who tells us that he had it from the lips of Constantine himself long afterwards when he was "honoured with his acquaintance and society". According to Eusebius, on a certain day the Emperor beheld a vision of a flaming cross in the heavens with the legend "Conquer by this." The time was shortly after mid-day "when the sun was beginning to decline". Lactantius, writing in the *De Mortibus Persecutorum*,[2] says that the vision appeared to Constantine, not at mid-day, but in a dream by night. Influenced by the vision the Emperor immediately caused a cross to be shaped for a battle-standard, using a long spear for the shaft and surmounting the whole with a crown and a cryptographic symbol of Christ.

It was a result, then, of this miraculous vision of the Cross, and under the protection of this standard, that Constantine overthrew Maxentius and fought his way to the mastery of Rome. The legend as related in the Old English *Elene* blends, or confuses, the events of three different years.[3] Since the Franks are mentioned in the account of the armies that threaten the Empire, we are carried back to the year 306, though Constantine's vision of the Cross which brings victory belongs to the year 312, and the victory itself to the year 322.

The legend of the journey of St Helena to Jerusalem, and the finding

---

[1] Book I, 28–31 (Migne, *Patr. Gr.*, xx 944–8).

[2] Migne, *Patr. Lat.*, vii 260–2.

[3] Cf. Cook, *Old English Elene, Phoenix, and Physiologus*, p. 85, note on line 7.

of the Cross, began to take form within a century after the events concerned. An early tradition had existed that from the time of Hadrian to
the reign of Constantine a statue of Jupiter had stood over the sepulchre of Christ, and a shrine of Venus on the site of the Cross.[1] After
his vision of the Cross Constantine gave orders that these shrines be destroyed and the places purified. According to Ambrose,[2] the Emperor's mother, Helena, desiring to visit these holy places, made a
journey to Jerusalem. While there she began a search for the wood of
the Cross at Golgotha. When the ground was dug, she found three
crosses of which she was able to identify the true Cross by the inscription affixed to it at the time of the Crucifixion. Later she searched for
the nails and found them. One of the nails she had set in a crown, and a
second in a bridle, and sent them to Constantine, who made use of
both. In the *Ecclesiastical History* of Rufinus,[3] and the *Epistle to Severus*
of Paulinus of Nola,[4] we find identification of the Cross by miracle re-
placing identification by the inscription. In both these accounts, as in
the *Elene*, persons recently dead are brought to life when the true
Cross is lifted over them.

It is on this story of Constantine's vision, and St Helena's finding of
the Cross, that Cynewulf based the poem called the *Elene*. And in that
poem he was attempting more than merely a versification of religious
tradition as he found it in the Latin *Vita*. He was quite obviously attempting to fashion his material according to the recognized demands
of a definite literary convention. Just as the unknown author of the
Andreas was guided in the telling of his tale of St Andrew by the essential design of an epic tale, so Cynewulf in the *Elene* reshapes his source
material wherever it lends itself to the heroic pattern, and to an expression of the heroic mood.

The introductory lines of the *Elene* place the events of the poem in
the sixth year of Constantine's reign.[5] In this opening passage the

[1] Cf. Jerome, *Epistle to Paulinus*, lviii 3 (Migne, *Patr. Lat.*, xxii 581).
[2] *Oration on the Death of Theodosius*, Chapters 43, 45–8 (Migne, *Patr. Lat.*,
xvi 1400–2).
[3] Migne, *Patr. Lat.*, xxi 475 ff.   [4] Migne, *Patr. Lat.*, lxi 326 ff.
[5] That is, in 312, since Constantine was acclaimed Emperor in Britain in
306. It is hardly necessary to point out the discrepancy between this date and
the statement in lines 1–7 of the *Elene*.

brief portrait of the Emperor contains many of the stock phrases of panegyric which characterize the conventional picture of the epic hero. He is a "mighty war-lord", "merciful to men", and a "defender of the folk in battle". He prospers in glory and power. As the poem begins he is facing war with the Northern tribes.

The description of the assembled forces of the Huns and Franks encamped on the banks of the Danube, and later engaged in battle with the Roman army, is the conventional martial scene so dear to Old English poets. In this instance it is somewhat unusually extended.[1] All the characteristic detail of the Germanic battle Cynewulf introduces into the material of the Latin *Vita*. We have the gathering of the clans, and the conventional symbols of carnage: the dark, cruel raven; the wet-winged eagle looking down on the gathered hosts; and the howling wolf, the "forest companion". The noise and movement of troops as the Roman forces advance to confront the foe are described with great vividness. We hear the rattle of shields and spears, the cries of the heralds, the tramping of horses' hoofs, the tumult of marching men, the clamour of scavenging bird and beast.

Face to face the two armies encamp on the Danube for the night. But Constantine is fearful as he surveys the forces of the Huns and the Hreth-Goths which so far outnumber his own. He has little hope of victory because of his lack of men. It is during this night that he sees the vision of the Cross with its encircling legend of victory. In the morning he has a replica fashioned and under the new standard moves forward to the attack.

The battle scene that follows is notable for epic realism. There is shock of troops and crash of bucklers. The storming warriors break through the shield-wall and drive home the sword, while overhead the ash spears, the "battle-adders", fly in clouds. Helmets and spear-points flash. War cries rise, and the howl of the wolf. The heathen are driven in flight. Some war took; some barely survived the battle, fleeing to strongholds among the rocky cliffs; some were drowned in the river depths. Of the forces of the Huns but few ever returned home.

After the victory Constantine returned to "his cities and his stately seat", and there summoned a council of wise men from whom he might learn what God it was "whose symbol so brightly revealed" had

[1] *Elene*, 18–68; 105–47.

brought him victory. Instructed in the Christian faith, he quickly adopt-
ed it, and was baptized. As Cynewulf tells the tale, the Emperor gave
himself fully to the service of the new religion. Through the Scriptures,
and the doctrine of scholars, he studied the records of the life and
ministry of Christ. His mind became increasingly concerned with the
story of the Crucifixion, and at length he sent his mother, Elene, to
Jerusalem to search for the Cross.

Just as Cynewulf had obviously taken delight in a detailed narrative
of the battle, so again he makes full use of the descriptive opportunities
implicit in St Helena's Mediterranean voyage.[1] The poet's panorama
is divided, as it were, into two scenes. The first is the preparation for
the voyage and the loading of the ships. The second is the sailing and
the voyage itself. Both are well done.

There is a busy sense of movement and bustle in the first scene. We
are shown the ships waiting at the shore, the sea-horses "ready at the
ocean's rim". To the harbour come men hurrying along the border-
paths, band after band, to load the vessels with buckler and lance, with
battle-sarks, with men in byrnies, with man and maid. It is a stirring
scene of embarkation. The voyage itself is one of the outstanding brief
sea-pictures in Old English verse. It is, of course, much less rugged in
mood than the ocean-realisms of the *Seafarer*, and, one need hardly say,
not to be compared with the full length voyage of St Andrew. But
there is sharp suggestion of sea-wind and white-crested billows, of
swelling sails and plunging bows, of a fleet of ships standing out to sea,
and ultimately dropping anchor in a foreign harbour as the voyage ends.

It is inherent in the nature of his source material that in later passages Cynewulf is not able to maintain the narrative vigour and descriptive realism of the battle and voyage scenes. Such scenes offered
material which lent itself well to his creative powers, and to the epic
stress he was attempting. But between St Helena's arrival at Jerusalem
and the actual beginning of the search for the Cross there is an interval
of some 400 lines in which the poet is wrestling with stubborn dialectic
material. One can see him endeavouring, not always successfully, to
avail himself of any opportunity to enliven this portion of his source
material. His decisions are not always wise. At one point[2] he is quoting from Isaiah i 2–3, and the prophet's pregnant statement, "The ox

[1] *Elene*, 225–55.   [2] *Elene*, 353–63.

knoweth his owner, and the ass his master's crib," is seized on by the poet for elaboration: "The weary cattle, that day by day men drive and beat, know their protector and take it not amiss, nor hate the friend that gives them food." Here Cynewulf, in attempting a development of the pastoral image, has sacrificed the compressed vividness of his original. The result is in notable contrast to the effective use of poetic elaboration that is illustrated by a finely wrought passage in the *Phoenix* (243–57) where the image of sprouting seed is expanded into a decorative miniature of the pastoral year.

The rather tedious dialectic of this portion of the poem has to do with St Helena's prolonged and controversial debates with the Jewish leaders before she is able to secure from them the information she needs to advance her search for the Cross. On her arrival at Jerusalem the Queen has called into conference all the wisest among the people who might have knowledge of the Christ who had been put to death upon the Cross. In the course of her interrogation of the gathered sages a group of 3,000 was cut, first to 1,000, and then to 500, but to no avail. Though threatened with death, all denied knowledge of the Cross which St Helena sought.

At last, however, a certain Judas, after repeated questioning and imprisonment, broke down and agreed to reveal the truth. Leading the way to Calvary, but ignorant of the precise spot on which the Cross had stood, Judas prayed for a sign. A vapour miraculously rising from the ground guided him to dig at a certain place. There twenty feet deep he found three crosses together. The true Cross was identified by the miracle of the dead body brought to life, as in the accounts of Rufinus and Paulinus already noted. By a second miracle the nails used in the Crucifixion were later discovered deep in the ground, where their gleaming radiance, like stars or jewels, made them visible through the earth.

We have seen that often in the saints' legends the appearance of the Devil upon the scene, when his power is threatened by acts of the saint, is the conventional symbol of the conquest of evil by good. Such an appearance occurs in the *Elene* just after Judas has recovered the Cross. The Devil laments his subjection to the power of Christ and bewails this latest humiliation, especially at the hand of one named

Judas. For it was a Judas who of old gave him his highest hope. Now a second Judas has humbled him greatly. He threatens to raise up a new king who will repudiate God and follow the Devil's teaching, a passage that has been interpreted by some as an allusion to the Emperor Julian, the Apostate, nephew of Constantine.

On the whole, the Devil of Cynewulf's *Elene* is by no means as sharply individualized as are the diabolic figures in some of the other Old English poems. He is neither the fallen Lucifer of *Genesis B*, nor the imitated Germanic warrior of the *Andreas*, nor one of the howling demons who make the fens hideous around the lonely hermitage of the English St Guthlac. He is the conventional symbol of evil, and his appearance in the poem is brief.

On the spot where the Cross was found St Helena later had a church erected, and the wood of the Cross placed there in a silver casket adorned with gold and gems. She sent for Eusebius to come to Jerusalem for the instruction of Judas, and for his consecration as Bishop under the new name of Cyriacus. Before returning to Rome St Helena commanded the people to observe as a feast day the date on which the Cross was recovered.

The final eighty-five lines of the *Elene* are given over to the personal passage and runic signature, and to the brief depiction of the Last Judgment which marks the end of so many Old English religious poems. It is a matter of interest that the runic signature ends with a passage of seven lines (1271–7) that Cynewulf may have imitated from Virgil's description of Aeolus and the Cave of the Winds.[1]

The depiction of the fires of Doomsday in the *Elene* is unique in Old English religious poetry. The conventional descriptions of Doomsday[2] picture a cataclysm of flame that brings the annihilation of earth and all that earth has brought forth. More than once in Old English verse fiery destruction by the flames of Judgment Day is compared with the watery devastation that came upon earth in the Flood.[3] But in the *Elene* the destroying flames of Judgment seem to merge into the punitive and purging fires of purgatory, and eternal punishment. All

---

[1] *Aeneid*, I 52–9.

[2] See the vivid description in *The Last Judgment*, ll. 930–1006, Chapter VI.

[3] Cf. *Christ*, 805–8; and 984–6.

souls, Cynewulf writes, shall be divided into three groups, and shall find their places at different depths in the flame. The uppermost group shall be the faithful for whom the fire shall be tempered as may be mildest and most easy to endure. The second group, soiled with sin, shall be chastened in the midst of the flames. Both these groups shall be purged and purified of every blemish like fine gold, and shall come in the end to God's presence. The third group, impious transgressors, shall be fast in the abyss of fire for ever. Never again shall they come to the mind of God. In no other Old English poem does the painting of the Judgment flames show so explicit a reflection of early patristic doctrine.

So ends this poem of St Helena's Finding of the Cross. The Cynewulfian personal passage which immediately precedes the runic signature is notable among the poet's references to himself. It seems probable that the *Elene* is the latest of his signed poems, for Cynewulf's mood is that of weariness and age, as of one drawing near the end of the journey. But it is also the mood of the devout Christian who has found in the Cross the central symbol of his longing and all his hope—as had the author of the *Dream of the Rood*. As Cynewulf finishes his poem he looks back upon the long and patient reading by which he has traced the history of the Cross before he could set it down with loving devotion for others to read. And he ends his legend, as had the author of the Latin *Vita*, with a prayer that "the doors of heaven may be opened, and their lot be assigned with Mary, for all who are mindful of this dearest of feast-days of the Cross".

ST HELENA FINDS THE TRUE CROSS

(Elene)

Then had passed   as the years departed
In ordered count   through the course of time
Two hundred three   and also thirty
Of winters for the world   since the Glory of kings,
The Ruling Lord   and Light of the righteous,
Was born on earth   in the image of man.
The year was the sixth   of Constantine's sway
Since he was raised up   in the Roman kingdom
To be battle-lord   and leader in war.
He was eager for praise,   defender of peoples,
Unto men merciful;   his princely might
Increased under heaven.   He was true king,
War-lord of peoples.   God prospered him
In glory and might   so that for many
Through all the earth   he became a comfort,
Defending the folk,   when against the foe
He took up weapons.

                He was threatened with war,
Tumult of battle.   The Hunnish tribe
And the Hreth-Goths also   assembled a host.
Fierce in strife   marched the Franks and the Hugas;
Bold men were they   and ready for battle.
War-spears glittered   and woven mail;
With shout and shield   they raised their standards.
The men of war   were openly mustered,
The clan was gathered,   the folk fared forth.
The wolf in the wood   sang his song of war,
Hid not his hope   of carnage to come.
The wet-winged eagle   clamoured and cried
As he followed the foe.   Straight through the cities

(1–31)

The greatest of battle-hosts   hasted to war
In hordes as many   as the Hunnish king
Might anywhere muster   of neighbouring men,
Mail-clad warriors.   The mightiest of armies
Went forth to battle   in bands made strong
With mounted legions,   till in a foreign land
They boldly camped   on the Danube's bank
Near the river's torrent   with tumult of men.
Fain would they conquer   the kingdom of Rome,
Plunder and waste it.   The approach of the Huns
Was known through the cities.   And Caesar bade
Against the fierce foe's   flying arrows
Summon the warriors   straightway to strife,
Bring men to battle   under the sky.
Straightway the Romans,   strong in might,
Were weaponed for battle   though their war-band was less
Than rode round the ruthless   king of the Huns.
    Then shields resounded   and war-wood sang;
The king with his troops   advanced to attack.
The raven clamoured   cruel and dark.
The host moved forward;   horn-bearers leaped;
Heralds shouted;   horses trod earth;
The army assembled,   the stalwart to strife.
    Then the king was affrighted,   shaken with fear,
When he beheld   the foreign foe,
The army of Huns,   the horde of the Hreth-Goths,
Who there at the Roman   empire's end
On the river's margin   mustered their host,
A countless force.   The Roman king
Endured heart-sorrow.   No hope had he
Of winning the battle   for want of strength.
He had too few warriors,   trusted comrades,
Against that overmight   of stalwart men.
There the army encamped,   eorls round their prince,
Near to the river   for the night-long time

(31–67)

After first they beheld   the march of the foe.
    Then to great Caesar   as he lay in slumber
Asleep with his train   was a vision revealed.
To him appeared   a beauteous Presence,
In man's shape   made manifest,
White and shining,   more fair of form
Than early or late   he beheld under heaven.
He started from slumber,   did on his boar-helm,
And straightway the herald,   fair heavenly form,
Spoke unto Caesar,   named him by name,
And the veil of darkness   vanished away:
    "O Constantine,   the King of angels,
Leader of nations   and Lord of fate,
Proclaims a compact.   Be not afraid
Though these foreign tribes   threaten with terror,
With hard battle.   To heaven look up,
To the Prince of glory.   There find support
And a token of triumph."

                              Straightway the king
Opened his heart   to the angel's bidding
And looked on high   as the herald bade,
Fair weaver of concord.   Clothed with treasure
O'er the roof of clouds   he beheld the Cross
Adorned with gold;   its jewels glittered.
The radiant Tree   was written round
With gleaming letters   of glowing light:
"With this sign thou shalt halt   the hostile host,
And crush the foe   in this perilous fray."
    Then the radiance faded   faring on high,
And the angel with it,   to the host of the holy.
The king was the blither,   the captain of heroes,
And the freer from sorrow   in his inmost soul
By virtue of that vision   so wondrous fair.
    Then Constantine,   the glorious king,
Protector of princes   and Giver of gifts,

                    (68–100)

N

War-lord of armies,   bade quickly work
And shape a symbol   like the Cross of Christ
As he saw that sign   revealed in the heavens.
He bade at dawn,   at the break of day,
Rouse the warriors   to the weapon-storm,
Lift high the standard,   the Holy Tree,
In the thick of the foe   bear the Cross before them.
 Loud o'er the legions   the trumpets sang.
The raven rejoiced;   the wet-winged eagle
Gazed on the struggle,   the cruel strife;
The wolf, woodland comrade,   lifted his wail.
Battle-terror was come.   Then was crashing of shields,
Crush of heroes   and hard hand-swing,
The slaughter of many,   when first they met
The flying darts.   Against the doomed
The stalwart fighters   with strong hand
Sent storms of arrows,   their battle-adders,
O'er the yellow shield   on the savage foe.
Stout-hearted they stormed,   fiercely attacking;
Broke through the shield-hedge;   drove home the sword.
Before the legions   the banner was lifted,
The war-song was sung.   Helmets of gold
And spear-points flashed   on the field of war.
The pagans perished;   peaceless they fell.
 Then headlong fled   the Hunnish folk
When the Roman war-lord   waging the fight
Bade lift on high   the Holy Tree.
Heroes were scattered;   some war took;
Some barely survived   in the bitter fight;
Some half-alive   fled to a fastness,
Sheltered themselves   in the stony cliffs,
Beside the Danube   defended a stronghold;
And some at life's end drowned   in the river-depths.
 Then the heroes exulted   pursuing the heathen
Until evening came   from the dawn of day;

(100–140)

Ash-spears flew,   their battle-adders.
The host was cut down,   the hated horde;
Of the Hunnish troops   but few returned home.
So was it clear   that the King Almighty
Awarded to Constantine   in that day's work
Fortune in battle,   glory and fame
And an earthly kingdom,   through the Holy Cross.
    Then the warden of armies   went again home
Exulting in booty   and honoured in war,
Now the battle was won.   The defender of warriors,
The battle-brave king,   with a throng of thanes
Returned to his cities   and his stately seat.
The warden of warriors   summoned his wisest
Quickly to council,   whoso had learned
Wisdom's riches   through ancient writings
And held all knowledge   in their inmost hearts.
The king triumphant,   prince of the people,
Began to ask   through that ample host
If there were any   of old or young
Who could tell in words   or say for truth
What God it might be,   Giver of glory,
"Whose beacon it was   so brightly revealed,
Most shining of symbols,   that shielded my people,
Awarded me war-might   in fight with the foe
And brought me honour   through the beauteous Tree."
    Not any then   could give him answer
Or clearly tell   of that Victor-Tree.
But the sagest there   before the assembly
Proclaimed it a token   of Heaven's King,
Of which was no doubting.   When they heard these words
Those taught through baptism   were happy of heart
(Though little their number);   their spirits were light
As they preached to Caesar   the Gospel's grace:
How the Splendour of kings,   Defender of spirits,
In the glory of Trinity   greatly extolled,

(140–177)

Was born upon earth;   how God's own Son
In the sight of many   was stretched on the Cross
In dreadful anguish;   and how He redeemed
From devils' dominion   the sons of men,
Sorrowing spirits,   and granted them grace
Through the same Cross that Caesar   saw in his dream,
A token of triumph   against hostile attack;
How the Glory of heroes   out of the grave
Upon the third day   rose from death,
The Ruler of all   the race of men,
And ascended to heaven.   Of sacred mysteries
Wisely they taught   the victorious king
As they themselves   had been taught by Silvester;
From whom the ruler   had the rite of baptism
And all his days fostered it   fearing the Lord.

 Then glad of heart   was the giver of treasure,
The battle-bold king.   New joy and bliss
Were granted his spirit.   The Guardian of heaven
Was his greatest comfort   and his highest hope.
By grace of the Spirit   the king began
By day and night   to make known God's law;
Famous in battle   the gold-friend of heroes
Gave himself fully   to the service of God.

 Then the mighty prince,   protector of peoples,
Bold in battle   and swift with the spear,
Learned through the Scriptures   and scholars' lore
Where the Lord of the heavens   was lifted up
With malice and hatred   on the Holy Tree
Mid the mob's commotion,   when the Ancient Foe
Misled and mistaught   the Jewish tribe
With cunning lies   till they crucified
God Himself,   the Creator of all.
And for that in misery   for evermore
They shall suffer curse.   Then the worship of Christ
Was in Caesar's heart.   He was henceforth mindful

(178–213)

Of the beauteous Tree; and he bade his mother
Fare o'er the floodway with a throng of folk
To the home of the Jews, with a host of warriors
Zealously search where the Tree of splendour,
The Holy Rood, was hid in the earth,
The Cross of heaven's King. Nor was Elene slow
To the voyage, nor slighted the word of her son,
The giver of good. Soon was she ready
For the joyous journey as the helm of hosts,
Of mail-clad warriors, had given command.
    Then a host of eorls made haste to the shore;
Sea-horses stood ready at the ocean's rim,
Bridled sea-stallions breasting the waves.
The lady's departure was plain to see
As she moved with her train to the tumbling breakers.
Many a stately man stood on the shore
Of the Wendel-sea. Swiftly they hurried
Over the border-paths, band after band.
They loaded the vessels with buckler and lance,
With men in byrnies, with battle-sarks,
With man and maid. O'er the sea-monsters' home
They drove their foaming deep-flanked ships.
Oft on the waves the stout wood stood
The blows of the billows. The ocean roared.
Never learned I early or late
Of lady who led on the ocean-lanes
Fairer band o'er the paths of the flood.
There might he see who beheld that sailing
Sea-wood scud under swelling sails,
Sea-steeds plunge and break through the billows,
Wave-ships skim. The warriors bold
Were blithe, and the queen had joy of the journey.
    When the high-prowed ships had come to their haven
Over the ocean in the Grecian land
They left their vessels much tossed of the tides,

(214–251)

Their old sea-homes,   at the ocean's shore
Fast at anchor   to await on the waves
The fate of the band,   when the battle-queen
With her troop of warriors   o'er the eastern ways
Should seek them again.   Then was easily seen
Woven mail   on many an eorl,
Choicest of blades,   bright battle-byrny,
Visored casque   and fair boar-crest.
There men of war   were on the march,
A convoy of warriors   around their queen.
The stalwart heroes,   heralds of Caesar,
Gaily fared   through the Grecian land,
Men of battle   in shining mail;
And many a gem   in its jewelled setting
Gleamed in that war-host,   the gift of a lord.
    Then the blessed Elene   in her bold heart
Was earnestly mindful   of the emperor's will
That across the plains   with her proven band,
A host in armour,   she should eagerly seek
The Jewish fatherland.   So it befell
In a little time   that the mighty troop
Famed in battle,   fierce with the spear,
In the greatest of companies   came to Jerusalem
Into the city   with their stately queen.
    There she bade summon   the city-dwellers,
The wisest in Jewry,   from far and wide
To come to council,   whoso most clearly
Were sage in expounding   through sacred law
The secrets of God.   And so were gathered
From the farthest borders   no little band,
Three thousand men   selected for learning
And wise in their mastery   of Moses' law.
Then the lovely lady   saluted the Hebrews:
    "Full well I know   through the words of the prophets
In the Books of God   that in days gone by

(252–290)

You once were precious   to the Prince of glory,
Zealous in deed   and dear unto God.
But lo! all wisdom   unwisely you spurned
Reviling Him   Who with radiant might
Thought to free you   from fiery torture,
From burning damnation   and the bonds of hell.
Upon His face   you spat your filth
Who created anew   the light of the eye
Healing your blindness   by His blessed spittle,
And from unclean spirits   set men free.
To death you doomed Him   Who Himself from death
Of your folk raised many   to their former life.
With darkened minds   you thought to mingle
Light with darkness,   lies with truth,
Hatred with honour.   In your impious hearts
You counselled evil.   Therefore the curse
Is come upon you,   on your sinful souls.
With darkened minds   you dared to judge,
You dared condemn,   that radiant Power;
You have lived in error   unto this day.

    "Go forth now quickly   and cull out men
Well versed in wisdom   and skilled in word,
Men noble of nature   who have your law
First and foremost   in their inmost hearts,
Who can make me answer   and tell me truly
Of every issue   I may ask of them."

    Then mournful of mind   those men of learning
Drew apart   oppressed with fear
And sad of spirit.   They eagerly sought
The wisest in council   to answer the queen
Both of good and evil   as she might ask.
In their throng they found   one thousand men
Of learned mind   who well remembered
Jewish tradition   of olden days.
In a swarming band   they crowded about her

(291-329)

Where the stately queen,   great Caesar's kin,
On a royal dais   all decked with gold
Sat in splendour.   She spoke to the eorls:
    "Hearken ye wise men   to words of wisdom,
Holy mysteries.   Lo! you have heard
The lore of the prophets: how the Prince of might,
The Lord of life,   in a child's likeness
Should be born among men.   Of whom sang Moses,
Warden of Israel,   speaking this word:
'To you shall be born   by a wondrous birth,
Glorious in might   a Child whose mother
Shall not bring forth   by man's embrace.'
Of Him sang David   a lordly song,
Solomon's father,   foremost of men;
The ancient prophet   uttered this word:
'Of old I beheld   the Lord of creation,
Giver of victories,   God of might,
Shepherd of glory.   The vision stood
At my right hand   and before my face,
Nor ever have I turned   mine eyes from Him.'
    "So also of you   Isaiah the prophet
Deeply musing   spoke before men
Through the spirit of God: 'I have raised up sons,
Begotten offspring;   I gave them glory,
Spiritual comfort.   But Me they spurned
And held Me in hatred.   They had no sense
Or wit of wisdom.   The weary cattle
That day by day   men drive and beat
Know their protector,   nor take it amiss,
Nor hate the friend   that gives them food.
But never was the nation   of Israel willing
To acknowledge Me,   though many a marvel
I did before them   in my days on earth.'
    "Lo! we have heard   through the Holy Books
That the Lord God gave you   glory unblemished,

(329–365)

Fullness of might,   declaring to Moses
How you should hearken   to the Heavenly King
And keep His counsels.   Quickly you wearied!
You have contended   against the truth
Despising the Shining   Shaper of all,
The Lord of lords;   you have lived in error
Against God's law.   Now go ye quickly
And search out those   who by wisdom's strength
Best have unriddled   the ancient writings,
The law of your people,   and may give reply
From the mind's depths   and make me answer."
    Then sad of heart   and troubled of spirit
The crowd went forth   as the queen decreed.
They found five hundred   exceeding sage
Picked from their people,   who most in mind
Had power of learning   and wisdom's lore.
These city-wardens   after a season
Were gathered together   in the great hall.
Then the lady looked on them   every one
And straightway began   to greet them with words:
    "Long have you followed   your foolish ways,
Ye vile and wretched,   scorning the Scriptures,
The law of your fathers;   never more than now
When your hearts rejected   the healing of your blindness
And you spurned the truth   that the Son of God
Was born in Bethlehem,   the Only-Begotten,
The Prince of princes.   Though ye knew the law,
The words of the prophets,   ye workers of sin,
You were not willing   to receive the truth."
    Then of one mind   they all made answer:
"Lo! we have learned   the Hebrew law
Which in former days   our fathers knew
At the ark of God;   and we can not grasp
Why so great is your wrath,   O lady, against us.
We know no sin   that we have sinned

(366–402)

Among this nation,   nor any evil
Against you ever."   Then Elene spoke
In discourse clear   addressing the host:
    "Go now swiftly   and seek afar
What men among you   have most in heart
Strength of mind   and wisdom's might
That they may truly   and fully tell
What thing soever   I may ask of them."
    Then they left the council   as the royal queen,
Mighty over cities,   had made decree.
Sad of spirit   they searchingly pondered
Thoughtfully seeking   what sin it was
That they on that soil   had done against Caesar,
Which the queen rebuked.   Then wise of word
One sage in council   spoke to the eorls,
Whose name was Judas: "Full well I know
That she will ask   of the Tree of triumph
Whereon once suffered   unspotted of sin
The Prince of all peoples,   God's own Son,
Whom wholly guiltless   of any evil
In former days   our fathers hung
On the high Cross   with bitter hatred,
A grievous thought!   Now great is the need
That we strengthen our spirits   not to disclose
The fearful crime,   where the Holy Cross
Was hidden in darkness   after His death,
Lest our ancient writings   be overthrown
And the law of our fathers   be confounded.
Not long thereafter   shall Israel's kindred
And Israel's worship   prevail on earth
If this be disclosed.   This also, of old,
My father's father   faithful and wise
(His name was Zaccheus)   said to my father,
His beloved son   (Simon his name,
He has gone from this world)   speaking this word:

(402–440)

'If in your lifetime   it ever betide
That you hear men ask   of the Holy Tree
Raising dispute   of the Glorious Rood
Whereon was hung   the Lord of heaven,
The King of truth,   the Prince of peace,
Be swift to answer,   beloved son,
Ere destruction seize you.   Nor ever thereafter
By taking thought   shall the Hebrew tribe
Maintain dominion   or rule over men.
But the glory shall grow,   the lordship shall live
For ever and ever   of those who delight
To love and worship   the Crucified King.'
        "To my wise father   I promptly replied:
'How could it happen   that with hostile mind
Our fathers laid hold   on the Holy One
To compass His death,   if they knew indeed
That He was the Christ,   the King of heaven,
God's True Son,   the Saviour of souls?'
        "Then sage of spirit   my forefather said:
'Consider, my son,   the greatness of God,
The Saviour's name.   It is not to be measured
By any mortal   nor can mind of man
Search it out   on the paths of earth.
Never did I follow   the ways of this folk,
But held me asunder   from all their sins;
I wrought no shame   upon my soul.
Often fiercely   I fought against evil
What time the sages   in council sat
And sought in their hearts   to hang on the Cross
The Son of God,   the Guardian of peoples,
The Lord of all,   of angels and men,
Noblest of sons.   But those wretched souls
Lost in their folly   could not inflict
Death upon Him   as they had deemed
With terrible tortures,   though a certain time

(441–479)

Upon the gallows   the Son of God
Gave up the ghost.   Then the Glory of glories,
The Lord of heaven,   was lifted from the Cross.
For three nights' time   He tarried in darkness
Deep in the grave;   then the Light of all light,
The Lord of angels,   living arose
On the third day   and unto His thanes
Revealed His presence   apparelled in splendour,
Shining in light,   the Triumphant Lord!
    'Then after a season   your brother received
Burning faith   and baptism's bath;
For his love of the Lord   Stephen was stoned.
Yet evil for evil   he gave not again
But meek in affliction   pled for his foes,
Made supplication   to the King of glory
To avenge not upon them   that dreadful deed
When at Saul's command   they slew him in hatred
Sinless of evil   and free of fault;
The Saul who with malice   brought many to torture,
Doomed many to death   of the folk of Christ.
Yet the Lord showed him mercy;   in later years
He became a comfort   to many a man.
The God of beginnings,   the Saviour of men,
Named him anew,   and ever thereafter
He was known as St Paul;   and none was better,
More learned than he,   of the teachers of law
Under shelter of heaven   of man or maid
Born in the world,   although at his bidding
Your brother Stephen   was stoned with stones.
    'So may you learn,   beloved man,
How ample in mercy   is the Lord of all,
Even though against Him   we work transgression
And wounds of evil,   if we make amends
For these foul offences   and cease from sin.
Therefore thenceforward   my beloved father,

(480–517)

And I too, believed   this gospel of love:
That the Guide of life,   the God of glory,
Bore mortal anguish   for man's great need.
Wherefore I admonish you,   dearest of men,
In secret counsel,   that you speak no evil
Or hate or blasphemy   in bitter answer
Against God's Son.   So shall you gain
The life eternal   allotted in heaven,
The best reward   of triumphs won.'
    "So did my father   in former days
Give me instruction,   a stripling lad;
Taught me the truth   with words of wisdom.
His name was Simon.   Decide ye now
What in your bosoms   to you seems best
To say in answer,   if this queen should ask
Of the noble Cross.   Now do you know
The musings of my heart   and all my mind."
    Then said unto him   the sagest among them:
"Never have we known   a man of this nation
Or another mortal   except now thee
To reveal in such wise   so secret things!
Do as it seemeth thee,   skilled in the law,
If thou be questioned   in this crowd of men.
He has need of knowledge   and wary word
And a wise man's prudence,   who can make reply
Before such council   to the noble queen."
    Then words were rife;   men reasoned the matter
From every side,   some this, some that;
They mused and pondered.   Many a thane
Came to the council;   heralds proclaimed,
Messengers of Caesar: "The queen commands
That you come to the palace   and there report
Your synod's decisions.   There is need of knowledge
Where many are gathered,   and wisdom of mind."
    Then were they ready   though wretched of heart,

(517–555)

The lords of the clan,   at the stern decree.
They went to the court   to proclaim to all
Their craft of learning.   The lady asked
The heart-sick Hebrews   of their ancient scriptures,
How once in the world   their wise men sang,
Their holy sages,   of the Son of God
Where the Lord would suffer,   the Creator's Son,
For His love of souls.   But they were stubborn,
Harder than flint;   nor would they confess
Aught of the mystery   or make answer
Of the things she sought;   but with set minds
They made denial   of all she asked,
Saying in their life-days   early or late
They had never had knowledge   of such a matter.
   Elene answered,   addressed them in anger:
"I say to you truly   and I tell no lie
If longer you persist   with wily deceit
To follow this falsehood,   who stand before me,
A pyre on the hill-top,   hottest of flames,
A withering fire,   shall snatch you away
And consume your flesh;   for you the falsehood
Shall purchase death.   Nor can you prove
The words you have sinfully   clothed with shame,
Nor conceal the event   or its secret power."
   Then they thought to die,   they had dread of the fire,
The ending of life;   and unto the queen
They delivered Judas   skilled in the scriptures,
Praising him as prudent   and wondrous wise:
"He can tell truth,   disclose fate's secrets,
And all our law   from beginning to end
As you fain would know.   His blood is noble;
He is wise in word-craft,   a prophet's son;
He has courage in council.   His nature is such
He has shrewd answers   and sharpness of wit.
He will clearly show forth   in all their fullness

(556–596)

His gifts of learning   to your heart's delight."

   Then she let them depart   in peace to their homes
Holding as hostage   Judas alone.
She bade him tell her   of the Holy Tree
Which had long been concealed   in a secret place;
She drew him apart   and in private addressed him,
The illustrious queen: "Two things are your lot,
Or life or death   as you may find dearer;
Now tell me promptly   which pleases you more."

   Judas made answer;   he could not at all
Avoid this sorrow   or avert her wrath;
He was wholly caught   in the power of the queen:
"How could it happen   with one who wanders
In waste places,   weary and starved,
Haunting the moorlands   as hunger's thrall,
If a loaf and a stone   are both before him,
The hard and the soft,   that he take the stone
To stay his hunger   and leave the loaf,
Turn to poverty   forsaking plenty
And spurn the better,   having choice of both?"

   Then with frank words   before the eorls
The blessed Elene   gave him answer:
"If you wish a home   in the heavenly kingdom
Among the angels,   life on earth
And reward in glory,   tell me at once
Where the Holy Rood   of the Heavenly King
Rests under ground,   which in grievous sin
Now for a season   you've concealed from men."

   Judas addressed her;   his spirit was sad,
Hot at his heart   with double woe,
That he must give over   such glorious hope
Of the heavenly land   and this life on earth,
If he did not tell her   of the Holy Tree:

   "How can I learn   what so long ago
Came to pass   in the course of time?

(596–633)

Many a winter   has vanished away,
Two hundred or more   in measured count;
I can not tell,   I know not the number.
Many a learned man   living before us,
Good men and wise,   have gone their way;
I was born long after   in later days.
That which I know not   I can not know,
Nor find in my mind   the things that befell
So long ago."

                    And Elene answered:
"How has it happened   among this people
That you hold in memory   many a tale
Of heroic feats   performed by the Trojans
In waging their battles?   That ancient war
Was earlier far   in the flight of time
Than this noble event.   Yet with full knowledge
You quickly recall   the count of their dead,
The slaughtered spearmen   who sank under shield.
Your writings recount   the cairn-covered graves,
The very places,   and the years that have passed."

    Then sorely troubled   Judas spoke:
"Needs must we long   remember, my lady,
That bitter struggle,   for our books set forth
The battles themselves   and the bearing of heroes.
But this other matter   from any man's mouth
We never have heard   save here, and now."

    Then the excellent queen   made answer to Judas:
"Overmuch you contend   against truth and right
In what you avow   of the Victor-Cross.
You told your kinsmen   of the Tree of life
Not long ago;   now you change to a lie."

    Then Judas responded   saying he spoke
In great trouble   and grievous doubt,
Thinking to suffer   more shameful ills.
And Caesar's kinswoman   said unto him:

                    (633-669)

"Lo! we have heard   through the Holy Books
Proclaimed to men   that the Child of God,
The Son of the King,   on Calvary
Was nailed on the Cross.   Now straight make known
All your learning,   as the Books relate
Of Calvary's site   where the spot may be,
Ere destruction seize you   and death for your sins,
That I may cleanse it   to the will of Christ
For a help to men   so that Holy God,
The Giver of glory   and Saviour of souls,
The Prince of might,   may prosper my purpose
And all the inward   hopes of my heart."
   Stubbornly Judas   said unto her:
"The spot I know not   nor the space of ground;
Nor aught do I know   of the matter at all"
   Then Elene answered   with angry heart:
"Truly I swear   by the Son of God
The Crucified Christ,   that before this people
You shall perish of hunger   except you purpose
To leave these falsehoods,   and tell me truth."
   Then she bade her retainers   take the sinner
And cast him down living   into a dry pit;
Her servants delayed not.   There in sorrow
Tortured with hunger,   trammelled with chains,
Lacking all food   he lay seven nights
In that bitter bondage.   On the seventh day
Weary and foodless,   enfeebled in strength,
Crippled with pain   he began to cry:
"I entreat and implore   by the Prince of heaven
That you grant me release   from this living death
Who here am humbled   by hunger's pangs.
Gladly will I tell you   of the Holy Tree;
By hunger subdued   I can hide it no longer.
Too grim is this thralldom,   too galling these bonds,
Too bitter my pangs   as the days passed by.

(670–705)

O

I can not longer   suffer this sorrow
Or continue concealment   of the Tree of life,
Though in former days   I was swayed by folly
And now have knowledge   of the truth too late."

   Then when the queen   in the midst of her company
Saw the man's bearing   she quickly bade
That they let him loose   out of his bondage
And the narrow prison   wherein he was penned.
Quickly they did it   and gently drew him,
As the queen appointed,   out of the pit.

   Stout of heart   they strode to a spot
Up on the hill   where the Lord was hung
Upon the gallows,   God's Own Son,
The Warden of heaven.   But weak with hunger
Judas knew not clearly   where the Holy Cross
Covered with earth   by the Devil's craft
Long time abode   fast in its bed
Secretly buried   and concealed from men.

   Then Judas straightway   though strengthless and feeble
Made entreaty   in the Hebrew tongue:
"O Saviour God   Who hast power of glory
Thy Holy Might   made heaven and earth,
The breaking waves   and the broad sea's bosom,
The mighty Creation;   Thy hands marked out
The bounds of earth   and the heavens above.
Lo! Thou art Ruler   reigning in triumph
Over the highest   of the angel hosts
Who wing through heaven   enwound with light
In the splendour of glory;   the spirits of men
May not mount up   from the ways of earth
With mortal body   to that radiant band,
Messengers of glory.   Them hast Thou made
And set to Thy service,   heavenly and holy.

   Unto that order are there six ordained
In perpetual bliss.   With pinions six

(705–742)

They are set about   and brightly adorned;
They shine in splendour.   Four of them serve
In ceaseless flight   before God's face
Eternally singing   in heavenly splendour,
With radiant voices   revering heaven's King,
The sweetest of chantings.   These are the Cherubim
In pure strains singing   these words of praise:
    'Holy is the Holy   God of archangels,
The Lord of hosts.   All heaven and earth
Are full of His glory;   His great might
Is marked with splendour.'   And two among them
A stately order   called Seraphim,
Safeguard the portals   of Paradise
And the Tree of Life   with a sword of flame.
Firm in their grasp   the sharp edge flashes,
The hard blade quivers,   with changing hue.
For Thou, Lord God,   dost govern for ever,
And of old didst hurl   from heaven on high
Guilty transgressors   filthy and foul.
That sinful rabble   perforce descended
To the dark home   and ruin of death.
Now in Hell's surges   hidden in darkness
They endure death-pangs   in the Dragon's clutch.
He defied Thy dominion!   In misery therefore
Full of all foulness,   outcast and vile
He shall suffer affliction   and sore constraint.
Fast in torment   and fettered in pain
He shall not escape   the weight of Thy word.
    "If it be Thy will,   O Ruler of angels,
That Christ shall reign   Who hung on the Cross,
Who of old through Mary   was born on earth,
The Lord of angels   as a little child,
Now Father of spirits   show forth Thy sign!
Were He not Thy Son   unsoiled of evil
Never had He worked   the wonders He wrought

(743–779)

In His life on earth,   and never, O Lord,
Wouldest Thou have roused Him,   Ruler of nations,
In splendour from death   in the sight of men
Were He not Thy Joy   through the gentle Maid.
   "As Thou didst hearken   to the holy man,
To the prayer of Moses,   O God of might,
When Thou didst lay bare   the bones of Joseph
Under the hill-slope   in that hour sublime,
So now I pray Thee,   O Joy of peoples,
By the bright Creation   if it be Thy will
That Thou mayest show me,   O Shaper of spirits,
The holy treasure   long hidden from men.
From its place of concealment   let a smoke arise
Under compass of heaven   curling in air,
O Lord of life!   So shall I better
Make strong my faith   and more firmly fix
The thoughts of my heart   and unwavering hope
On the crucified Christ,   that He is indeed
The Saviour of souls   and Israel's King
Eternal, Almighty,   over heavenly mansions
Ruling for ever   in glory and grace."
   Then from that spot   rose up a smoke,
A steam under heaven;   and the heart of the man
Was blissful within him.   The wise man and blessed
Clapped his hands   to heaven above.
Sage in spirit   Judas spoke:
   "Now I know   in my stubborn heart
That Thou art in sooth   the Saviour of men.
To Thee, God of nations,   enthroned in glory
Be thanks eternal   that through Thy grace
To me so sinful,   so sad of spirit,
Thou hast now discovered   the secrets of Time.
O Son of God   I beseech Thee now,
Thou Giver of good,   of old begotten,
Proclaimed to men   as the Glory of kings,

(780–816)

That no more Thou remember   the many transgressions
Which again and again   I have sinned against Thee.
Grant me to be numbered,   O God of might,
In the roll of Thy kingdom   to rest with the saints
In the bright city   where Stephen, my brother,
Is adorned with glory   because he held dear
His compact with Thee   though they stoned him with stones.
He has guerdon of battle,   unending bliss,
And the wonders he wrought   are writ in the Writings."
    Then joyous of spirit   with eager strength
He began to dig   and delve in earth
Under the turf   for the Tree of glory,
Till twenty feet deep   in a chamber of darkness
He found there hidden   under the hill
Three crosses together   in a gloomy grave
Covered with dirt   where in former days
The impious rabble,   the Jewish race,
Overspread them with earth.   Against God's Son
They stirred up hatred   as they never should
If they had not hearkened   to the hateful urging
Of the Author of evil.   Then his heart was happy,
His spirit strengthened   and his mind made glad,
Through the blessed Cross   when he saw that beacon
Resting in holiness   under the earth.
    With his hands he grasped   the Tree of glory
And by many aided   lifted it up
From its grave in the ground.   Then the stranger-guests
And all the host   made haste to the city.
The stalwart heroes   courageous of heart
In the sight of all   before Elene's knee
Set the three crosses.   The queen in her soul
Had joy of the work.   She began to question
On which of the crosses   was crucified
The Son of God,   the Saviour of men:
    "Lo! we have heard   in the Holy Books

(817–853)

Plainly told   that the Prince of glory
And two beside Him   suffered the cross;
He Himself was the third.   All the sky grew dark
In that terrible hour.   Now tell, if you can,
On which of these crosses   was crucified
The Lord of angels,   the God of glory."
Nor could Judas tell her   for he knew not truly,
Or inform her fully   of the Victor-Tree
On which our Saviour,   the Son of God,
Was crucified.   But he bade that the crosses
Mid the noise of the host   be raised on high
In the midst of the city,   there to remain
Till the King Almighty   unto the multitude
Made known by a marvel   the glorious Cross.
    With musing hearts   the heroes triumphant
Sat them down there   chanting a song
Around the three crosses   till the ninth hour came
And their minds by a marvel   were again made glad.
For there came from the neighbourhood   in great numbers
A gathered company,   no little crowd,
Who bore on a bier   with a band of mourners
A young man lifeless;   his soul had fled.
It was the ninth hour.   Then Judas was joyous
And gladdened in spirit.   Upon the ground
He bade lay down   the dead man's corpse,
The lifeless body.   Deeply brooding,
Imbued with wisdom,   the warden of truth
Upheld two crosses   o'er that house of clay.
It was dead as before   and fast on its bier;
The limbs were cold   and clothed with constraint.
Then the third Cross holy   was raised on high.
The corpse lay waiting   till the Cross of the Prince
Was raised above it,   the Rood of Heaven's King,
True Token of triumph.   Then straightway he rose
Endowed with spirit,   both body and soul.

(854–890)

Then sweet was the praise   which the people offered
As they worshipped the Father,   serving God's Son.
To Him be given   glory and thanks
By every creature   for ever and ever!
Firmly in mind   the people remembered,
As well they should,   the wonder God wrought,
The Guide of life,   for man's lasting good.
    But the lying demon,   the Devil from hell,
The loathsome Monster   mindful of evil,
Winging through air came   clamouring loud:
"What man is this   who mangles my following,
Adds to old hatred   and harries my realm?
This strife is unending.   Sinful souls
Within my dominions   no longer remain
Now this Foe is come   whom I counted undone.
It is He who hath robbed me   of every right
And all my holdings,   no happy lot!
The Saviour hath wrought me   many a mischief,
Many a deed   of enduring hate.
In Nazareth nurtured   and nourished to manhood
He stripped me for ever   of all my store.
    "I may not prosper.   His dominion is wide
Over all the earth.   My might is diminished
Under the heavens.   No need have I
To exalt the Cross   with eager delight!
Lo! oft has the Saviour   shut me in
To mournful sorrow   in that straitened home
By Judas aforetime   I was filled with hope;
By a second Judas   I am sorely humbled,
Fleeced of all good,   a friendless foe.
But soon I shall find   through incitement to evil
Escape from the bondage   of that bitter abode.
I shall call up against thee   another king
Who shall scourge thee sorely   forsaking thy teaching
And following after   my evil ways.

(890–930)

He shall send thee down　to the worst and the darkest
Of fearful tortures　till afflicted with pain
Thou shalt firmly forswear　the Crucified King
Whom once thou didst follow."
　　　　　　　　　　　　Then Judas the wise
Boldly made answer.　His breast was filled
With the Holy Spirit,　with a flaming love
And wisdom welling　from a prophet's lore;
Sage in judgment　he spoke this word:
　"Thou needest not so eagerly,　Lord of evil,
Stir up strife　and renew distress,
Mindful of sin.　The Mighty King
Who hath wakened many　by His word from death
Shall cast thee down,　Thou doer of evil,
Deprived of honour　to the pit of pain.
Thou shalt know the more fully　how in folly of old
Thou didst abandon　that beauteous joy
And brightest of beacons,　the love of the Lord,
Abiding thereafter　in bitter torment
In a bath of fire　kindled with flame;
And there for ever,　O Evil of heart,
Thou shalt suffer damnation　with never an end."
　Then Elene heard　how friend and fiend
Blissful and evil,　blessed and vile,
Stirred up strife　on either side.
And her heart was the gladder　when Elene heard
How the Lord of sin,　the Scather from hell,
Was overmatched;　she wondered much
At the wisdom of Judas,　that he so wanting
In so little time　was so filled with faith
And was granted such knowledge.　She gave thanks to God,
The Warden of glory,　that her wish was fulfilled
Through the Son of God　with both these boons:
In the sight revealed　of the Tree of triumph,
And also the faith　which she knew full well

(931–966)

Was a glorious gift   in the hero's heart.
   Thereafter were published   among that people
And widely rumoured   throughout the realm
The glorious news   to the great vexation
Of all who belittled   the law of the Lord.
It was spread through the cities   and told in the towns
As far as the sea coast   circled them round
That the Cross of Christ   long compassed in earth
Was found again,   the fairest of beacons
That ever was lifted   early or late
Holy under heaven,   the joy of Christians
But the greatest of sorrows   for the sinful Jews,
The worst of destinies,   if only in the world
They could have changed it.
                       Then the queen gave bidding
Through the host of eorls   that heralds in haste
Speed on a journey.   Over the deep sea
They must needs return   to the lord of the Romans
And tell the hero   the happy tidings
That by grace of God   the glorious Cross
Uncovered in earth   was come to light
Where of old it was hidden   ages ago
To the grief of the saints   and good Christian folk.
   Then the heart of the king   was happy within him,
His mind made glad,   at the glorious news.
And many were gathered   in golden raiment
Travelling from far   to ask of those tidings.
The greatest of comforts   was come to the king,
A laughing heart,   at the happy news
Which the couriers carried   o'er the eastern ways:
How his valiant warriors   with their victor-queen
Across the swan-road   had safely come
To the Grecian shore.   Then Caesar bade
That again with all speed   they make ready to sail.
The warriors delayed not   hearing his word,

(967–1002)

The prince's bidding.   He bade them give greeting
To the valiant Elene   if those valorous men
Should survive the sea   and journey in safety
To the Holy City.   And Caesar commanded
That the messengers bid her,   to profit them both,
That she build on the hill-slope   a house of God,
A church on Calvary   to the will of Christ
For a help to men   where the Holy Rood
Was found again,   the fairest of trees
That ever earth-dwellers   had known on earth.

   And so she did   when those dear-loved men
O'er the ocean waves   from out the west
Brought many a message   of loving good will.
The queen bade seek   men dowered with skill,
The best who could cunningly   build in stone,
To rear God's temple   on that spot of ground.
According to the word   of the Warden of heaven
She had the Rood garnished   with gold and gems,
Skilfully set   with precious stones
And enclosed with clasps   in a casket of silver.
There from that time   the Tree of life,
Best Tree of triumph,   has had its abode
In beauty unbroken.   It will always be
A ready help   for hapless souls
Who suffer affliction,   sorrow and woe.
There shall they quickly   find comfort and aid
And heavenly grace   through the Holy Rood.

   Then after an interval   Judas received
The bath of baptism   and being made pure
Was true unto Christ   and loved of the Lord.
Fixed in his heart   his faith was firm
When the Holy Spirit,   the Comforter, came
To abide in his breast   and prompt to repentance.
He chose the better,   the bliss of glory,
And refused the worse,   the rites of false faith;

¦ (1003–1041)

He put down error   and worship of evil.
And the Lord Everlasting,   the Wielder of might,
God the Creator,   was gracious to him.
So was he baptized   who many a time
Had despised the light;   his spirit was stirred
To the better life   and celestial glory.

   Lo! Fate had ordained   in his days on earth
That he should be loyal   and dear to the Lord,
Pleasing to Christ.   So was it published
When Elene sagely   sent for Eusebius,
Wise Bishop of Rome,   to be brought to their aid
With his train of heroes   to the Holy City,
To ordain Judas   in Jerusalem
Into the priesthood   as the people's bishop
For his great gifts chosen   by the Spirit's grace
To the Church of God;   and counselled by wisdom
He called him Cyriacus,   and named him anew.
Throughout the nation   the Bishop was known
By the better name,   "the law of the Lord".

   Then Elene's mood   was greatly mindful
Of the noble matter   of the nails that pierced
The feet of our Healer,   and likewise His hands
Whereby the Almighty,   Master of heaven,
Was hung on the Cross.   The Christian queen
Made query about them   and bade Cyriacus
That once again   he accomplish her will
In this wondrous matter   by the Spirit's might,
And by grace disclose it.   She boldly declared
And told the Bishop: "O protector of men,
Thou didst show me truly   the glorious Tree
Of the King of heaven   whereon was hung
By heathen hands   the Healer of souls,
God's Own Son,   the Saviour of men.
An eager longing   for the nails doth now
Fill my heart.   I would have thee find them

(1041–1080)

Where deeply buried,   embosomed in earth,
They are hidden in darkness.   My heart is grieving,
Rueful and sad,   nor shall ever know rest
Till the Father Almighty,   Redeemer of men,
The Lord of hosts   holy from heaven,
Shall fulfil my desire   and show forth the nails.

"Now, best of heralds,   with humble heart
Send up thy prayers   to the Prince of glory
In the shining heavens;   and seek of Him,
The Lord of warriors,   Warden Almighty,
That He may bring thee   to this buried treasure
That lies there secret   and concealed from men."

Then the holy Bishop   with heart inspired,
Made strong in spirit,   went forth with joy
Joined with much people   praising God.
On Calvary's hill   he bowed his head,
Spoke his heart's musings   by the Spirit's might,
And in great humility   called upon God
That the Lord of angels   in his urgent need
Might to him make manifest   that secret matter
Where he most surely   might search for the nails.

And there as they gazed   the God of all comfort
Showed them a sign,   a flash of flame
Where the noblest of nails   in cunning concealment
Through the evil of men   had been buried in earth.
There came then suddenly   brighter than the sun
A flickering fire.   The folk beheld
The Giver of good   show forth a marvel
Where shining from darkness   like heavenly stars
Or golden jewels,   deep in the ground
The nails covered over   were kindled with light.

Then the host exulted,   their hearts rejoiced,
They glorified God   with one accord,
Though undone by the Devil   they long had lived
In the coils of error,   cut off from Christ.

(1080–1120)

They said: "We have seen   this token of triumph,
This wonder of God   Whom we once denied
With lying falsehood.   Now come to light
And clearly revealed   is the course of events.
Glory to God   in heaven on high!"

   Then again was made blissful   the heart of the bishop
Who was stirred to repentance   by the Son of God.
Shaken with terror   he took the nails,
Carried them straightway   to the noble queen.
All was fulfilled,   all the will of the woman
As the excellent queen   had asked of him.
There was sound of weeping,   but not for woe
Were their faces wet   with the welling flood;
Tear drops fell   on the twisted nails;
The will of the woman   was fairly fulfilled.

   In her lap she laid them   with fervent faith
And with gladsome joy   adored the gift
Which to her had been granted   to soothe her grief.
She gave thanks to God,   the Giver of triumph,
That her eyes so surely   might see the truth
Which was augured of old   from the world's beginning
To comfort the folk.   Her heart was filled
With the grace of wisdom;   the Holy Ghost,
The heavenly Spirit,   abode in her breast
Housing within   in her noble heart.

   So the Son of God,   Almighty, Triumphant,
Protected and loved her   from that time forth.
Eagerly then   in her inmost soul
She sought the right   and a road to glory.
And the Lord of hosts,   Our Father in heaven,
God Almighty,   granted her help;
So the queen accomplished   her will in the world.
It was prophesied   and sung by the prophets
From the very beginning   in days gone by
As it afterwards happened   in each regard.

(1120-1156)

Then the queen began   by grace of the Spirit
Eagerly seeking   with earnest care
To what service she might   most meetly and best
Devote the nails   to mankind's advantage,
And what in this matter   might be God's will.
She bade summon quickly   a wise man to counsel
Who by might of knowledge   had insight of mind;
She asked what he deemed it   best to do
And well and faithfully   followed his teaching.

He said: "It is fitting,   O fairest queen,
That you keep God's sayings   secret and holy,
And eagerly accomplish   the King's commands,
Since God, the Saviour,   has granted to you
Strength of spirit   and wisdom's art.
Do you bid the most royal   of earthly rulers,
Holder of fortresses,   fasten the nails
On his horse's bridle   for a bit to the steed.
Among many nations   its fame shall be known
Over all the earth,   when in strife thereby
He shall beat down the foe   where bold-hearted fighters
Girded with weapons   go forth to war
And strive for triumph   foe against foe
On either hand.   He shall have strength
In all his battles,   success in strife,
Everywhere peace   and rest after war
Who reins his white steed   with this best of bridles
When the stout in strife   in the storm of darts,
Battle-bold heroes,   bear shield and spear.
For every man   against menacing danger
It shall be a resistless   weapon in war.

"The prophet sang of it,   sage in spirit,
With deep discernment   and wisdom's wit.
He spoke this word: 'It shall be well known
That the horse of the king   in the press of heroes
Shall be graced with bit,   and with bridle-rings.

(1156–1194)

That sign shall be holy   and sacred to God.
Fame shall he win   and honour in war
Who reineth that steed.'"
                              Then Elene straightway
Before the eorls   brought it all to pass.
She bade men deck   and adorn the bridle
Of the royal ring-giver,   ruler of men,
And sent to her son   o'er the ocean-stream
That glorious offering   as a gracious gift.
     Then she bade summon   to the holy city,
Within the borough,   those she knew were best
Among the Jews   of that race of men.
And the queen began   to admonish the band
Of well-beloved   that they firmly fulfil
The service of God;   with peace among themselves
And loving kindness;   that they live without sin
All the days of their life;   keep their leader's commands
And all Christian customs   according as Cyriacus,
Sage in learning,   should set them forth.
     So was the bishopric   fairly founded.
To him from afar   came the limb-sick and lame,
The halt and the weak,   the bloody with wounds,
The blind and the lepers,   the lowly and sad;
And there they found healing   at the bishop's hands,
Salvation for ever.   And Elene made him
Gifts of great treasure   when ready to go
To her home again;   and she gave command
To all God's servants   throughout the realm,
To man and maid,   that with soul and strength
They should always honour   in their inmost hearts
That dearest of days   when the Holy Cross
Was found again,   the fairest of trees
That ever grew from ground   with increase of leaves.
     The season of Spring   was over and spent
Save for six nights   ere summer began

(1194–1228)

On the Kalends of May.   May hell's door be closed
And the entrance to heaven,   the angels' realm
And eternal bliss,   be open for ever,
And his lot appointed   with the Lady Mary
For every man   who keepeth in mind
The most hallowed feast,   under heaven, of the Cross
Which the Great Lord of all   clasped with His arms. Finit.

  Thus, old and death-bound   through this doomed flesh,
I have wondrously gathered   and woven this lay.
At times I have pondered   and patterned my thought
In the anxious night-watches.   I knew not the truth
Concerning the Rood   till with radiant power
Wisdom made wider   the thoughts of my mind.
Soiled by past deeds   and shackled with sin
I was vexed with sorrows,   bitterly bound,
Burdened with cares,   till the King of might
Through His radiant grace   granted me knowledge
To comfort old age,   a glorious gift;
Instilled it in mind,   made steadfast its light,
Made it more ample,   unfastened the flesh,
Unlocked the spirit,   gave the gift of song
Which I've used in the world   with gladness and glee.
Full oft I took thought   of the Tree of glory,
Not once alone,   ere I learned the truth
Of the radiant Cross   as I read it in books,
In the fullness of time   to set forth in writing
The tale of that Standard.
        Until then was strife,
C The *hero* perishing   haunted with care,
  Though he shared in the mead-hall   many a treasure
Y And appled gold.   He bewailed his *woe*;
N A *death-bound* soul   he suffered sorrow,
E Secret fear,   while his *horse* before him
  Measured the mile-paths,   proudly prancing,
W Decked with jewels.   *Joy* has fled,

      (1229–1264)

Mirth, with the years.　　Youth has vanished
U　And olden pride.　*Our* portion was once
The splendour of youth;　　now the days of our years
After time appointed　　have passed away.
L　Life's joy has waned　　as the *waters* flow,
The hurrying floods.　　For all under heaven
F　*Wealth* is transient.　　The treasures of earth
Wane neath the clouds　　most like to the wind
When it rises loud　　in the hearing of men,
Ranging the heavens,　　faring in fury,
And then all suddenly　　is barred in silence,
In its narrow prison　　strictly constrained.
　　So all this world　　shall vanish away
And on all she brought forth　　the fire shall seize
When the Lord Himself　　with legions of angels
Shall come to Judgment.　　A just doom
Shall each man hear　　from the mouth of his Judge.
He shall pay the penalty　　for all vain words
Spoken aforetime,　　and presumptuous thoughts.
Then shall the folk　　in the grasp of fire
Be sundered in three;　　all such as lived
From the beginning　　on this spacious ground.
Uppermost in the fire　　shall be faithful souls,
The army of blessed ones　　eager for glory;
But this they may sustain,　　suffering lightly
Free from torture,　　a valiant train.
For them the flame　　of the fire shall be tempered
As may be mildest　　and most easy to bear.
　　But sinful souls　　soiled with evil,
Sorrowful spirits,　　in the middle shall be chastened
In the hot surges　　compassed with smoke.
　　And those of the third group,　　accursed transgressors,
False foes of mankind,　　a criminal host,
Shall be in the abyss　　of blazing fire,
In the grip of the gleeds,　　made fast in flame

(1265–1302)

P

For their former deeds.   Nor ever thereafter
From that gulf of torment   shall they come again
To the mind of God,   the King of glory;
Those bitter foes   from the fierce fire
Shall be cast down   to the depths of hell.
      Unlike is the lot   of those other twain!
For they shall see God,   the Giver of triumph;
They shall be purified,   and purged of sin
Like to fine gold   that in fire is cleansed
Of every blemish,   in the oven's flame
Refined and molten.   Those men shall all
Be shorn and severed   of every evil,
Of all foul faults   by the Judgment flames.
They shall then know peace   and perpetual blessing;
The Lord of Angels   shall be loving and mild
Since they scorned all evil,   the works of sin,
And sang their praises   to the Son of God.
Therefore now   they shall shine in splendour
Like to the angels,   and enjoy for ever
A goodly heritage   and their glorious King.   Amen.

(1302–1321)

CHAPTER V

CHRISTIAN ALLEGORIES

FOREWORD

ALLEGORY is often used as an effective method of moral and religious instruction. Indeed, it is an artistic medium so persuasive in its
devices for making truth clear and convincing that Christian literature
and Christian art owe much to its pervasive influence. The medieval
Church found it a useful means of clarifying and stressing religious
exposition, and it is deeply inwrought in Scripture and in many pages
of the patristic writings. Even a cursory study reveals the extent to
which it governed the multitudinous detail of Church carving and
sculpture. It is to be expected, then, that the spirit of allegory, and
many of the Christian symbols it had created, would be reflected in the
Early English religious poems that express so ardently the faith of the
medieval Church.

We have already noted this influence of allegory in some of the religious poems previously considered, notably in certain of the *Advent
Lyrics*, and in much of the detail of Cynewulf's *Ascension*. But nowhere
else in Old English verse has the creative spirit of allegory so completely entered into both structure and substance of poetry as in three
poems of the Exeter Book: the *Phoenix*, the *Panther*, and the *Whale*. The
Phoenix is a poem of 677 lines, complete in itself. But the *Panther* and
the *Whale*, transcribed later in the Exeter manuscript, are parts of an
Old English *Bestiary*, or *Physiologus*, the *Panther* comprising lines 1–74,
the *Whale*, lines 75–162. The remainder of this *Bestiary* deals with a
bird that is usually identified as a partridge. But, since this portion of
the poem, because of a missing manuscript leaf, consists of two fragments of fourteen lines in all, this identification cannot be regarded as
absolutely established. It is made probable by the fact that the Panther,
Whale, and Partridge appear together, and in that order, in many
manuscripts of the Continental *Physiologus*. Perhaps more important,
the Old English text offers material that accords well with the interpretation of the partridge fable derived by the Greek naturalist from
Jeremiah xvii 11.

The first of the three poems, the *Panther*, has an introductory passage on Nature's variety in kinds of bird and beast, which would seem

to mark the poem as the first of a series. The third poem, the *Partridge*, is followed in the manuscript by the word *Finit*, which seems to mark it as ending a series. Because of these details, and the further fact that the Panther, Whale, and Partridge can represent the whole of nature, in representing earth, sea, and air, it is generally believed that the three poems constituted a complete, though very abbreviated, Old English *Physiologus*. It is obviously based on portions of the Greek and Latin *Bestiaries* which had grown up on the Continent by the fifth century, and were later to be translated into the vernacular tongues.

THE PANTHER

In the Old English poem, as in the Greek *Physiologus*, the Panther wears an air of medieval strangeness quite in contrast to the portrait of the Whale. This, in part at least, results from the qualities assigned to the Panther in the allegorical role he is to play. One reads in the opening lines that he is gentle and kindly, amiable and well-disposed to all except to the Dragon, against whom he wages eternal warfare. When the beast has had his fill of feasting, he slumbers until the third day, when he rises glorified from sleep. From the mouth of the Panther comes a melody and a fragrance "more sweet than the sweet smell of blossoming spices". Men throng the roads in their desire to follow that fragrance.

As in his original, the poet makes haste to unriddle the allegory for his readers lest they go astray: the Panther is a symbol of Christ and His love for all, except only the Author of evil. His sleep, and rising again on the third day, are Christ's death and Resurrection. The melody and fragrance that issue from His mouth are the Gospel of God's grace to man. The multitudes that throng the roads, pouring out of city and town to follow the fragrance, are the faithful who believe in Him.

It has been suggested that the original choice of the Panther to represent Christ, a choice seemingly so inappropriate, may have been derived from the Septuagint text of Hosea v 14, where the word "panther" held the place of the "lion" and "young lion" of the authorized version. In any case, once the beast was chosen, the allegory was firmly imposed upon him. The effect is an impression of quaint and curious

lore as if one were listening to old travellers' tales of long ago and far
away.

THE WHALE

The allegorical masquerade of the Panther is in marked contrast to
the realistic description of the Whale. For the Great Whale provides
his own allegory, and has done so from the days of the legends that re-
appear in the tales of Sindbad the Sailor down to the days of Melville
and Moby Dick. The legend of the Whale as set forth in the Old English
Physiologus is undoubtedly of very early date, and there is at least one
mark of confusion and contamination in the text of the fable as we find
it in the Exeter Book. The disappearing island on which sailors land
and kindle a fire, only to have it sink beneath their feet and carry them
with it, is in the Greek *Physiologus* not a whale, but a huge sea-monster
known as a shield-turtle. In the Old English poem the disappearing
island is similar to that of the Greek original, but it is plainly identified
by the poet as a whale. Yet somewhere behind the material which the
Old English poet uses the great sea-turtle still lurks, for the name
Fastitocalon, by which the whale is called in the Old English poem,
seems clearly a corruption of the Greek name for the shield-turtle.[1]

Not only is the Old English sea-monster called a whale, but the description is unmistakable. The element that is chiefly stressed is the
huge size of the sea-beast as he swims with open jaws, by a sweet odour
luring into his cavernous mouth whole schools of smaller fish. In this
matter of the Whale's size the Old English *Physiologus* is quite in accord
with ancient legend. Strabo and Pliny greatly exaggerated the size of
whales, and later writers such as Basil and Ambrose compared them to
mountains and islands.

The appearance of the Whale as it lies like an island motionless and
partly exposed at the surface of the sea is described with detail that
again seems to hint at old tradition. It looks, the Old English poet tells
us, "like a rough rock or a great mass of tossing sea-weed surrounded by
sand dunes at the sea-shore, so that mariners think they gaze at an
island". These details of appearance seem cognate to the description in
Sindbad's first voyage of the great fish on which "the sand has accumu-

[1] Cf. Cook, *The Old English Elene, Phoenix, and Physiologus*, Introduction,
pp. lxxxi–lxxxv.

lated so that it has become like an island, and trees have grown upon it". In the Old English poem the sailors moor their high-prowed ships by anchor ropes "to the land that is not land".[1] Disembarking, they make camp without thought of peril and kindle a fire. The flames leap high and joy returns to sea-weary men. When the Whale, "crafty in evil", feels that the sailors are firmly established, then suddenly "Ocean's Guest plunges downward in the salt wave seeking bottom, and in that hall of death drowns sailors and ships."

The poets' translation of the allegory is generally similar to that given in the Greek *Physiologus*, but in the Old English version of the fable it is an enlarged significance and a broader application to life that is stressed. In the Greek original the image of the deceiver who drags the unwary down to the depths is borrowed from Proverbs v 3–5, where the reader is warned against the luring wiles of the harlot. "Her feet go down to death; her steps take hold on hell." However, the author of the Greek fable, directly addressing his reader, is quick to add the more general warning: "If thou shalt depend upon the hope of the devil, he will plunge thee with himself down to the hell of fire."

It is this more general interpretation of the allegory that is stressed in the Old English poem. The Great Whale is Satan. The jaws which he snaps shut on the unwary are the gates of hell, the yawning Hell-mouth represented in the drawings of the Junius MS. that was used so often later on the medieval stages of mystery and miracle play. The Whale's sweet odour is the lure of worldly pleasures, the lusts of the flesh. The seductive wiles of Satan, and his victims' spiritual blindness mistaking evil for good and danger for safety, are the prelude to that final, sudden plunge to the depths of hell.

THE PHOENIX

The most skilful and artistic use of allegory in Old English poetry is found in the *Phoenix*. But the *Phoenix* is more than an allegorical fable.

---

[1] Cf. Milton's use of the story in *Paradise Lost*, I 200–8. The fact that Milton's Leviathan is slumbering in the *Norway foam* when the sailors anchor suggests that Milton may have been following the version of Olaus Magnus, *Historia de gentibus septentrionibus*, Rome, 1555.

It is perhaps the most graceful and finished of all the Old English
religious poems that have survived to us. Fashioned after a Latin poem
on the Phoenix usually attributed to Lactantius, the Old English poem
has by many been claimed for Cynewulf. Other than the usual linguistic and metrical tests, the results of which are not conclusive, there is
little evidence bearing on the question of authorship. The subject-
matter of the poem would certainly have delighted such a poet as
Cynewulf, and the style and manner are in general those we have come
to associate with the work of the Cynewulfian school. The most
definite conviction that emerges from a study of the poem is that its
unknown author was perhaps the most gifted of the Old English religious poets.

There is one passage in the *Phoenix* which associates it with the
Ascension, and the *Last Judgment*. In the signature passage of the *Ascension*
Cynewulf contrasts destruction in the flames of Doomsday with the
devastation formerly wrought by the waters of the Flood. As earth's
treasures were once overwhelmed by the Deluge, in the latter day they
shall be consumed by the fires of Judgment. So runs the thought.[1] It is
undoubtedly derived from 2 Peter iii 6–7, and may also represent a
knowledge of St Augustine's *De Civitate Dei*, xx 16, which seems to reflect the Scriptural passage. This same contrast is found in the *Last
Judgment*.[2] It is, however, in the *Phoenix* that it receives its most elaborated expression.[3] While these parallelisms cannot be regarded as evidence of the dependence of any one of these poems on the others, it is
noteworthy that the thought occurs in two Cynewulfian poems, one of
them signed, and has its most carefully wrought expression in the
Phoenix.

The poem begins with a landscape description of the Earthly Paradise in which the Phoenix lives. The delineation reflects Oriental tradition, and some of the details have analogues in the Biblical Genesis
ii 8–10; Ezekiel xlvii 7–9, 12; and Revelation xxii 1–2. In general,
however, the landscape is that of Lactantius: a far distant tableland
whose fertile soil is enriched by sweet fountains that monthly overflow,
where the land is green with trees that bear in every season, where in

---

[1] *Christ*, 805–14.   [2] *Christ*, 984–6.   [3] *Phoenix*, 41–9.

serene, unchanging weather no leaf withers or fruit decays, and where nothing noxious or noisome ever intrudes. It lies near the gates of the heavenly Paradise through whose open portals can be heard the hymns of the blessed.

The Phoenix that dwells in this land of wonder and delight is the symbol of an ancient Egyptian cult of sun-worship. The bird was associated in legend with the rites of Heliopolis in the service of Ra, the sun god. This symbolic association of the Phoenix and the sun was central in the early myth and traces of it survive in Lactantius and in the Old English poem where the poet's description of the Phoenix watching, as the stars grow dim, for the rising of the sun is an illustrative passage. The poem continues with an elaborated picture of the bird that is based on the Latin text. Twelve times it engages in its "water-play", bathing in the pleasant fountains of Paradise and drinking of their waters.[1] Then returning to a lofty tree it watches while the world becomes beautiful in the growing sunlight. When the sun has risen high, and the earth is illumined with its blaze, then the Phoenix is moved to adoration, winging with swift pinions into the sky, singing and carolling in joy and worship. This vivid touch reflects clearly the spirit of the pagan myth underlying the Christian allegory.

There is another passage of natural, rather than Christian, implication for which the Old English poet is not indebted to his Latin original. In lines 243–57 he employs the symbol of seed-grain for the idea of resurrection, thinking less in Christian terms than in terms of the succession in nature by which life continues through repeated re-births in a kind of natural immortality. It is a thought that was at the heart of such natural religions as the ancient cult of sun-worship. Though it is quite distinct from the Christian development of the idea of resurrection which the poet stresses in the *Phoenix*, it lends itself easily to association with it, and is so associated in the well known lines

[1] In the late-eleventh-century version of the Phoenix myth (MS. CCCC 198 of Corpus Christi College, Cambridge) the allegory in this detail is definitely clarified and sharpened. This late version of the fable states that the Earthly Paradise contained the *fons vitæ*, or fountain of life, and that it was in this fountain of life that the Phoenix bathed.

of 1 Corinthians xv 35–8. It finds expression in the works of Origen, Tertullian, and other early Christian writers.[1]

From the germinal idea of the rebirth of life from sprouting seed the poet develops an extended pastoral image. Some of the pastoral detail, in the manner of a Virgilian simile, is obviously chosen less as a constituent part of the central image than because of its easy and natural association with it. But the poetic whole is sensitively written. It is the most graceful simile in the *Phoenix*; its artistry is in its deft evoking of the pastoral scene: the gathering and storing of grain in the harvest; the wealth of food hoarded for the months of frost and snow and winter's furious might; the return of the warm sun of spring, the symbol of life; and once again the sowing of the grain to sprout and grow into new harvests. It is a brief, but expressive, painting of the pastoral scene through the changing seasons of nature. But it grew in the poet's mind from the thought of sprouting seed and the rebirth of life.

The burning and rebirth of the Phoenix is closely imitated from Lactantius, except in one important respect which we shall consider later. At the end of every thousand years the aged bird flies to a remote region of Syria where it lodges in a tall tree, fairest blooming of all on earth. There in a season of clear, unclouded weather, when the winds are stilled and the sun shines hot, the Phoenix builds a nest fashioned of fragrant herbs and spice-bearing sprigs and blossoms. As the bird sits upon its nest the heat of the sun kindles it into flame, and in a steam of sweet odours the Phoenix is consumed. But the ashes of the pyre fuse into the likeness of an apple from which grows a wondrous fair worm, as if come from an egg. From this develops the appearance first of an eagle's young, then of a full-grown eagle, then of a bird bright with many brilliant hues, as it was before. The Phoenix is reborn.

The one respect in which the Old English poem differs markedly from Lactantius in this account of the bird's death and rebirth has to do with the ashes of its former body. In Lactantius the Phoenix gathers the remnants of bone and ash and with oil, frankincense, and myrrh moulds them with its beak into a ball. This ball it carries to Heliopolis and

[1] Cf. Cook, *The Old English Elene, Phoenix, and Physiologus*, p. 115, note on line 243.

there offers it upon an altar in the Temple of the Sun. Obviously, this detail of the pagan myth cannot be brought into accord with the Christian allegory for which the Old English poet is employing the legend. In his rehandling of the material, therefore, the references to Heliopolis and this rite of sun worship are suppressed. The Old English Phoenix gathers together the remains of its former body and blends them with savoury herbs, but carries them back to its native dwelling in the Earthly Paradise and there buries them.

There is in the Old English poem another much less important, but interesting, suppression of the material of Lactantius. In the description of the building of the funeral nest the Latin poet has listed the names of various oils and ointments which the Phoenix uses in fashioning its nest: cinnamon and balm, odorous acanthus, incense-gum and cassia, nard and myrrh. The Anglo-Saxon poet, perhaps because of the intrusive Eastern flavour of these names, has replaced the list with a general, but widely inclusive, reference to "all sweetest spices and fragrant herbs", and to the "sweetest blossoms and odours of earth."

In the second half of the Old English *Phoenix* we have explicit interpretation of the Christian allegory of the bird's death and resurrection. The flight of the Phoenix from the Earthly Paradise to the remote region in Syria is the loss of Eden by our first parents in the Fall of Man. The high tree in which the Phoenix nests is God's grace and mercy to men. The sweet spices and fragrant herbs which are used in the building of the nest are the words and deeds of righteousness. These Christian virtues are particularized by the poet: God's warrior is one who is faithful in prayer and constant in alms-giving, avoiding evil, keeping the law, seeking strength from the Lord. "Such," says the poet, "are the shoots, the pleasant herbs, which the wild bird plucks for the shaping of his nest." The flames that consume the Phoenix are the fires of Judgment. The rebirth of the Phoenix is the soul's resurrection to eternal life.

However, as is not unusual in a poem of this type, the spirit of allegory is not to be bound in unvarying patterns. Here and there the equations of the allegory are altered, and the implications changed. For example in lines 508–14, and again in 552–61, the thought is of man's resurrection by the grace of God. But in 646–7 the Phoenix is

explicitly identified with Christ, and the fine description of the
Phoenix returning to the Earthly Paradise attended by rejoicing flocks
of all the race of birds[1] lends itself easily to an allegory of the Ascension.[2]

The use of the Phoenix as an allegorical symbol of man's faith in
immortality has roots in the Book of Job where a reference to the
bird is implicit in Chapter xxix 18. And it is to the Book of Job that
the Old English poet specifically appeals for authority as he brings his
allegory to an end. He is describing the coming fires of Judgment. They
shall hold no terror for the faithful. For blessed souls, coming from
their earthly exile, shall bring with them the "sweet spices and winsome fragrance" of good deeds. They shall be adorned with glory and
shall live in light. "Let no man think," exclaims the poet, "that I
fashion this poem with falsehoods. Hear ye the words, the wisdom, of
Job!" The eighteen lines that follow[3] are directly elaborated from
two passages in Job, one of which[4] is the assertion of Job's faith in
resurrection set forth in the well-known verses: "For I know that my
Redeemer liveth and that He shall stand at the latter day upon the
earth; and though after my skin worms destroy this body, yet in my
flesh shall I see God."

The *Phoenix* is a work of art that gives brilliant evidence of the creative influence of medieval Christianity successfully remoulding for
new purposes an ancient pagan fable. One finishes the poem with a conviction that here, in unusual degree, a talented writer has achieved a
sustained and graceful control of poetic symbols for the embodiment
of a central truth of the Christian faith. In spite of the poet's pains-
taking elaboration of the details of his allegory, his poem aspires to,
and approaches, that high creative level at which the miracle of poetic
fusion occurs, and the symbol, for the moment, becomes one with the
truth it expresses.

[1] *Phoenix*, 335–60.
[2] That the shining flocks of birds are intended by the poet as symbols of the
hosts of righteous souls who accompany their risen Lord is clearly shown by
lines 591–4 of the *Phoenix*.
[3] *Phoenix*, 552–69.   [4] Job xix 25–6.

THE PANTHER

(Physiologus 1—74)

   Many are the creatures,   the manifold kinds,
Throughout the earth   whose natures we may not
Fully interpret,   or tell their numbers,
So wide-spread are they   over the world:
These teeming legions   of birds and beasts
That range the world   as far as the waters,
The roaring ocean   and salt sea-streams,
Brightly encircle   the bosom of earth.
   Lo! we have learned   of a wondrous beast
Living in far lands,   famed among men,
In mountain caverns   making his home.
His name is Panther,   as men who know
In their writings tell   of the lonely rover.
   He is full of kindness,   friendly to all
Save the Dragon only   with whom for ever
He wages eternal,   unceasing war
By every means   of hurt he can muster.
He's a winsome creature   most wondrous fair,
Of varied hues.   As holy men tell
How Joseph's coat   was coloured with dyes
Of every shading,   each shining more fair,
More excellent than the others   to the eyes of men,
So the coat of this beast   is wondrous bright,
Glowing in beauty   and gleaming with hues
Each than the others   more rich and more rare.
   He is mild and loving,   unique of nature,
Meek and gentle   and kindly of mood.
None will he assail   save the venomous Serpent,
His Ancient Foe   whom I spoke of before.
   When, fain of his fill,   he tastes of food,
After each meal   in the mountain caverns

He seeks his rest   in a secret spot.
There the Great Warrior   a three days' while
Heavy with sleep   sinks into slumber;
And on the third day   endowed with glory
The Mighty One wakens   straightway from sleep.
Out of the beast's mouth   melody cometh,
Loveliest music;   and after that strain
A fragrance rises   from the fields of earth,
A breath more winsome,   sweeter and stronger
Than any savour,   than flowering spice
Or fruits of the forest;   more excellent far
Than all earthly treasures.   Then out from the towns,
From kingly dwellings   and castle halls,
Men in multitudes   throng the roads
Hurrying onward   in crowding hosts,
Warriors in battle-gear;   even the beasts
After that sweet strain   fare towards the fragrance.
    So is the Lord God,   Giver of joys,
Kindly to every   creature of earth
With all loving gifts,   save alone to the Dragon,
The Author of venom,   the Ancient Foe
Whom once He bound   in the bottomless pit,
Fettered him there,   by force constrained him
In the grip of the flames.   Then He rose from the grave,
The God of angels,   the Giver of triumph,
On the third day   after He died for men.
That was sweet fragrance   winsome and fair
Over all the world;   and unto that odour
Righteous men gathered   from every region
Through all the limits   and lands of earth.
    Thus spake of old   St Paul the wise:
"Manifold and abounding   are the blessings of earth
God gives unto men   for salvation and grace,
The Almighty Father   and only Hope
Of every being   in the heavens above,
And the world below."   That is lovely fragrance!

(36–74)

THE WHALE
(Physiologus 75–162)

Now I will fashion   the tale of a fish,
With wise wit singing   in measured strains
The song of the Great Whale.   Often unwittingly
Ocean-mariners   meet with this monster,
Fastitocalon,   fierce and menacing,
The Great Sea-Swimmer   of the ocean-streams.

  Like a rough rock   is the Whale's appearance,
Or as if there were swaying   by the shore of the sea
A great mass of sedge   in the midst of the sand dunes;
So it seems to sailors   they see an island,
And they firmly fasten   their high-prowed ships
With anchor-ropes   to the land that is no land,
Hobble their sea-steeds   at ocean's end,
Land bold on the island   and leave their barks
Moored at the water's edge   in the wave's embrace.

  There they encamp,   the sea-weary sailors,
Fearing no danger.   They kindle a fire;
High on the island   the hot flames blaze
And joy returns   to travel-worn hearts
Eager for rest.   Then, crafty in evil,
When the Whale feels the sailors   are fully set
And firmly lodged,   enjoying fair weather,
Suddenly with his prey   Ocean's Guest plunges
Down in the salt wave   seeking the depths,
In the hall of death   drowning sailors and ships.

  Such is the manner of demons,   the devils' way,
Luring from virtue,   inciting to lust,
By secret power   deceiving men's souls
That they may seek help   at the hands of their foes
And, fixed in sin,   find abode with the Fiend.
Sly and deceitful,   when the Devil perceives

Out of hell-torment   that each of mankind,
Of the race of men,   is bound with his ring,
Then with cunning craft   the Dark Destroyer
Takes proud and humble   who here on earth
Through sin did his will.   Seizing them suddenly
Shrouded in darkness,   estranged from good,
He seeks out hell,   the bottomless abyss
In the misty gloom;   even as the Great Whale
Who drowns the mariners,   sea-steeds and men.

   A second trait has he,   the proud Sea-Thrasher,
Even more marvellous: when hunger torments
And the fierce Water-Monster   is fain of food,
Then the Ocean-Warden   opens his mouth,
Unlocks his wide jaws,   and a winsome odour
Comes from his belly;   other kinds of fish
Are deceived thereby,   all eagerly swimming
To where the sweet fragrance   comes flowing forth.
In unwary schools   they enter within
Till the wide mouth is filled.   Then swiftly the Whale
Over his sea-prey   snaps his grim jaws.

   So is it with him   in this transient time
Who takes heed to his life   too late and too little,
Letting vain delights   through their luring fragrance
Ensnare his soul   till he slips away,
Soiled with sin,   from the King of glory.
Before them the Devil   after death's journey
Throws open hell   for all who in folly
Fulfilled the lying   lusts of the flesh
Against the law.   But when the Wily One,
Expert in evil,   has brought into bonds
In the burning heat   those cleaving to him
Laden with sins,   who during their life-days
Did his bidding,   on them after death
His savage jaws   he snaps together,
The gates of hell.   Who gather there

(113–152)

Q

Know no retreat,   no return out thence,
Any more than the fishes   swimming the sea
Can escape from the grip   of the Great Whale.
   Therefore by every means   (should every man
Serve the Lord God)   and strive against devils
By words and works,   that we may behold
The King of glory.   In this transient time
Let us seek for peace   and healing at His hands,
That we in grace may dwell   with Him so dear
And have His bliss   and blessedness for ever!

(152–162)

THE PHOENIX
(Phoenix)

Lo! I have learned   of the loveliest of lands
Far to the eastward,   famous among men.
But few ever fare   to that far-off realm
Set apart from the sinful   by the power of God.
Beauteous that country   and blessed with joys,
With the fairest odours   of all the earth;
Goodly the island,   gracious the Maker,
Matchless and mighty,   who stablished the world.
There ever stand open   the portals of heaven
With songs of rapture   for blessed souls.

The plain is winsome,   the woods are green,
Widespread under heaven.   No rain or snow,
Or breath of frost   or blast of fire,
Or freezing hail   or fall of rime,
Or blaze of sun   or bitter-long cold,
Or scorching summer   or winter storm
Work harm a whit,   but the plain endures
Sound and unscathed.   The lovely land
Is rich with blossoms.   No mountains rise,
No lofty hills,   as here with us;
No high rock-cliffs,   no dales or hollows,
No mountain gorges,   no caves or crags,
Naught rough or rugged;   but the pleasant plain
Basks under heaven   laden with bloom.

Twelve cubits higher   is that lovely land,
As learned writers   in their books relate,
Than any of these hills   that here in splendour
Tower on high   under heavenly stars.
Serene that country,   sunny groves gleaming;
Winsome the woodlands;   fruits never fail
Or shining blossoms.   As God gave bidding

(1–35)

The groves stand for ever   growing and green.
Winter and summer   the woods alike
Are hung with blossoms;   under heaven no leaf
Withers, no fire   shall waste the plain
To the end of the world.   As the waters of old,
The sea-floods, covered   the compass of earth
And the pleasant plain   stood all uninjured,
By the grace of God   unhurt and unharmed,
So shall it flourish   till the fire of Judgment
When graves shall open,   the dwellings of death.
   Naught hostile lodges   in all that land,
No pain or weeping   or sign of sorrow,
No age or anguish   or narrow death;
No ending of life   or coming of evil,
No feud or vengeance   or fret of care;
No lack of wealth   or pressure of want,
No sorrow or sleeping   or sore disease.
No winter storm   or change of weather
Fierce under heaven,   or bitter frost
With wintry icicles   smites any man there.
No hail or hoar-frost   descends to earth,
No windy cloud;   no water falls
Driven by storm.   But running streams
And welling waters   wondrously spring
Overflowing earth   from fountains fair.
   From the midst of the wood   a winsome water
Each month breaks out   from the turf of earth,
Cold as the sea-stream,   coursing sweetly
Through all the grove.   By the bidding of God
The flood streams forth   through the glorious land
Twelve times yearly.   The trees are hung
With beauteous increase,   flowering buds;
Holy under heaven   the woodland treasures
Wane not nor wither;   no failing bloom,
No fruits of the wildwood,   fall to earth;

(35–75)

But in every season   on all the trees
The boughs bear their burden   of fruit anew.
Green are the groves   in the grassy meadow,
Gaily garnished   by the might of God.
No branch is broken,   and fragrance fair
Fills all the land.   Nor ever comes change
Till the Ruler whose wisdom   wrought its beginning
His ancient Creation   shall bring to its end.

　In that woodland dwelleth,   most wondrous fair
And strong of wing,   a fowl called Phoenix;
There dauntless-hearted   he has his home,
His lonely lodging.   In that lovely land
Death shall never   do him a hurt,
Or work him harm   while the world standeth.

　Each day he observes   the sun's bright journey
Greeting God's candle,   the gleaming gem,
Eagerly watching   till over the ocean
The fairest of orbs   shines forth from the East,
God's bright token   glowing in splendour,
The ancient hand-work   of the Father of all.
The stars are hid   in the western wave,
Dimmed at dawn,   and the dusky night
Steals darkly away;   then, strong of wing
And proud of pinion,   the bird looks out
Over the ocean   under the sky,
Eagerly waiting   when up from the East
Heaven's gleam comes gliding   over the wide water.
Then the fair bird,   changeless in beauty,
Frequents at the fountain   the welling streams;
Twelve times the blessed one   bathes in the burn
Ere the bright beacon comes,   the candle of heaven;
And even as often   at every bath
Tastes the pleasant water   of brimcold wells.

　Thereafter the proud one   after his water-play
Takes his flight   to a lofty tree

(75-112)

Whence most easily   o'er the eastern ways
He beholds the course   of the heavenly taper
Brightly shining   over the tossing sea,
A blaze of light.   The land is made beautiful,
The world made fair,   when the famous gem
O'er the ocean-stretches   illumines the earth
All the world over,   noblest of orbs.
    When the sun climbs high   over the salt streams
The gray bird wings   from his woodland tree
And, swift of pinion,   soars to the sky
Singing and carolling   to meet the sun.
Then is the bearing   of the bird so fair,
Its heart so gladsome   and so graced with joy,
It trills its song   in clear-voiced strain,
More wondrous music   than ever child of man
Heard under heaven   since the High-King,
Author of glory,   created the world,
The earth and the heavens.   The music of its hymn
Is sweeter than all song-craft,   more winsome and fair
Than any harmony.   Neither trumpet nor horn,
Nor melody of harp   is like to that lay,
Nor voice of man,   nor strain of organ music,
Nor swan's singing feathers,   nor any pleasant sound
That God gave for joy to men   in this mournful world.
So he hymns and carols   with joyous heart
Until the sun   in the southern sky
Sinks to its setting.   Then in silence he listens;
Thrice the wise-hearted   lifts his head,
Thrice shakes his feathers   strong in flight,
Then broods in silence.   Twelve times the bird
Notes the hours   of night and day.
    So is it ordained   for the forest dweller
To live in that land   having joy of life,
Well-being and bliss   and all the world's beauty,
Till the warden of the wood   of this life's winters

(113–152)

Has numbered a thousand. Aged and old
The gray-plumed is weary   and weighted with years.
Then the fairest of fowls   flies from the greenwood,
The blossoming earth,   seeks a boundless realm,
A land and lodging   where no man dwells;
And there exalted   over all the host
Has dominion and rule   of the race of birds,
With them in the waste   resides for a season.
Swift of pinion   and strong in flight
He wings to the westward,   heavy with years.
Around the royal one   throng the birds,
Servants and thanes   of a peerless prince.
And so he seeks out   the Syrian land
With a lordly following.   There the pure fowl
Suddenly leaves them,   lodging in shadow
In a woodland covert,   a secret spot
Sequestered and hidden   from the hosts of men.

There he takes lodging   in a lofty tree
Fast by its roots   in the forest-wood
Under heaven's roof.   The race of men
Call the tree Phoenix   from the name of the fowl.
Unto that tree,   as I have heard tell,
The Great King has granted,   the Lord of mankind,
That it alone   of all tall trees
Is the brightest blooming   in all the earth.
Nor may aught of evil   work it a harm;
For ever shielded,   for ever unscathed,
It stands to the end   while the world standeth.

When the wind lies at rest   and weather is fair,
And heaven's bright gem   shines holy on high,
When clouds are dispersed   and seas are tranquil
And every storm   is stilled under heaven,
When the weather-candle   shines warm from the south
Lighting earth's legions,   then in the boughs
He begins to form   and fashion a nest.

(152–189)

His sage heart stirs   with a great desire
Swiftly to alter   old age to youth,
To renew his life.   From near and far
He gleans and gathers   to his lodging-place
Pleasant plants   and fruits of the forest,
All sweetest spices   and fragrant herbs
Which the King of glory,   Lord of beginnings,
Created on earth   for a blessing to men,
The sweetest under heaven.   So he assembles
In the boughs of the tree   his shining treasures.
There in that waste-land   the wild bird
In the tall tree's top   timbers his house
Pleasant and lovely.   And there he lodges
In that lofty chamber;   in the leafy shade
Besets his feathered body   on every side
With the sweetest odours   and blossoms of earth.

When the gem of the sky   in the summer season,
The burning sun,   shines over the shades
Scanning the world,   the Phoenix sits
Fain of departure,   fulfilling his fate.
His house is kindled   by heat of the sun;
The herbs grow hot,   the pleasant hall steams
With sweetest odours;   in the surging flame,
In the fire-grip, burns   the bird with his nest.
The pyre is kindled,   the fire enfolds
The home of the heart-sick.   The yellow flame
Fiercely rages;   the Phoenix burns,
Full of years,   as the fire consumes
The fleeting body.   The spirit fades,
The soul of the fated.   The bale-fire seizes
Both bone and flesh.

But his life is reborn
After a season,   when the ashes begin
After the fire-surge   fusing together
Compressed to a ball.   The brightest of nests,

(189–227)

The house of the stout-heart,   by force of the flame
Is clean consumed;   the corpse grows chill;
The bone-frame is broken;   the burning subsides.
From the flame of the fire   is found thereafter
In the ash of the pyre   an apple's likeness,
Of which grows a worm   most wondrous fair,
As it were a creature   come from an egg,
Shining from the shell.   In the shadow it grows
Fashioned first   as an eagle's young,
A comely fledgeling;   then flourishing fair
Is like in form   to a full-grown eagle
Adorned with feathers   as he was at first,
Brightly gleaming.   Then is beauty reborn,
Sundered from sin,   once more made new;
Even in such fashion   as men, for food,
Bring home in harvest   at reaping time
Pleasant fare,   the fruits of earth,
Ere coming of winter   lest rain-storms waste;
Find joy and strength   in their garnered store
When frost and snow   with furious might
Cover earth over   with winter weeds:
From these grains again   grow riches for men
Through the sprouting kernels,   first sowed pure seed;
Then the warm sun in Spring-time,   symbol of life,
Wakes the world's wealth   and new crops rise,
Each after its kind,   the treasures of earth.
   Even so the Phoenix   after long life
Grows young and fashioned   with flesh anew.
He eats no food,   no fare of earth,
But only a drop   of honey-dew
Which falls in the midnight;   thereby the Phoenix
Comforts his life   till he comes again
To his own habitation,   his ancient seat.
   Beset with his sweet herbs,   proud of plumage,
The bird is reborn,   his life made young,

(227–266)

Youthful and gifted   with every grace.
Then from the ground   he gathers together
The nimble body   that the bale-fire broke;
With skill assembles   the ashy remnants,
The crumbling bones   left after the blaze;
Brings together there   bone and ashes
And covers over   with savoury herbs
The spoil of the death-fire,   fairly adorned.

 Then he takes his departure,   turns to his home,
Grasps in his talons,   clasps in his claws,
What the fire has left;   joyously flying
To his native dwelling,   his sunbright seat,
His happy homeland.   All is renewed,
Life and feathered body   as it was at first
What time God placed him   in that pleasant plain.
He brings there the bones   which the fiery surges
Swallowed in flame   on the funeral pyre,
The ashes as well;   and all together
Buries the leavings,   ashes and bone,
In his island home.   For him is renewed
The sign of the sun   when the light of heaven,
Brightest of orbs,   most joyous of jewels,
Over the ocean   shines from the east.

 Fair-breasted that fowl   and comely of hue
With varied colours;   the head behind
Is emerald burnished   and blended with scarlet.
The tail plumes are coloured   some crimson, some brown,
And cunningly speckled   with shining spots.
White of hue   are the backs of the wings,
The neck all green   beneath and above.
The strong neb gleams   like glass or gem;
Without and within   the beak is fair.
The eye is stark,   most like to stone
Or shining jewel   skilfully wrought
In a golden setting   by cunning smiths.

(267–304)

All round the neck   like the ring of the sun
Is a shining circlet   fashioned of feathers.
Wondrously bright   and shining the belly,
Brilliant and comely;   over the back
Splendidly fashioned   the shield is spread.
The fair bird's shanks,   its yellow feet
Are patterned with scales.   'Tis a peerless fowl
Most like in appearance   to a peacock proud,
As the writings say;   neither sluggish or slow,
Torpid or slothful,   as some birds are
Heavily winging   their way in the sky;
But swift and lively   and very light,
Fair and goodly   and marked with glory.
Eternal the God   who grants him that grace!
    Then from that country   the Phoenix flies
To seek his homeland,   his ancient seat.
He wings his way   observed of men
Assembled together   from south and north,
From east and west,   in hurrying hosts.
A great folk gathers   from far and near
To behold God's grace   in the beauteous bird
For whom at Creation   the Lord of all
Ordained and stablished   a special nature,
A fairer perfection   beyond all fowl.
Men on earth   all marvel in wonder
At the fair fowl's beauty,   inscribing in books
And skilfully carving   on marble stone
When the day and the hour   shall exhibit to men
The gleaming beauty   of the flying bird.
    Then all about him   the race of birds
In flocks assemble   on every side,
Winging from far ways,   singing his praises,
Hymning their hero   in fervent strains;
Around the Phoenix   in circling flight
They attend the holy one   high in air,

(305–340)

Thronging in multitudes.   Men look up,
Marvel to see   that happy host
Worship the wild bird,   flock after flock,
Keenly acclaiming   and praising as King
Their beloved lord;   joyously leading
Their liege to his home;   till at last alone
He swiftly soars   where that blissful band
May not follow after   when the best of birds
From the turf of earth   returns to his homeland.
　　So the blessed bird   after his death-bale
Enters once more   his ancient abode,
His fatherland fair.   Leaving their leader
The birds sad-hearted   return to their home,
Their prince to his palace.   God only knows,
The Almighty King,   what his breed may be,
Or male or female;   and no man knows,
But only the Maker,   the ancient edict,
The wondrous causes   of that fowl's kind.
　　There blessed abiding   the bird has bliss
In the welling streams   and the woodland grove
Till a thousand winters   have waxed and waned,
And again life ends   as the bale-fire burns,
The ravaging flames;   yet he rises again,
Strangely, wondrously   wakened to life.
Therefore drooping   he dreads not death,
Dire death-pangs,   but ever he knows
After the fire's force   life refashioned,
Breath after burning,   and straight transformed
Out of the ashes   once more restored
Unto bird's form   his youth is reborn
Under sheltering skies.   He is himself
Both his own son   and his own dear father;
Ever the heir   of his former remains.
The Almighty Maker   of all mankind
Has granted him wondrously   once more to be

(341–378)

What before he was,   with feathers apparelled
Though fire clasp him   close in its grip.
    So each blessed soul   through sombre death
After his life-days   of sore distress
Gains life everlasting,   knowing God's grace
In bliss never-ending;   and ever thereafter
Resides in glory   as reward for his works.
The traits of this bird   clearly betoken
Christ's chosen thanes,   how on earth they thrill
By the Father's grace   with a gleaming joy
In this perilous time,   and attain thereafter
Bliss on high   in the heavenly home.
    We have learned that our Maker   in fullness of might
Shaped man and woman,   and set their home
In the winsomest region   of all the world,
Paradise named   and known among men.
In their new-born bliss   they lacked no blessing
As long as they heeded   the Holy One's word,
Their Maker's command.   But evil assailed them,
The envious hate   of the Ancient Foe
Who offered as food   the fruit of the Tree;
And they both in folly   ate of the apple,
The fruit forbidden,   against God's will.
Bitter their misery   after the eating,
Bitter that banquet   for their daughters and sons!
With sorrow their teeth   were set on edge
After their guilt.   They gained God's wrath
And fearful anguish.   For the taste of that fruit,
Breaking God's bidding,   their children paid
A heavy penance.   With grieving hearts
They must needs give over   that lovely land
Through the Serpent's guile.   Sorely he snared them,
Our first forefathers,   in those former days
Through his cunning craft;   they were banished afar,
In the Valley of Death   found a dreadful abode,

(479–416)

A bitterer dwelling.   The better life
Was hidden in darkness,   and the holy plain
Through the Fiend's seduction   was bolted fast
For many a winter,   till the Joy of men,
Help of the helpless,   Lord of light
And all our Hope,   by His advent hither
Loosed again   those locks for men.

   Like unto that   is the flight of the Phoenix,
As scholars tell us   and the writings teach,
When, full of years,   he forsakes his seat,
Heavy with winters   and weary of soul
Finds refuge and rest   in the woodland grove;
And there with the loveliest   sprigs and spices
Builds a new dwelling,   a nest in the wood.
He hath great desire   to gain new life,
To be reborn   through the blaze of fire,
To live after death;   a longing to go
After the fire-bath   back to his home,
His sun-bright seat.   Even so our first parents,
Our forbears, forsook   that Eden so fair;
Left lovely behind them   the home of glory,
And trod a long path   to the power of the fiends
Where the hateful monsters   harried them sore.

   Yet were there many   who heeded their Maker
With reverent worship   and righteous deeds.
To them the Lord,   High-King of heaven,
Was mild and gentle   with merciful heart.
That is the high tree   in which the holy
Have their habitation,   nor ever a whit
May the Ancient Foe   injure with venom
Or aught of evil   in this perilous time.

   There God's warrior   weaves his nest,
Safe from assault,   by virtuous deeds:
Deals alms to the needy;   seeks aid of the Lord;
Flees from the vices   of this fleeting world,

(417–457)

Dark deeds of sin;　observes God's law
Fearless-minded;　faithful in prayer
With pure heart bows　on bended knee.
He flees all evil,　every foul sin,
In fear of the Lord,　longing and striving
For all good works.　God is his shield
In every season,　Giver of good,
Shaper of victory.　Such are the shoots,
The pleasant herbs,　which the wild bird plucks,
Gathers together　from far and wide
To his fair abode　where, firmly shielded
From every evil,　he shapes his nest.

　So in their households　the soldiers of God
Work His will　with mind and with might,
Striving for glory.　Eternal and strong
God repays them　guerdon and blessing.
Of these fair shoots　is their dwelling fashioned
In the City of Glory　for reward of their works,
That with hearts overflowing　and fervent wills
They zealously heeded　God's holy teachings,
By day and by night　adoring their Lord,
With faith undimmed　preferring their Dear One
To worldly wealth.　It is not their wish,
Their joyous hope,　that they long may live
In this fleeting world.　With fervent zeal
The blessed soul strives　for eternal bliss,
A home in heaven　with the High-King,
Until the end comes　of his earthly days.

　Then Death lays hold　of every man's life,
That greedy warrior　with weapons girt,
And swiftly buries　in the bosom of earth
The fleeting body　bereft of the soul,
Where long it lies　with clay covered over
Till the flame of the fires　of Judgment Day.

　Then the hosts of men　shall be gathered together

(457-492)

When the Father of angels,   the Lord of all,
Shall call to assembly.   The King of triumph
Shall judge with justice.   All in the earth
Shall rise to Judgment   when the Righteous Lord,
The Prince of angels,   Saviour of souls,
With the sounding trumpet   shall speak to men
Over the spacious earth.   Then shadowy Death
By the grace of God   shall end for the blessed.
The good shall gather   in hurrying hosts
When this sinful world   burns in its shame
Consumed by the fire.   Men's hearts shall fear
When the flames despoil   earth's fleeting riches,
When the fire consumes   the treasures of earth,
Greedily grasps   the appled gold,
Greedily swallows   the wealth of the world.
   Then for mankind   shall come to light
This bird's fair token   in that revealing time
When the Almighty   shall raise up all men
Out of their graves;   shall gather the bones,
Body and limbs   and the breath of life,
Before the knees of Christ.   Brightly the King,
Fair Gem of light,   from His lofty seat
Shall beam on the holy.   Blessed is he
In that fearful hour   who finds favour with God!
   Then go glad-hearted   the pure of sin;
Souls pass back again   into their bodies
While high to the heavens   the bale-fires burn.
Bitter for many   that fearful blaze
When blessed or sinful,   body and soul,
Each from the grave   goes to God's Judgment
Shaking with fear.   The fire rages
Consuming the sinful;   but blessed souls
After their exile   are garbed in good works,
The deeds they have done.   These are sweet spices,
The winsome herbs   wherewith the wild bird

(492–529)

Besets his nest   till it burns with fire,
And the Phoenix with it   flames in the sun;
Then after the burning   the bird is reborn!
So every soul   shall be swathed in flesh,
Shall be young and fair,   who fervently strives
By his deeds on earth   that on Judgment Day
The King of glory,   Almighty God,
Gracious and mild   may show him mercy.

   Then holy spirits   shall carol and sing,
The souls of the righteous   shall raise their hymns,
Pure and chosen   praising the King
Strain after strain.   They shall mount to glory
Fragrant with good deeds,   sweetly perfumed.
Then the souls of men   shall be purged of sin,
Brightly refined   in the flame of the fire.

   Let no man ween   that I weave this lay,
Fashion this poem,   with false report;
Hear ye the words,   the wisdom of Job!
With heart inspired   with breath of the Spirit,
Exalted in honour,   he spake these words:
"In my inmost heart   I have no fear
To die in my nest,   needy and weary
A lowly wayfarer   on the long journey,
Covered over with clay   in the bosom of earth
Bewailing past deeds;   then after death,
Like the Phoenix fowl,   by the grace of God
Once more rising   to life renewed
And bliss with the Lord   where His beloved
Adore their Dear One.   Never for ever
Shall I need to know   an end of that life,
That light and blessing.   Yea, though my body
Moulders and rots   as it rests in earth
A relish to worms,   yet the Ruler of all
After death's fullness   shall free my soul
And wake it to glory.   That hope never wanes

R   (530–568)

In the thoughts of my heart   that I have in the Lord
Firm hold on lasting   and living joy."
    So the wise Seer,   God's prophet of old,
Sage of heart   sang of his rising,
His resurrection   to life everlasting;
That we the more clearly   may comprehend
The glorious truth   which the bright bird betokens
By his death in the blaze.   Remnants of bone,
Ashes and embers   he gathers together
After the burning,   clasps in his claws
And sunward soars   to the courts of the King.
There he remains   for many a winter
With form refashioned   and youth made new;
Nor there may any   in all that land
Menace with mischief.   So after death,
Through the might of the Maker,   bodies and souls
Journey together   in fragrance fair,
Most like that bird,   to eternal bliss
Where the Sun of Righteousness   shines in splendour
High o'er the hosts   in the City of Glory.
    Then on the souls   of the blessed shall shine
High in the heavens   the Saviour Christ;
And flashing birds   shall follow Him there
Brightly restored,   rejoicing in bliss
In that happy home   for ever and ever,
The souls of the chosen.   No subtle fiend
May injure with evil;   but ever on high
Apparelled in light   they shall live for ever
Like the Phoenix fowl,   glowing with grace
In God's protection.   Splendidly gleaming
Every man's works   in that winsome home
Before the face   of eternal God
Shall shine forever   like to the sun.
    There bright crowns   of blazing gems
Wondrously woven   shine on the saints;

(568–604)

Around their heads glowing   a glory gleams.
God's royal diadem   richly adorns
Each of the righteous   with radiant light
In the heavenly life   where lasting joy,
Ever living   and ever new,
Faileth never;   but they live in light
Arrayed in glory,   adorned with grace,
With the Lord of angels.   In that joyous land
They shall know no sorrow,   no want or woe,
No days of hardship,   or wasting hunger,
No pangs of thirst,   pain or old age;
But the Great King shall give them   every good thing.
   There the band of the blessed   shall worship the Saviour,
Hymning the might   of the heavenly King,
Praising the Lord,   a happy host
Making sweet melody,   singing in chorus
Around the holy   high throne of God.
Blithely they honour   the best of Princes,
Saints and angels   in sweet accord:
"Glory to Thee,   True God of splendour!
And thanks for grace   new-given to man,
And all Thy goodness!   Great is Thy wisdom,
Beyond all measure   Thy strength of might,
High and holy.   The heavens are filled
With Thy wondrous glory,   Almighty God,
Splendour of splendours,   with angels above
And on earth below.   Preserve Thy servants,
Lord of Creation,   Father of all,
Ruler of heaven,   reigning on high."
   So righteous souls   purged of all sin
In the City of Glory   acclaim His grace,
Singing in splendour   the praise of their King:
"For Thee alone   is eternal honour
World without end!   Nor was ever beginning
Or birth of His blessedness!   Born a Child

(604–639)

Here upon earth,   yet high in heaven
Holy abode   His bounteous might,
His glory undying.   Though pangs of death
He bore on the Cross,   His bitter Passion,
Yet on the third day   after His death
By His Father's grace   He was given new life.
So the Phoenix fowl   with youth refashioned,
When out of the ashes   he wakes again
To the life of life   perfected in form,
Is a symbol of the power   of the Son of God;
Just so our Saviour   granted us grace,
Enduring life,   through His body's death
Even as the Phoenix   in eager flight
Bears in his wings   the winsome herbs,
The sweetest and fairest   fruits of earth."

There are the songs   as the writings say,
The hymns of the holy   in heaven above
Whose minds are set   on the merciful Lord.
In those realms of glory   they bring unto God
A winsome fragrance   of words and works
In that life of light.   Praise to the Lord
In His glorious kingdom,   fullness of grace,
Power and honour   world without end.
He is rightly the Ruler   of heaven and earth
In that lovely City,   apparelled in splendour.

To us He has granted,   the Giver of light,
That on earth we may win   by worthy deeds
Blessings in heaven,   where we may abide
In that holy kingdom   enthroned on high,
And live in the gladness   of light and peace;
Have an abode   of genial joy;
Know happy days   beholding the Lord
Merciful and mild   for ever and ever,
And sing Him paeans   of eternal praise
In bliss with the angels.   Alleluia!

(640–677)

CHAPTER VI

THE SECOND ADVENT

FOREWORD

VISIONS of Doomsday and the Last Judgment furnish material which naturally had repeated expression in Old English religious verse. Not infrequently these themes are present, even in poems on other subjects, as concluding passages or epilogues. The *Elene*, we have seen, ends with just such an apocalyptic vision. Cynewulf's signatures of *Juliana* and the *Ascension* exhibit the use of this material to compose the characteristic passsages in which, like bits of mosaic work, he set the runic letters that spelled his name. Nor is this constant thought of the ending of the world, and what lies beyond, any matter for wonder. It was an inevitable expression of the vitality of the Christian faith, and it was stimulated by the widespread belief that the Second Advent was not something far off in time, but near at hand. There were not a few who believed and prophesied that the year 1000 would see the Second Coming of Christ. Various collections of Old English sermons afford evidence of this general state of mind, as the well-known Blickling homily, *The End of the World is Near*, gives particular illustration.

Doomsday and Judgment, then, together with visions of the damned in hell and the blessed in glory, constituted material that was constantly being reshaped, at length or in brief, and was available to fashion the epilogue of almost any poem on a Christian theme. Because of the nature of the subject matter, some of the sincerest and most eloquent verse that has survived to us springs from this apocalyptic mood. For detailed and elaborated treatment of Doomsday and the Last Judgment we must turn to two poems which are particularly and completely devoted to these themes. One is a poem the text of which is usually known as *Judgment Day II*,[1] translated in the present volume with the title *Doomsday*. The second poem is the third section of the so-called *Christ*,[2] in this volume translated as the *Last Judgment*.

[1] Cf. Dobbie, *The Anglo-Saxon Minor Poems*, Introduction, lxix–lxxii, and pp. 58–67.
[2] *Christ*, 867–1664.

251

DOOMSDAY

The *Doomsday*, a poem of 306 lines, is found in MS. 201 in the library of Corpus Christi College, Cambridge. This eleventh-century MS. is chiefly a collection of homilies and other ecclesiastical documents, among which are the *Doomsday* and four shorter poems including a Pater Noster and a Gloria. The *Doomsday* has its source in the Latin poem *De Die Judicii*,[1] which has been attributed both to Bede and to Alcuin. The dependence of the Old English poem on this source is noted in the manuscript, at the beginning of *Doomsday*, by the rubric: *Incipiunt versus Bede presbiter De die judicii*, and by quotation of the opening verses of the Latin poem. A scribal comment at the conclusion of the Old English poem marks it as the end of the Latin source also. A weakening of the technique of alliteration in the *Doomsday* suggests that it is a late poem, perhaps as late as the middle of the tenth century.[2] An influence of the poem is reflected in an anonymous Latin homily of that period which dealt vigorously with the terrors of the Last Judgment.[3]

The *Doomsday* follows rather closely the structure and material of its Latin source. Though the poem is 306 lines long, as compared with the 157 lines of the Latin,[4] the increased length is chiefly a result of translation from the terse style of the original to the more expansive style of Old English verse, rather than of any considerable addition of new matter. The poet's skill is revealed in his expert handling of the borrowed material. The details of landscape in his introductory lines are rendered with admirable lyric grace, and the introduction of the Doomsday theme by the prophetic darkening of the mood of nature in the face of the approaching storm is a romantic touch, deftly handled.

This Corpus Christi version of the Doomsday theme has definite marks of difference from other Old English apocalyptic visions. Many of the details, of course, follow the formal pattern for such a poem. The list of conventional signs of approaching Doomsday are repro-

---

[1] The Latin text is printed in Lumby's *Be Domes Daege*, Publications E.E.T.S., 65, pp. 22–6.

[2] See Dobbie's comments on the metrical characteristics of the poem, *The Anglo-Saxon Minor Poems*, Introduction, pp. lxxi–lxxii.

[3] Printed in Napier's *Wulfstan*, pp. 134–43.

[4] Excluding the final nine lines of prayer.

duced here as in the *Last Judgment* of *Christ*, 867–1664. So are also many of the details which depict the torments of the damned and the joys of the blessed. Nevertheless, from the beginning of the poem one is conscious of a difference. The heart of this difference lies, perhaps, in the fact that the Old English *Doomsday* is personal and penitential in mood, whereas the scenes of the *Last Judgment* constitute a universal and epic panorama of the Judgment that is coming on the world, and upon all mankind.

This penitential note is struck at the very beginning of the poem in the author's reference to the "mournful" verses to which his heart turns in this hour of contrition. His mood quickly finds expression in familiar images of confession and remorse: the beating of the breast, the outpouring of tears, the prostration in the dust. This section of the poem shows a definite influence of the *Soul and Body* poems which formed a familiar medieval type of religious composition, and which had representation in Old English poetry in two poetical addresses of the Soul to the Body, one found in the Vercelli MS., one in the Exeter Book.

We find in the Corpus Christi *Doomsday* the familiar stress on the soul's need of repentance during this earthly life. Later is too late. It is during these mortal years that eternal healing for the hapless soul can be won. It is noteworthy that in this poem the term "Leech", rather than the more usual "Healer", is twice used in reference to the Saviour. He is the Physician to whom the soul may bring for treatment the wounds of sin. In one passage, indeed, the professional implications of the term are developed by an exhortation of the soul to pray for "plasters and lotions, for gentle leechdoms" from the Lord of life.

This phraseology is unusual in the religious poems and is coupled here with expressions of faith in the kindly and gentle mercy of the Heavenly Leech. The poem paraphrases Isaiah xlii 3 in an assurance that "the Lord Christ will not quench with water the lukewarm smoke of the smouldering flax," neither will the Ruler of angels "heavily bruise the foolish heart". The mood of this portion of the poem is the mood of one who is well acquainted with "leechdoms", and who has a gentle sympathy with the afflicted and distressed.

But when the poet comes to the description of the sufferings of lost souls this gentle note has vanished. There are few paintings of hell in Old English verse more horrible in rehearsal of the torments of the damned than is the vision in this Corpus Christi *Doomsday*. There "no little spark of light shall shine." In this black and smothering darkness serpents feed upon the souls of the sinful, and, in unique addition to the conventional horrors of the scene, lost spirits wander in realms of loathsome filth, with a "vast flowing of foul stench".

One other passage in the poem shows an equal skill in vivid descriptive power. In telling how, in the latter day, all the fatal pleasures of earth shall vanish, leaving the soul surrounded by the torments of hell, the poem presents such personified figures as stride through the lines of later Morality plays representing the Virtues and Vices. Drunkenness and Feasting shall flee away. Laughter and Revelry shall depart together. Lust and Greed and Vice shall hasten into the darkness.

To the list of unusual features in the Corpus Christi *Doomsday* must be added scenes from the final description of the joys of the blessed. Here the poem stands alone among all the Old English apocalyptic visions. In this heavenly scene blessed souls, received and honoured by the Father and His Loving Son, and adorned with "heavenly garlands", take their place with the angelic hosts and the assemblies of the saints, with the fellowships of the patriarchs and prophets, and with the Apostles, in a garden of red roses. There, as if in a medieval painting, or an illuminated manuscript page, God's Peerless Beloved, Mary, Most Blessed of Maidens, the Lady who bore the Lord of all, walking between the Father and Son, shall lead a throng of white-robed maidens in a fair company through the lovely, bright kingdom of the Glorious Father. Need we wonder, with this vision so vivid in its loveliness and peace, that the poet ends his poem by echoing the question of his Latin original: "What can there be of hardship in this life if thereby we may come to dwell eternally in light, and live in bliss for ever?"

THE LAST JUDGMENT

The *Last Judgment* is found in the Exeter Book immediately following Cynewulf's signed poem on the Ascension. It has been suggested,

because of the poem's many six-beat lines, and an apparent Saxon influence in its vocabulary, that the *Last Judgment* may be, like *Genesis B*,
a translation of an Old Saxon original.[1] On the other hand, the poem
has been associated with the preceding *Ascension* and *Advent Lyrics*, and
the combined three sections regarded as a single poem, known as the
Christ and signed in the middle with the Cynewulfian runes. As we
have already noted,[2] this view rests on a number of doubtful assump-
tions, and it is safer to look on the *Last Judgment* as a separate poem. It
stands out in Old English verse as an unusual poem of fluent rhythms
and poetic vigour.

The poem is derived from a number of sources of which the principal one is an alphabetic Latin hymn on Doomsday quoted by Bede in
his *De Arte Metrica*, the *Apparebit repentina dies magna Domini*.[3] Though
brief in comparison with the 798 lines of the *Last Judgment*, this
hymn may be considered a source of the Old English poem in the sense
that it establishes the structure. The material of the alphabetic couplets of the Latin hymn is of course greatly expanded in the Old English,
and five of the couplets (B,L,P,Y,Z) are not used at all. But the Latin
original clearly sets a pattern in brief, which is followed in considerably expanded form in the *Last Judgment*.

Upon this skeleton the author builds up his poem with matter taken
from other sources. Christ's stern indictment of man's ingratitude,[4]
for example, is borrowed by almost literal translation from a sermon
of Caesarius of Arles. Material is taken also from Ephraem Syrus,
from Gregory's homilies, and from various Scriptural sources. In one
sense, then, the *Last Judgment* is a mosaic of borrowings. But such a
statement gives an inadequate impression of the Old English poem.
For these borrowings have been so fused by religious faith that the
result is a new poetic unity. There are, moreover, sections of the
poem which do not rest on any of the sources mentioned and which
illustrate well the skill of the Old English poet in the shaping of his
theme.

The *Last Judgment* possesses descriptive energy of a high order. It is

[1] Binz, *Untersuchungen zum altenglischen sogennanten Christ*, Basel, 1907.
[2] See Foreword, Chapter II.   [3] Cook, *The Christ of Cynewulf*, pp. 171–7.
[4] *Christ*, 1379 ff.

the sustained flight of vision and emotion that is unusual. We have seen that Early English religious poetry has many briefer treatments of these apocalyptic themes. But the poet of the *Last Judgment* takes off for extended flight, and his inspiration does not fail. Old English verse has few paintings of such sustained creative energy as the poetic panorama that begins with the sounding trumpets of Doomsday, and continues to the final fury of the Judgment flames, when "the stain of the world's sin shall be burned away in their billowing surges."

Many of the details in this cosmic panorama are, of course, supplied by the sources on which the Old English poet draws. Isaiah xiii 9–11 and Mark xiii 24–7 provide him with many of the conventional signs of the approach of Doomsday. Matthew xxiv 30 furnishes the suggestion for the image of the Cross that towers over the universe at Judgment. This striking image is so developed by the poet of the *Last Judgment* that the Cross becomes the source of all light to illumine Creation. As the sun and moon fail, and the stars disappear, the radiance of the Cross, red with the Saviour's blood, shines through the heavens, and the eyes of all the resurrected hosts turn to gaze. Sinners shall see in the Cross a woe and a menace. Righteous souls shall behold it with joy. This vision of the Judgment scene reveals a splendour and elevation of conception unmatched in Old English apocalyptic descriptions.

An unusual feature of the *Last Judgment* is the introduction into it of a somewhat extended depiction of the Crucifixion. For it is on Judgment Day, writes the poet, that mankind shall know clearly Who it was that suffered on the Cross. Many in terror shall recognize too late that it was the Lord of all Creation Who hung on the Rood. In some wondrous way all nature had known and recognized; but impious and ungrateful men failed in perception. This thought leads the poet to introduce a list of natural phenomena that gave evidence of nature's knowledge that the Lord of all was on the Cross: the earthquake and darkening of the sun, the splitting of walls and rocks, earth's giving up her dead, the trees that ran with bloody sap. In these lines the poet is not only borrowing from Scripture but is also following, somewhat freely, a homily of Gregory. The reference to the trees that ran bloody sap under the bark occurs in the apocryphal 2 Esdras v 5, but the portent there is in connection, not with the Crucifixion, but with an apocalyptic vision.

One of the most eloquent scenes in the *Last Judgment* is that in which Christ demands an accounting from sinners. "How is the account unequal between us two?"—this is the thought which introduces a stern indictment of man's ingratitude.[1] This material the poet has borrowed from the *De Judicio et Compunctione* of Ephraem Syrus, and in even greater detail from a homily by Caesarius of Arles.[2]

The *Last Judgment* ends, as do the *Phoenix* and the *Doomsday*, with a description of the joys of the blessed. The material of these concluding lines is not unusual. It forms the conventional picture of the land of happiness rich in all delights, and free from every noxious and evil thing. Again and again the authors of these Old English religious poems slip sweetly into the familiar rhythms in which the dream of celestial blessedness was so often set forth. The details of this heavenly vision apparently had their Scriptural source in Revelation xxi 4: "And God shall wipe away all tears from their eyes, and there shall be no more death, neither sorrow, nor crying, neither shall there be any more pain; for the former things are passed away." During the early Christian centuries this list was fashioned and re-fashioned, with constant addition of detail, in the writings of the Church Fathers, and in such poets as Lactantius.

In the final lines of the *Last Judgment*[3] the poet is once again borrowing from Gregory[4] and from a sermon of St Augustine.[5] The outstanding feature of this concluding passage is its felicity in fusion of imagery and rhythm. Both phrasing and poetic pattern are governed by a sustained antithesis in which an absolute perfection is set in contrast with the earthly flaws by which in this life the ideal is inevitably conditioned. An extended use of balanced elements shapes the pattern of the poetic structure. The poet has consistently reserved his successive phrasings of ideal beauty and perfection for the second half-line in the alliterative arrangement, and the result is the shaping of his Latin prose sources into new poetic and rhetorical design.

[1] *Christ*, 1459 ff.   [2] Migne, *Patr. Lat.*, XXXIX 2207.
[3] *Christ*, 1649–64.   [4] Migne, *Patr. Lat.*, LXXIX 657–8.
[5] Migne, *Patr. Lat.*, XL 1351.

It is well that we conclude our reading of these eloquently fashioned poems of Early Christian England with the strains of apocalyptic vision that bring the *Doomsday* and *Last Judgment* to a close. For in the joyous detail of these lyric passages we catch the timeless stir of man's outreaching spirit. Here is the most secret shaping of his heart's desire, his haunting hunger for truth and righteousness, his dream of eternal peace. Here is the song of angels, the bliss of the saints, the heavenly Paradise of blessed souls. Here is the vision of an ideal loveliness that cannot fade, in a Kingdom that is not of this world.

DOOMSDAY

(Be Domes Daege)

Lo! I sat alone   in a leafy bower
Deep in a wood   and sheltered in shade
Where welling waters   wandered and murmured
In the midst of a meadow,   all as I tell.
There pleasant plants   were budding and blooming
In a throng together   in that gay expanse;
The trees of the wood   were tossing and sighing
In a storm of wind;   the heavens were stirred,
And my sad spirit   was sorely troubled.
    Then all suddenly,   fearful and sad,
I commenced to sing   those mournful verses,
All as you said;   I remembered my sins,
The transgressions of life,   and the long hour
Of the dark coming   of death in the world.
Grievously I dread   the Great Judgment
Because of the evil   I have done on earth;
In terror I fear   God's wrath eternal
Upon myself   and all sinful souls,
When the Almighty King   shall divide mankind
Assigning His judgment   by His secret might.
I remembered also   the glory of God
And of all the saints   in the heavenly scene,
Likewise the evil   and doom of the damned.
All this I remembered   deeply mourning,
And mourning spoke,   troubled in mind:
   "Open all ye fountains,   in hot floods
Overflowing the face   with sudden tears
While I, a sinner,   smite with fist
And beat my breast,   bowing my body
Unto the earth   in the place of prayer,
Naming over   the sorrows I've earned.

(1–32)

I bid you desist not   nor cease from tears;
Suffuse with weeping   my sorrowful face;
Overflow it straightway   with salt drops
And reveal my transgression   to Eternal God.
Let naught endure   in the depths of the heart
Of wicked sins   that once were hid
Of breast and tongue,   of all the body,
That shall not be clear   and disclosed in words.
This is a healing   for the hapless soul,
And the best of hopes   for him who grieves,
That on earth he bewail   the wounds he suffers
To his Heavenly Leech,   who alone may heal
Blundering spirits   and free the bound.
Never with His right hand   will the Ruler of angels
Heavily bruise   the foolish heart,
Nor will the Lord Christ   quench with water
The lukewarm smoke   of the smouldering flax.
Did not the thief   give thee plain example,
Who was put to death   with Christ on a cross,
How greatly availing,   how glorious in worth,
Is true repentance   of transgression and sin.
The thief on the cross,   in vice and crime
All weighed down   with evil deeds,
With death at hand   addressed his prayer
Unto his Master   with earnest heart.
With his few words   filled with faith
He obtained salvation   and timely help
And with his Saviour   entered in
Through the peerless portals   of Paradise.
   Lo! now I ask thee,   O anxious heart,
Why delay so long   to confide in thy Leech;
Or why art thou silent,   O sinful tongue,
When there still is time   to obtain forgiveness
While the Almighty   with attentive ear,
The God of heaven,   will hear thee gladly?

(33-70)

For the Great Day cometh   when God shall judge
The limits of earth,   when all alone
Thou shalt give account   unto God, the Creator,
And make thy reckoning   with the Mighty Lord.
  I bid thee be prompter   with penitent tears
To turn the anger   of the Eternal Judge.
Why grovelest thou in dust,   O guilty flesh,
Filled with crime?   Why dost thou not cleanse
With gushing tears   thy grievous sins?
Why dost thou not pray   for plasters and lotions,
For gentle leechdoms,   from the Lord of life?
Now must thou grieve   with gushing tears
The while there is time   and a tide for weeping;
For wholesome is it   that here on earth
Men weep and repent,   doing God's will.
Glad is God's Son   if thou suffer sadness
And judge thyself   for thy sins on earth;
And never will Heaven's Prince   punish offences
More than one time   for any man;
Nor shalt thou reject   this wailing and weeping
Or the time for forgiveness   still granted to thee.
  In thy mind remember   how great is the torment
That befalls the wretched   for their former deeds,
When with awful terror,   in exalted might,
The King shall pass judgment   on all mankind
For their former deeds;   and what fore-tokens
Shall herald the Coming   of Christ to earth.
The earth shall tremble,   the hills also
Shall sink and perish,   the mountain peaks
Bow down and topple,   the terrible roar
Of the fierce sea confound   the minds of men.
The heavens on high   shall be darkened and dimmed,
Blotted and black,   a shadowy chaos;
Forsaking their stations   the stars shall fall;
The sun shall darken   with the dawning of day,

S   (71–108)

The moon have no might   to scatter night's shades;
And then shall come hither   from heaven above
Tokens of death;   the wretched shall dread.
Unnumbered hosts   shall appear in the heavens,
A mustered multitude   compassing round
All the angel band,   girding about
With power and glory   the Great Creator,
The Lord Everlasting.   Shining in light
The Dispenser of glory   shall sit on His throne
Crowned with splendour.   From all sides swiftly
We shall be summoned   before His face
That each may receive   from the Lord Himself
The judgment due,   as his deeds deserve.
    I bid thee, man,   that thou remember
How grim the terror   before God's throne.
The greatest of hosts   shall stand aghast,
Confused and confounded,   helpless and fearful.
Then shall assemble   from the sheltering sky
All the angel troop   round Eternal God.
A great proclamation   shall muster for judgment
The offspring of Adam,   all dwellers on earth
Ever brought forth   or born of woman,
That ever were,   or ever would be,
Or that ever were destined   for a day to come.
    Then before all   shall all be revealed:
Men's hidden thoughts,   and all that the heart
Devised of evil,   or the tongue invoked
Of hurtful wrong,   or the hand of man
Accomplished of crime   in dark dens,
Of deeds on earth.   All the evil that ever
Man shamed in the world   to make known to another,
Or reveal to any,   shall be known to all,
And all set forth   that man long concealed.
    Besides all this   the heavens on high
Shall be wholly filled   with poisonous fire.

(109–146)

It shall rush over all   nor shall there be rescue,
Nor may any restrain   the strength of its might.
All that to the eye   seems endless and boundless
Neath the circling sky   shall alike be filled
With red fire.   The blazing flame
Shall blow and crackle,   cruel and red;
It shall hurtle and surge   for the scourging of sinners.
The avenging blaze   shall never forbear,
Nor then grant mercy   to any man,
Except on earth   he be purged of evil
And come to judgment   thoroughly cleansed.
There many a nation,   numberless peoples,
Will fiercely beat   their guilty breasts
With their fists, in fear,   for their sinful lusts.
    There the poor shall come   and the princes of earth,
The rich and the pauper   all racked with fear.
The wealthy and the needy   shall know one law
And all together   shall be gripped by dread.
The furious flood   of surging fire
Shall ravage and burn   those wretched souls,
And ready worms   shall rend and slit
The hearts of the sinful.   Nor may any presume
In his own strength   when he stands at the Judgment.
But dread shall deluge them   all together,
The heart's secrets   and sorrowful tears;
And there shall stand stiffened,   most like to stone,
All the honourless band   foreboding evil.
    What doest thou, O flesh,   what performest thou here?
What pangs in that hour   shalt thou deplore?
Woe to thee now   that servest this world,
That livest here gladly   in wanton delights
Goading thyself   with sensual spurs!
Why dost thou not fear   the fiery terror,
For thyself dreading   the agonies dire
Which the Lord of old   allotted for fiends,

(147–183)

For accursed souls, as a woeful reward?
Lo! in their greatness they go beyond
The mind and the speech of any man.
No tongue can utter or tell in words
To any on earth those awful pangs,
Those places filled to the depths with fire
In the midst of the terrible torment of hell.
　　In menace there are mingled together
Smoking fires and bitter frost,
Cold and fierce heat in the midst of hell.
At times, without measure eyes weep tears
For the blast of that furnace filled with bale.
At times, there also in the cruel cold
The teeth of men chatter. In this grim exchange
The souls of the wicked are whirled for ever
Amid black night and the bitter reek
Of seething pitch. There no sound stirs
Save only weeping and wild lament,
Naught else ever! Nor is ever seen
The face of any save only the fiends
Who torture the fallen. There naught is found
Save cold and fire and loathsome filth.
There with nose they can smell naught
Save a vast flowing of foul stench.
There wailing lips shall be filled with fire,
With vomiting blaze of baleful flame.
With cruel teeth the worms shall tear them
And gnaw their bones with burning tusks.
Above all this the wretched breast
Will be harrowed and haunted with bitter care,
Because the depraved flesh, in this time of peril,
Heaped on itself so many sins
It was doomed to death in the dark dungeon
Where those dreadful tortures for ever endure.
　　Not any little spark of light shall shine

(184–219)

For miserable sinners; no mercy there,
No peace or hope or hush of silence
Shall gladden a whit that weeping host.
All solace shall vanish, nor shall aught avail
To furnish defence from that fearful plight.
No glimpse shall be seen there of any gladness
But only most torturing terror and fear,
Grieving hearts, sore gritting of teeth.
On every side shall be cruel sorrow,
Wrath and weariness and wasting disease;
And sinful souls in the surging flame
In that blind gulf shall wander and burn.
   Then the fatal joys of this world shall fade,
All together gliding away.
Drunkenness and Feasting shall take flight,
Laughter and Play shall depart together;
Lust shall go hence, and Greed fare far;
Vice shall vanish and every excess,
Guiltily hastening into the gloom.
And Sleep shall fly careworn and feeble,
Torpid with slumber, slinking away.
What is now unlawful shall then overlay
With ravaging black flame the wretched for ever.
The dearest in life shall be loathsome then,
And its sins shall whirl the weary soul
Sorely forever in sorrow and grief.
   Lo! he shall be happy and more than happy,
And world without end the happiest of wights,
Whoso successfully may then escape
Such torture and ruin, and happy in heart
Prosper in the world before his Prince
And afterwards have the heavenly kingdom,
The greatest of hopes. There night with its gloom
Never hides the gleaming of the heavenly light.
Sorrow comes not nor sadness nor wearied age,

(220–256)

Nor does any toil there   ever befall,
Or hunger or thirst   or haggard sleep;
No fever or sickness   or sudden death,
No crackling of fire   or loathsome cold.
There shall be no weariness   nor any woe,
Destruction or care   or savage torment;
No lightning flash   or fierce storm,
Winter or thunder   or whit of cold;
No heavy showers   of hail and snow,
No lack or loss,   no dread of death,
No want or misery,   nor any mourning.

   But peace and plenty   shall reign together,
Excellence   and everlasting good,
Grace and glory   and life and love
And beauteous concord.   Better than all
Eternal God   shall graciously grant them
All good things.   There present for ever
The Father receives them,   honours them all,
Blesses and glorifies,   guards them well,
Fairly adorns them,   freely loves them,
And orders all things   from His throne on high.

   His loving Son,   the Lord of triumph,
Shall allot to each   everlasting reward,
Heavenly garlands   (a glorious gift),
Amid the excellent   host of angels
And all the assemblies   and throngs of the saints.
Amid those fellowships   they shall be mingled
Among the patriarchs   and holy prophets
With happy hearts   in the heavenly realms
Where are the apostles   of the Mighty Prince.
Surrounded there   with wealth of red roses
They shall shine eternally.

                    There a maiden troop
Of white ones shall wend   wound with blossoms,
The loveliest of bands,   and leading them all

(257–292)

God's peerless Beloved,   the Virgin pure,
The Lady who bore   the Lord of all,
Brought forth God   for us on earth.
That is Mary,   the Best of Maidens,
Of all most blessed;   between Father and Son
She shall lead them all   through the lovely bright kingdom
Of the Glorious Father   in a fair company
Among the great keepers   of that lasting kinship,
The wardens of the heavenly   realms on high.
    What can there be of hardship   here in life,
If thou wilt say truth   to him who seeks,
If thereby thou mayest   amid that host
For all eternity   live in delight,
And in heaven above   in those blessed mansions
Have bliss for ever   world without end?

(292–306)

THE LAST JUDGMENT

(Christ 867–1664)

Suddenly in the midnight   on mortal men
The Great Day of the Lord God   shall come with might,
Filling with fear   the fair Creation,
Like a wily thief   who walks in darkness,
A robber bold   in the black night
Who suddenly assails   men fast in slumber,
Lying in wait for the unwary   and the unprepared.
   So on Mount Sion   a mighty host
Shall gather together   faithful to God,
Bright and blithe;   they shall know bliss.
From the four regions   of earth's realm,
From the uttermost corners   of earth's kingdom,
All-shining angels   in unison sounding
Shall blow their trumpets   in a great blast.
The earth shall tremble,   the mould under men.
Loud shall resound   the strains of the trumpets
Swelling clear   to the course of the stars.
They shall peal and sing   from south and north,
From east and west   over all creation.
They shall wake from death   the sons of warriors,
All mankind,   from the ancient earth
To the terror of Judgment,   telling them rise,
Start up straightway   from their deep sleep.
   Then shall be heard   a grieving host
Sad of spirit   and sore distressed
In their woe bewailing   the deeds of life,
Trembling in terror,   most appalling of portents
To man ever manifest   early or late.
Whole hosts of spirits   shall be gathered together,
Angels and devils,   the shining and the dark;
Both shall assemble,   the white and the black,

(867–897)

And unto them both   shall be place appointed,
For angels and for devils   a different home.
    Suddenly on Mount Sion   from the south and east
Shall come from the Creator   light like the sun
Shining more bright   than men may imagine,
Gleaming in splendour,   when the Son of God
Through the arching heavens   hither appears.
Then comes the wondrous   presence of Christ,
The glory of the Great King,   from the eastern skies,
Cordial and kind   to His own people,
Severe to the sinful,   wondrously varying:
Unto the blessed   and the forlorn unlike!
    To all the good   He is gracious of aspect,
Winsome and blithe   to that holy band,
Joyous and loving,   a gentle Friend.
'Tis a pleasant sight   and sweet to His dear ones,
That shining beauty   gentle in joy,
The Coming of the Saviour,   the King of might,
To all who earlier   here on earth
Pleased Him well   by their words and works.
    But to transgressors,   to guilty souls
Who come before Him   destroyed by sin
He shall be fearful   and frightful to see.
This may serve as a warning   of woe for sinners
That a man of wisdom   need feel no dismay,
No whit of dread   in the Day of Doom.
In the face of that terror   he shall not fear
When he sees the Shaper   of all Creation
Moving to Judgment   with wondrous might,
And round Him circling   on every side
The angel multitude   in shining muster,
Hosts of the holy   throng upon throng.
    There is din through the deep Creation.   Before the Lord
The greatest of raging fires   flames over earth.
The hot blaze surges,   the heavens shall fall;

(897–932)

The steadfast light   of the stars shall fail.
The sun shall be blackened   to the hue of blood
Which shone so brightly   for the sons of men
Over the ancient earth.   The moon herself
That by night illumined   mankind with her light
Shall sink from her station;   so also the stars
Swept by the whirlwind   through the storm-beat air
Shall vanish from heaven.

                                     With His angel host
The Lord of kings   shall come to the Judgment,
The glorious Ruler;   His gladsome thanes,
The hosts of the holy,   shall attend their Lord
When the Prince of men   amid pangs of terror
Himself shall seek out   the peoples of earth.

    Then loud shall be heard   through the wide world
The sound of heaven's trumpet;   on seven sides
The winds shall rage   raving in uproar;
They shall wake and wither   the world with storm;
They shall fill with fear   the creatures of earth.
Then shall be heard   the heaviest of crashes,
Mighty and deafening,   a measureless blast,
The greatest of tumults,   terrible to men.

    There the doomed hordes   and hosts of mankind
Shall turn away   to the towering flames
Where consuming fire   shall seize them alive,
Some above, some below,   filled full of flame.
Then shall be clear   how the kin of Adam
Full of sorrow   weep in distress,
Nor for little cause,   those hapless legions,
But for the greatest   of all griefs
When the dark surge of fire,   the dusky flame,
Seizes all three: the seas with their fish,
The earth with her hills,   and the high heavens
Bright with stars.   The destroying fire
In fiercest fury   shall burn all three

                    (933–969)

Grimly together.   And all the earth
Shall moan in misery   in that awful hour.
   So the greedy spirit,   the despoiling brands,
Shall search through earth   and her high-built halls;
The wide-known blaze   burning and greedy
Shall fill the world   with a terror of flame.
Broken city-walls   shall crumble and crash;
Mountains shall melt,   and the high cliffs
Which in olden days   shielded the earth
Stout and steadfast   against the floods,
Barriers against the waters,   the breaking waves.
   In that dread hour   the death-fire shall clutch
Every creature   of bird and beast.
The fire-dark flame   shall fare through earth
A raging warrior.   As waters of old,
The rushing floods,   flowed over earth,
In that hour shall burn   in a bath of fire
All the fishes   cut off from the sea;
All beasts of the deep   shall wretchedly die.
Water shall burn like wax.   And then shall be
More of marvels   than man can imagine:
How the storm and the stun   and the wild wind
Shatter the wide Creation.   Men shall wail
And weep lamenting   with woeful voices,
Abject and wretched   and wrung with regret.
The dark flame shall seethe   men ruined by sin;
The gleeds shall swallow up   golden jewels,
The ancient treasure   of the kings of earth.
   Then shall be clamour and care,   cries of the living,
Wailing, loud weeping,   men's pitiful plaints
Mid the din of heaven.   Souls dark with sin
Shall nowhere on earth   ever gain peace
Or any escape   from those scathing flames.
But the fire shall seize   on all in the earth;
It shall burrow fiercely,   in fury explore
(970–1003)

The corners of earth   without and within,
Till the blast of the flames   shall have burned away
The stain of the sin of the world   in its billowing surge.
    Then Mighty God   in His majesty
On glorious Mount Sion   shall come unto men;
He shall shine in holiness   King of heaven
In wondrous glory   o'er His gathered bands;
And round about Him   the best of companies,
His holy legions,   shall gleam in light,
The blessed army   of the angel host.
In their inmost hearts   they tremble in terror
In fear of the Father.   No wonder it is
That sin-stained souls   lamenting in sorrow
Are smitten with terror   when sinless spirits,
The band of archangels   shining and bright,
Radiant creatures,   cower in fear
Of the Judgment of God.   The most dreadful of days
Shall come on the world   when the Glorious King
Shall chasten with power   all peoples of earth,
Bidding men rise up   out of their graves,
Summoning all   to the Great Assembly.
    Straightway all   of Adam's kin
Shall be clothed with flesh,   shall come to an end
Of their rest in earth;   each of mankind
Shall rise up living,   put on body and limbs,
Made young again   at the Coming of Christ.
Each shall have on him   of evil or good
All his soul garnered   in years gone by,
Shall have both together,   body and soul.
Then the manner of his works,   and the memory of his words,
The hidden musing   of his inmost heart,
Shall come to light   before heaven's King.
    Then shall mankind   be renewed and increased
Through the might of God.   The legions of men
Shall rise to Judgment   when the Lord of life

(1004–1042)

Looses Death's bond.   The heavens shall burn;
The stars shall fall;   the greedy flames
Shall waste the world   and spirits shall turn
To their long home.   Over all the earth
The deeds of men   shall be manifest,
Nor can any mortal   before his Maker
Hide his hoard,   the thoughts of the heart,
Nor cloak his deeds.   On that Great Day
To God shall be clear   how all on earth
Earned life everlasting;   there shall come to light
What late or early   he wrought in the world.
Not a whit shall be hid   of the musings of men
But the Day shall lay bare   the hoard of the breast,
The thoughts of the heart.   He must early take heed
Of his soul's good   who would bring unto God
A radiant beauty   when the blazing flames,
Hot and greedy,   before the Great Judge
Test how souls   have been held against sin.

   Then the trumpet's strain   and the shining standard,
The fiery heat   and the heavenly host,
The throng of angels   and the throes of fear,
The Day of terror   and the towering Cross
Upraised as a sign   of the Ruler's might,
Shall summon mankind   before the King,
Every soul   that early or late
Was fashioned in flesh   with limbs and body.

   Then the greatest of legions,   living and young,
Shall go before the face   of the Lord God.
By need and by desire   known by their names
They shall bring to God's Son   the hoard of the breast,
The jewels of life.   The Father will learn
How safely his sons   have guarded their souls
In the former land   where they lived on earth.

   Those shall be bold   who bring unto God
A shining beauty.   Their strength and joy

(1042–1077)

Shall be greatly abundant   to bless their souls,
To reward their works.   Well is it with them
Who find favour with God   in that grim hour!
    There sin-stained men   in anguish of spirit
Shall see as their fate   the most fearful of woes:
It shall bring them no grace   that the brightest of beacons,
The Rood of our Saviour   red with His blood,
Over-run with bright gore,   upreared before men,
With radiant light   shall illumine the wide Creation.
No shadows shall lurk   where the light of the Cross
Streams on all nations.   Yet shall it stand
As a woe and a menace   for evil men,
Sinners who gave   no thanks to God
That for Man's transgressions   He grievously hung
On the holy Tree,   where with love our Lord
Bought life for men   with His ransoming body
(Which had wrought no evil   nor any wrong)
Whereby He redeemed us.   For that He ordains
A stern requital   when the red-stained Rood
Shall shine in splendour   in the place of the sun.
    Upon it shall gaze   in grief and terror
Dark workers of evil   undone by sin;
They shall see as a bane   what was best of all
Had they only perceived it   to be their good.
In anguish of soul   they shall see on their Lord
The ancient scars   and the open wounds
Where the plotters of evil   pierced with nails
The white hands   and the holy feet.
There from His side   they shed His blood;
Water and blood flowed   both together,
Streaming out   in the sight of men,
Running red   as He hung on the Rood.
    All this they may see   clear and unclouded:
How He cruelly suffered   for love of mankind,
For the saving of sinners.   The sons of men

(1078–1118)

Shall surely know   how the false denied Him,
How the damned insulted Him,   spat in His face,
Reviled with abuse;   on His blessed visage
Struck Him with outstretched   hand and fist.
On His head the blind-hearts,   fools and sinners,
Cruelly fashioned   a crown of thorns.
   Then men beheld   how the mute Creation,
The all-green earth   and the heavens above,
Lifeless creatures,   bewailed in woe,
Felt with fear   the pangs of the Lord
When savage scathers   laid sinful hands
On their Creator.   The sun was put out,
Darkened with misery.   Men beheld
The richest of hangings   in Jerusalem,
The Temple's glory   that drew men's gaze,
Cleft asunder   and cast to earth
In pieces twain: the veil of the Temple
Woven in beauty   of wondrous hues
Was shorn in two   as if a sharp sword-edge
Had slashed it through.   Then split asunder
Stones and walls   over all the world;
And the earth also   shaken with terror
Trembled in tumult;   the tossing sea
Made known its might,   broke from its bonds
And overflowed   the fields of earth.
   In their bright stations   the stars forsook
Their shining splendour.   In that self-same time
Heaven perceived   Who raised it high
And set it with gems.   It had sent its herald
When the King of Creation   was born on earth.
   Lo! sinners beheld   on the day He suffered
A mighty wonder   when earth gave up
Those lying within.   Living again
All rose up   whom she fast confined,
The dead and buried   who had done God's will.

(1118–1159)

And Hell knew also,   the Scourger of sin,
The Creator was come,   the Ruler of all,
When she gave up the horde   from her hot bosom;
Men's souls were gladdened,   their sorrow dispelled.
   And the sea made known   Who set its depths
On its broad bed,   the glorious King;
It gave firm passage   for the feet of God
When He walked the waves;   the ocean-currents
Dared not to sink   God's feet in the flood.
   And the trees proclaimed   Who fashioned their fruits,
Not few but many,   when Mighty God
Ascended a Tree   where He suffered torture
For the sake of sinners,   a dreadful death
For a help to men.   Many trees were moist
With bloody tear-drops   under the bark
Red and abundant;   the sap turned blood.
   No man has wisdom   to say for sooth
How inanimate creatures   that can not feel
Yet were aware   of the woe of our Lord.
Those that are fairest   of all earth's forms
And the high-built frame   of heaven above,
All grieved for that One   in the grip of fear;
Although by their natures   devoid of knowledge
They wondrously weened   when their Lord went forth,
Spirit from body.   But mind-darkened men
Harder of heart   than stones of flint
Knew not their Maker,   their Ruler, had ransomed
Men by His might   from the tortures of Hell,
The Almighty God.   Yet from the beginning,
From the world's creation,   by wisdom of wit
The Lord's prophets,   learned and holy,
Had often forecast   the Christ-Child's coming:
How the Precious Stone   would be sent unto men
For a help and comfort   to all mankind
Through all the world,   the Author of glory,

(1159–1197)

The Lord of bliss,   through the Blessed Maid.
   What can he hope   who will not heed
The mild and merciful   teaching of God
And the bitter pain   He bore for men,
That we might gain   a home in glory
World without end?   Woe to that man
In the grim Day   of the Great Judgment
Undone by sin,   who must gaze on the gashes,
The prints, of God's Passion!   With heavy hearts
They shall see the worst   of bitter woes:
How God Himself   in His great mercy
With His body bought them   ransom from sin
That they might live   delivered from evil,
And gain His eternal   abundance of bliss.
For that gracious gift   they gave no thanks.
Therefore suffering   they shall see as a torture
The signs of salvation   that shine on the good!
   Then Christ shall sit   on His kingly throne,
The God of heaven   on His high seat;
The Father Almighty,   the Shining Shaper,
The Lord of the skies,   shall allot to men
All just rewards   as their works deserve.
   On His right He shall summon   the righteous folk
For the choicest of virtues   chosen of Christ,
All who obeyed Him   with eager hearts
In their days on earth.   But unto transgressors
God shall assign   a more grievous fate:
He shall bid them depart,   the band of the sinful,
On His left; unmasked   they shall tremble and moan
In terror before Him   as foul as goats,
An unclean host   without hope of mercy.
Judgment shall be apportioned   in the presence of God
To the races of men   as they wrought on earth.
   Then shall be seen   on the souls of the blessed
Three clear signs   that in words and works

T   (1198–1235)

They heeded well   the will of their Lord.
    The first sign is seen   when they shine with light,
In grace and glory   high over earth.
On the souls of the pure   the deeds of the past
Shall burn more bright   than the light of the sun.
    A second sign is seen   when they receive God's grace
In celestial glory;   with eyes made glad
They behold their reward   in heavenly splendour
Blessed with angels,   brightest of joys.
    The third sign is seen   when the happy throng
Beholds the host   of the damned in darkness
Suffering pain,   sin's punishment:
The surging flames   and stinging serpents
With bitter fangs,   the band of the burning;
From which for the blessed   grows blissful joy.
    For when they see others   suffer the pain
Which they by the mercy   of God have missed,
The more grateful thanks   they give the Creator
For the bliss and the glory   on which they gaze;
That He redeemed them   from Hell's perdition
And gave them grace   of eternal joy.
Hell is locked for them,   heaven laid open!
So souls are rewarded   who have heeded well
The will of the Lord   with loving hearts.
    But for the others   all their desire
Shall go unfulfilled.   They shall see on themselves
Too much of woe,   the weight of sin
And deeds of wickedness   done in the past.
Pain shall cling   to their sorrowing spirits,
The throes of ruin,   in three ways:
    First, they shall see   the worst of afflictions
Flaming before them,   grim fires of hell
Prepared for their punishment.   Imprisoned therein
They suffer for ever   exile and curse.
    A second affliction   shall befall the guilty,

(1236–1273)

The lost, who endure   the darkest of shames:
God shall see on their souls   their burden of sin.
The radiant host   of the angels of heaven
And all the seed   of the sons of men,
And the Foul Fiend,   shall behold their faults,
Their dark transgressions   and all their guilt.
All eyes shall see   through their bodily substance
The sin on their souls.   The foul flesh
Shall become transparent   as it were clear glass
Through which most easily   men may gaze.
    A third affliction   shall befall the doomed:
Their pangs of remorse   when they see the pure
Gladdened with blessings   because of good deeds
Which they, the unhappy,   disdained to do
In their days on earth;   an anguish of sorrow
That so freely of old   they fell into sin;
They shall see the better souls   shining in bliss.
Not their own torment only   shall be their torture
But the bliss of the others   shall be a bane,
Since in former days   they disdained those joys
So unique and so fair   through the false delights,
The vain lusts,   of the vile flesh.
Then confounded   and filled with shame
They shall wander dizzily,   bearing their burden
Of foul transgressions   for the folk to see.
    Better were it then   had they been repentant
Before one man   for their wicked sins,
For all their vices   and every evil,
To God's priest confessing   in grief and fear
Conviction of sin.   Nor can the confessor
See through the flesh   as deep as the soul,
To know if men tell him   truth or a lie
When reciting their sins.   Yet he may have healing
For every evil   and unclean act
Who confesses transgression   before one man.

(1273–1309)

But no one can hide   on that hard Day
A sin unatoned;   there all men shall see it.
    Alas! in this life   could we only see
With our bodily eyes   the sin on our souls,
Our evil musings,   our unclean thoughts,
Then no one ever   could tell to another
With how great effort   each would strive
By every art   for eternal life,
And seek without ceasing   to cleanse his soul
Of the stains of sin,   to bridle his will,
To heal the fault   of a former wound
What little time   of life may be;
That unashamed   in the eyes of all
He may live blameless   his life among men
While body and soul   may be together.
    But here we must sagely   search through the breast
With the eyes of the mind   to the evil within;
For those other eyes,   the gems of the head,
Can in no way reach   to the realm of the spirit
To behold if evil   or good be within
That in the grim time   we find favour with God.
    Then over all hosts   He shall shine in splendour,
In lucent flame,   from His lofty throne.
Before all angels   and all peoples
First shall He speak   to the blessed souls.
With loving heart   and holy word
Heaven's High-King   shall promise them peace,
Shall give them comfort   and grant them grace,
Sending them safe   and signed with the Cross
Into the land   of angels' delight,
There to abide   in bliss for ever:
    "Enter with friends   my Father's kingdom,
Blessing with bliss,   bright beauteous home
Prepared and waiting   from before all worlds
Until you might look   on that wealth of life

(1310–1345)

In the heavenly land,   sweet joy with His loved ones.
All this you earned   when you aided the wretched,
With kind heart welcoming   the world's poor.
Humbly in My name   they asked your mercy
And you gave them shelter,   granted them help,
Clothes to the naked,   food to the needy;
Those that lay sick   in sore pain,
Suffering grievously   gripped by disease,
For them you soothed   and stayed their spirits
In kindly mood.   This you did unto Me
When with love you sought them   and cheered their souls
With lasting comfort.   Long shall you joy
And delight in your guerdon   with God's beloved."
   But in unlike fashion   with menace of fear
All-Ruling God   shall begin to speak
To the evil horde   on His left hand.
They can hope from their Maker   no whit of mercy,
Of life or love;   they shall find reward
Befitting their record   of words and works.
A righteous judgment   full of fear
Shall be their portion.   God's compassion
Shall be withdrawn   on the Day of Doom
From the hosts of men.   That stubborn horde
In stern words   He shall charge with sin,
There before Him   bidding them bring
A clear accounting   for the life He loaned them,
A joy to sinners.   God shall speak
As if to one man,   yet shall He mean
All the whole host   of sinful souls:
   "Mine, O man,   were the hands that made you,
Gave you understanding   shaped you of clay
With living spirit;   lovingly set you
Above all creatures   with beauty and form
Fashioned like Mine;   gave you fullness of power
And wealth in wide lands.   No whit of woe

(1346-1384)

Nor any darkness   had you need to endure.
Yet for all this good   you gave Me no thanks!
   "When I had shaped you   so winsome and shining
With wealth of power   to rule the world,
Then I placed your home   on the pleasant earth
That in Eden's bounty   and shining bloom
You might live in bliss.   But you would not listen
To the word of life;   you forsook My law
At your Foe's behest,   obeyed the wily Fiend,
The murdering Monster,   rather than your Maker.
   "Now I pass over   that ancient account
How at the first   you fell into sin
Debasing with evil   what I gave as a boon.
When I had granted   so much of good
And it seemed to your soul   but little delight
Except you gained power   co-equal with God,
Then you grew alien   to all that joy
And cast out afar   to the fiends' desire.
Mournful of mood,   sinful and sad,
Shorn of blessing   and every bliss,
The glory of Paradise   forced to forgo,
Into this dark world   you were driven out.
Long have you lived there   in lasting affliction,
Trouble and toil   and dark death;
And after your going hence,   beyond help,
Needs must you perish   in the pit of hell.
   "Then My heart rued it   that My handiwork
Should fall to the fiends,   that the sons of men
Should suffer damnation,   a sorrowful fate
And an unknown home.   Myself I descended
A son to his mother;   yet was her maidhood
All unstained.   I only was born
To comfort the wretched.   They wrapped Me about
With weeds of the lowly,   laid Me in darkness
Wound with dark clothing.   For the world I endured it!

(1385-1423)

"To men I seemed little; on a hard stone I lay,
A babe in the manger, to banish death
And the hot woe of hell that in life everlasting
You might shine holy and blessed through the pangs I bore.

"It was not for pride but in poor estate
I suffered pangs on earth and cruel pain,
That I thereby might be like you
And you might be made in semblance like Me,
Freed from sin. My head and face
Bore brutal blows for the love of men.
On My cheek was spittle from sinners' mouths.
For Me they blended a bitter drink
Of gall and vinegar. Grievously I felt
The malice of foes before the folk.
Men sinfully smote Me, held not their hands,
Scourged Me with scourges; with humble heart
For you I suffered their abuse and scorn.
Around My head they wreathed a crown
Rough and spiny, a ring of thorns,
Pressed it upon Me with pitiless hands.

"Then was I hanged on the high Rood,
Fastened to the Cross. Forth from My side
With spears they spilled My gore to the ground
That you might be freed from the Fiend's dominion.
Unsoiled of sin I suffered torture,
Sore affliction, until from the flesh
I gave up the spirit, the living soul.
Behold the prints where they pierced My hands,
My feet likewise, whereby made fast
I hung on the Cross. Still in My side
Plain to see is the bloody scar.

"How is the account uneven between us two!
I bore your pain that blessed and happy
You might have bliss in My kingdom above.
By My death for you I dearly bought

(1424–1462)

Eternal life   that released from sin
You might live forever   in radiant light.
My body lay buried,   hidden below
Deep in the grave   —which had done no evil—
That you might be blessed   in heaven above
Shining bright in My kingdom   with the angel band.

  "Why did you forfeit   that life so fair
Which in love of men,   to comfort the lowly,
With My own body   I graciously bought?
So witless you grew   that you gave no thanks
Unto your Ruler   Who had ransomed you.
I beg nothing   for the bitter death
I bore for you;   but bring Me your life
Which, racked with torture,   I ransomed with Mine.
That life I demand   which you marred with evil,
Slew with sin,   to your own shame.

  "The tabernacle of your body   which I builded for you
And sweetly hallowed,   a home for joy,
Why did you wilfully   soil it with sin,
With foul lusts   and grievous transgression?
That body which I freed   from the clutch of fiends
And bade it shun   wrongdoing and sin
Working evil   you soiled with shame.

  "Why did you hang Me   on a Cross of your hands
Where I hung more heavily   than that once of old?
Lo! this seems the harder.   More bitter to Me
The Cross of your sins   I unwillingly suffered
Than was that other   I ascended of old
Of My own will,   when the woe of mankind
Brought rue to My heart,   when I raised you from hell,
If only you had guarded   the gift I gave.

  "Poor was I in the world   that you might have wealth in heaven,
Wretched was I in your kingdom   that you might be rich in Mine.
But for all this you said   no thanks to your Saviour!
My brothers in the world   I bade you cherish,

(1463–1498)

With the fortune I gave you   befriend the poor.
But you did it not.   You denied the needy
To enter in   under your roof
Withholding all things   with hard heart,
Clothes to the naked,   food to the famished.
Though weary and ailing   they asked for water,
Dry, impoverished,   parched with thirst,
Coldly you spurned them.   You sought not the sorrowing,
Gave them no comfort,   no kindly word
To cheer their minds.   This you did unto Me,
The King of heaven.   Eternal torture
You shall suffer terribly,   torment with fiends."
    Then before all souls   the Lord Himself
Shall proclaim to that doomed folk   a dreadful decree,
Full of sorrow;   He shall say to the sinful:
    "Go now accursed,   of your own will cut off
From the joy of angels,   to unending flame
Prepared for Satan   and his companions,
The black Devil   and his dark crew,
Hot and fierce;   therein shall ye fall!"
    Bereft of all things   they may not dishonour
The command of heaven's King.   Headlong they'll fall
Into the grim pit;   they fought against God!
The Lord of heaven   will be stern and strong,
Fearful and wrathful;   nor shall any foe
On the paths of earth   abide in His presence.
    His right hand shall swing   His victorious sword
And into the depths   the devils shall fall,
Into the black flame   the band of the sinful,
Under earth's surface   the souls of the doomed,
To the home of fiends   the host of the wicked
To perish damned   in the house of pain,
Death-hall of the Devil.   Nor ever again
Shall they come to the mind of God   or escape from their sins.
    There foul with evil   and fast in flame

(1499–1538)

They suffer damnation.   The vengeance of sin
Shall be present and plain;   it is torture eternal.
Nor can the hot pit   from the tribes of hell
In the night never ending   burn away evil,
Nor ever the soil   of sin from the soul;
But the deep pit imprisons   the dreary-hearted
And bottomless binds   their souls with dark;
With ancient flame   and chilling fear,
With dreadful serpents'   deadly fangs,
With numberless torments,   it tortures that folk.
    This we may see   and say at once,
Tell for a truth,   that he has lost
His soul's warden,   wisdom of life,
Who has no concern   if his soul be wretched
Or if it be happy   where his home shall be
After his going hence.   In his heedless folly
He feels no fear   of committing sin;
Nor has he one whit   of regret in heart
That the Holy Ghost   has gone from him for ever
Through his foul transgressions   in this fleeting time.
    Then dark at the Judgment   the sinner shall stand
Palsied with fear   and pallid as death,
For wickedness accursed.   Unworthy of life
The faithless transgressor   shall be filled with fire,
Overwhelmed with fear   in the presence of God,
Haggard and pale   with the hue of the damned,
The sign of his guilt.   The children of sin
Shall pour out their tears   when there is no time,
Grieving for their transgressions.   They shall sorrow too late
For a help to their souls   when the Lord of hosts
Will no longer take heed   how hapless sinners
Lament their lost treasure   in that revealing time.
No room for regret   shall be granted to man
That he may have healing   who will not strive
To earn salvation   while he lives on earth.

(1539–1574)

In that Day to the good   no woe shall be awarded,
No joy to sinners,   but each shall receive
His proper reward   in the presence of God.

   Who fain would receive   life from the Lord
Must needs bestir him   while body and soul
May be together.   Let him gladly cherish
His soul's grace,   working God's will.
Let him be wary   in words and works,
In manners and musings,   so long as this world
Still shines for him,   gliding through shadows,
That he may not forfeit   in this fleeting time
His crown of bliss,   his count of days,
His grace of good works,   his reward of glory,
Which the King of heaven   in that holy time
Shall righteously give,   a guerdon of triumph
To all whose hearts   have hearkened to God.

   Then heaven and hell   shall be filled with souls
Of the sons of men.   The abyss shall swallow
The foes of God.   The darting flame
Shall consume the wretched,   the children of sin.
It shall never allow them   release from the fire
To safety and joy,   but the burning shall bind them
In immutable bondage,   destroying their souls.

   Fearful meseemeth   that the sons of men
Give no heed,   when they yield to transgression,
What God has prepared   to punish the wrong
Of evil-doers.   Then life and death
Shall swallow up sinners.   The house of pain
Shall be present and open   for perjured spirits;
Sinners shall fill it   with their black souls.
The guilty assembled   shall be set apart,
The base from the blessed,   to the tortures of hell
To punish their wrong.   There robbers and thieves,
Adulterers and liars   need not look for life;
The forsworn shall see   the reward of their sin,

(1575–1611)

Hard and devouring.   Hell shall take
The band of the faithless   banished by God
To the fiends for destruction.   They shall suffer doom
In awful anguish.   Woe unto him
Who, soiled with his sins,   must be severed from his Maker
On the Day of Doom   unto death below,
Into the hot fire   with the fiends in hell
Under locks of flame;   they shall yield their limbs
To be bound,   and to be burned,
And to be scourged,   as a penance for sin.
   Then the Holy Ghost   by the might of God
At the Lord's behest   shall lock up hell,
Greatest of death-halls   filled with fire
And the host of fiends—   worst of afflictions
For devils and men,   a house of moaning!
There may not any   ever escape
From their icy bonds.   They broke God's word,
The Books' bright bidding.   For that they abide
In night never-ending;   stained with their sin
They shall suffer sorrow   and endless pain
Who scorned the grace   and the glory of heaven.
   But the chosen souls   shall bring before Christ
Their bright treasures;   their bliss shall live
In the Day of Doom.   They shall joy with God
In the sweet life   assigned to the saints
In the heavenly kingdom.   That is the home
That knows no ending,   but there for ever
The pure have delight   in praising the Lord,
Dear Warden of life,   in light encompassed,
Swathed in peace,   shielded from sorrow,
Honoured with grace,   endeared unto God.
Always for ever   the angel band
Bright with glory   shall blissfully joy
In the worship of God.   The Warden of all
Shall have and shall hold   the hosts of the holy.

(1612–1648)

There is song of angels   and bliss of the saints,
The Saviour's dear presence   shining more bright
On all His beloved   than light of the sun.
There is love of dear ones;   life without death;
Exultant multitudes;   youth without age;
The splendour of heaven's hosts;   health without pain;
For the souls of the righteous   rest without toil.
There is glory of the saints;   day without darkness
Bright with blessing;   bliss without sorrow;
Accord among friends   without envy for ever
For the happy in heaven;   love without hate
In that holy throng.   No hunger there nor thirst,
Nor sleep nor sickness   nor burning sun,
Nor cold nor care.   But the band of the blessed,
Most shining of legions,   shall delight for ever
In the grace of the King   and glory with God.

(1649–1664)

INDEX

290